# Overcoming Global Inequalities

# OVERCOMING GLOBAL INEQUALITIES

*Immanuel Wallerstein,*
*Christopher Chase-Dunn, and*
*Christian Suter, coeditors*

**Political Economy of the World-System Annuals, Volume XXXIV**
*Immanuel Wallerstein, Series Editor*

LONDON AND NEW YORK

First published 2015 by Paradigm Publishers

Published 2016 by Routledge
2 Park Square, Milton Park, Abingdon, Oxfordshire OX14 4RN
711 Third Avenue, New York, NY 10017, USA

First issued in paperback 2016

*Routledge is an imprint of the Taylor & Francis Group, an informa business*

Library of Congress Cataloging-in-Publication Data

Structures of the World Political Economy and Future Global Conflict and Cooperation (Conference) (2013 : University of California, Riverside)
   Overcoming global inequalities / edited by Immanuel Wallerstein, Christopher Chase-Dunn, and Christian Suter.
       pages cm. — (Political economy of the world-system annuals ; volume XXXIV)
   Papers originally presented at a conference on Structures of the World Political Economy and Future Global Conflict and Cooperation, held in April of 2013 at the University of California-Riverside.
   Includes bibliographical references.
   ISBN 978-1-61205-675-3 (hardcover : alk. paper) — ISBN 978-1-61205-676-0 (library ebook)
   1. Equality—Congresses. 2. Equality—Economic aspects—Congresses. I. Wallerstein, Immanuel Maurice, 1930– II. Chase-Dunn, Christopher K. III. Suter, Christian, 1956– IV. Title.
   JC575.S776 2013
   305—dc23
                                                                    2014017033

Designed and Typeset by Straight Creek Bookmakers

ISBN 13: 978-1-61205-688-3 (pbk)
ISBN 13: 978-1-6120-5675-3 (hbk)

# CONTENTS

# INTRODUCTION

## GLOBAL INEQUALITIES AND THEIR CHALLENGES IN WORLD-HISTORICAL PERSPECTIVE

**Immanuel Wallerstein, Christopher Chase-Dunn, and Christian Suter**

This volume examines the changing nature of global inequalities and efforts that are being made to move toward a more egalitarian world society. The authors are world-historical sociologists and geographers who place the contemporary issues of unequal power, wealth, and income in global historical perspective. The geographers examine the roles of geopolitics and patterns of warfare in the historical development of the modern world-system. And the sociologists examine endeavors to improve the situations of poor peoples and nations and to engage the challenges of sustainability that are linked with global inequalities. This is cutting-edge research from engaged social scientists intended to help humanity deal with the challenges of global inequality in the twenty-first century.

Some see recent developments in the world political economy as fundamental departures from the structures of the past, while others view these recent changes as rather similar to those that have occurred in earlier centuries. The international division of labor in the world economy has been in turmoil with the deindustrialization of older industrial regions and the rise of new centers of production and accumulation. The wave of financialization over the past several decades sent the global economy into a crisis in 2008. Rising food prices and high unemployment have led to an increase in anti-authoritarian social movements and waves of protest in the Global South and to unsustainable levels of sovereign debt and pressures for greater austerity in the Global North.

What are the implications of these developments for the future of global conflict and cooperation? Western powers have been involved in wars in the Middle East. The "rogue" states of Iran and North Korea refuse to give up their development of nuclear weapons. And a group of semiperipheral countries, including China, South Korea, Brazil, and Russia, continue to vie for a more prominent place on the world stage. There are struggles within international organizations between the old world powers and those that are rising. Thus, the world-system seems to be evolving toward an increasingly multipolar political structure in which the ability of the United States to generate hegemonic consensus and order has declined.

The world-systems perspective is often identified with a focus on what are now called Global North/South relations. While it has been claimed that the world is now "flat," it seems obvious to most observers that huge inequalities continue to be an important characteristic of an emerging global society. Theorists of a recent stage of global capitalism claim that nation-states are much less important than before and that a global society is emerging in which class relations are increasingly structured by the processes of corporate globalization. It is alleged that this is a new or recent development, having succeeded a situation in which class relations were primarily organized within national societies. The world-systems perspective contends that class relations have been transnational all along and that the core/periphery hierarchy, in which national societies are categorized as being located within the zones of core, semiperiphery, and periphery, continues to be a fundamental aspect of the global system.

There were large inequalities of power and wealth organized as the colonial empires of European core states for centuries, and in the nineteenth century a huge income inequality emerged between the core and the noncore of the global system. This gigantic Global North/South inequality continues to exist despite decolonization and all the rhetoric about developing the Global South.

Since the Protestant Reformation, the institutions of global governance have evolved in response to a series of world revolutions in which local rebellions and social movements have clustered together in time to challenge the powers that be. The elite groups that best succeeded at managing rebellion from below are the ones that were most successful at accumulating capital and occupying the commanding heights of the global system. The contemporary period is one in which the hegemony of the United States is increasingly in question and a new constellation of social movements and counter-hegemonic regimes is challenging the incumbencies of global power.

This volume contains papers that were originally presented at a conference on structures of the world political economy and future global conflict and cooperation, which was sponsored by the Political Economy of the World-System (PEWS) Section of the American Sociological Association and the World Society

Foundation of Zurich, Switzerland. This conference was held in April 2013 at the University of California, Riverside, and was organized by the Institute for Research on World-Systems (IROWS) at UC Riverside and by the World Society Foundation.[1]

The World Society Foundation and the PEWS Section encouraged researchers to investigate the evolution of the world economic and political structures in the twenty-first century, contending scenarios for the future of global conflict and cooperation, and particularly the relationship between the two.

Part I contains chapters that examine the historical and contemporary nature of global inequalities. In Chapter 1 Manuela Boatcă analyzes how the global stratification system reproduces inequalities by focusing on the institutional nature of citizenship as an ascriptive characteristic that is increasingly becoming commodified as those with inferior statuses try to move up in the global hierarchy. In Chapter 2 Gary Coyne examines how national language-training policies reflect, resist, and exacerbate global and within-country linguistic inequalities. Chapter 3 is an inquiry by Lindsay Marie Jacobs and Ronan Van Rossem into the extent to which political and economic power represent alternative dimensions of the global structure of power, and whether political power is a good strategy for countries that want to improve their position in the economic hierarchy. In Chapter 4 Jeffrey Kentor and Matthew R. Sanderson examine the extent to which different kinds of dependence on foreign investment are related to greater violence within countries. In Chapter 5 Jason Struna interrogates the idea that the working class is becoming transnationalized with the rise of capitalist globalization.

Part II contains chapters that examine geopolitics and warfare as forms of struggle in the modern world-system. In Chapter 6 Patrick Bond examines the extent to which the semiperipheral BRICS nations (Brazil, Russia, India, China, and South Africa) constitute a challenge to US hegemony and/or the logic of global capitalism. In Chapter 7 Raymond J. Dezzani and Colin Flint examine the role warfare has played in the global competitive system since the nineteenth century.

Part III contains chapters that focus on social movements and national development efforts. In Chapter 8 James Fenelon analyzes the global indigenous movement and the alternatives it poses for the future of global society. In Chapter 9 Jennifer Givens and Andrew Jorgenson study the effects of two different dimensions of global integration on the carbon emissions of national societies. In Chapter 10 Şahan Savaş Karataşlı, Sefika Kumral, Ben Scully, and Smriti Upadhyay use data from newspaper articles regarding protests and other forms of unrest to examine the class nature of the 2011 outbreak of global resistance. And in Chapter 11 Harold R. Kerbo and Patrick Ziltener compare efforts to reduce poverty and inequality in Cambodia with what has happened in other Southeast Asian countries.

The reproduction of a very hierarchical structure of global inequality clashes with the increasing awareness of those in the Global South that they are truly disadvantaged in global society. Human rights and democracy remain contested concepts, but the different versions of these modern ideologies have been embraced by the vast majority of the peoples of the Earth. These facts shed strong light on the inadequacies of the notion of "might makes right" and the failure of the existing institutions of global governance to live up to their own definitions of legitimacy. Thus the twenty-first century is going through another period of world revolution and interimperial rivalry that is similar in some ways to what happened in the first half of the twentieth century. Hopefully a better world can emerge without the painful mass violence that happened in the twentieth-century "age of extremes."

## Note

1. For more information on the World Society Foundation and its activities, please check out our website: www.worldsociety.ch/. The PEWS website is at www2.asanet.org/sectionpews/index.html. The IROWS website is at http://irows.ucr.edu. The other publication coming out of this conference is Christian Suter and Christopher Chase-Dunn, eds., *Structures of the World Political Economy and the Future of Global Conflict and Cooperation: World Society Studies 2014* (Münster/Berlin/Wien/Zurich: Lit Verlag, 2014).

# PART I

Historical Development of Inequalities

# 1

# COMMODIFICATION OF CITIZENSHIP

## GLOBAL INEQUALITIES AND THE MODERN TRANSMISSION OF PROPERTY[1]

**Manuela Boatcă**

## Abstract

Conventional sociological understandings conceive of modern social arrangements as being defined by achieved characteristics. By contrast, recent legal and sociological scholarship on global inequalities has shown how citizenship—an ascribed characteristic—is a central mechanism ensuring the maintenance of high between-country inequality in the modern world-system. In line with this newer literature, this chapter argues that the widening of the worldwide inequality gap is paralleled by an increase in the commodification of citizenship. To this end, it looks at the emergence of official economic citizenship (or "citizenship by investment") programs as well as at the illegal trade in EU passports ("buy an EU citizenship" schemes) in Eastern Europe and the Caribbean as similar strategies of eluding the ascription of citizenship through recourse to the market. Citizenship is thus shown to be a core mechanism not only for the maintenance of global inequalities, but also for ensuring their reproduction in the postcolonial present.

## Introduction

Time and again, canonical sociology has presented and analyzed citizenship as a counterbalance of social inequalities. From Max Weber through Talcott Parsons and up to Bryan Turner, the institutionalization of citizenship was seen as part of a sequence of social change characteristic of the West, which entailed progress from bondage to freedom and from ascribed to achieved positions in the inequality structure, ultimately defining the alleged transition from tradition to modernity. In stark contrast to the former view, recent legal and sociological scholarship on global inequalities has, on one hand, advanced a conceptualization of national citizenship as a form of inherited property (Shachar 2009). On the other hand, it has provided empirical data for the claim that citizenship remains the main determinant of a person's position within the world inequality structure today (Korzeniewicz and Moran 2009). While conventional sociological understandings conceive of modern social arrangements as being defined by achieved characteristics, such approaches conclude the very opposite: it is precisely due to its ascribed character that citizenship has functioned as a central mechanism ensuring the maintenance of high between-country inequality in the modern world-system in the past and can do so today. Thus, membership in the political community of citizens has made for the relative social and political inclusion of the populations of Western European nation-states under both jus soli and jus sanguinis arrangements. At the same time, however, it has accounted for the selective exclusion of the colonized and non-European populations from the same social and political rights throughout recent history (Boatcă 2011).

In line with the newer literature on global inequality, I will therefore argue that the widening of the worldwide inequality gap is paralleled by an increase in the commodification of citizenship. I will illustrate this by zooming in on two similar strategies of eluding the ascription of citizenship through recourse to the market: first, the emergence of official economic citizenship programs ("citizenship by investment") in Eastern Europe and the Caribbean and, second, the trade in EU passports ("buy an EU citizenship" schemes).

## "City Air Makes One Free"

Especially in his section on the city in *Economy and Society*, but also at various points in his sociology of religion, Max Weber clearly traced the rise of citizenship as an institutionalized association of an autonomous status group (*Stand* in German) of *individual* burghers subject to the same law back to the ancient Greek *polis* and the medieval Occidental city (Weber 1978, 1240). According to him, the revolutionary innovation differentiating the Central and Northern European cities from all others had been the principle that "city air makes man free," according to which slaves or serfs employed for wages in the city soon became free from obligations to their master as well as legally free. Consequently, in time, status differences between free and unfree city dwellers gave way to equality of individual citizens before the law. Although this was characteristic of medieval Occidental cities, antecedents could be found in ancient Greece and Rome, but also in the Near East and in Russia, where town-dwelling slaves or serfs could purchase their freedom. According to Weber, this possibility not only intensified the economic effort of unfree petty burghers, thus spurring capital accumulation through rational operation in trade or industry, but also constituted a preliminary stage in the achievement of political equality (Isin 2002; Weber 1978, 1238).

As the revolutionary innovation differentiating the Occidental city from the Oriental Rest, the principle that "city air makes man free" carried the additional meaning of a sequence of social change that, as it progressed from bondage to freedom, gradually abandoned ascribed criteria of social stratification in favor of achieved characteristics, ultimately describing an ideal-typical transition from tradition to modernity.

According to Weber, the intended meaning and purpose (*Sinn* in German) of the institutionalization of citizenship in the modern (Occidental) state—"the first to have the concept of the 'citizen of the state' (*Staatsbürger*)"—is that of providing "a certain counterbalance to the social *inequalities* which are *neither* rooted in natural differences nor created by natural qualities but are produced, rather, by social conditions." Taking into account the fact that "the inequality of the outward circumstances of life, particularly of *property*, ... can never be eliminated altogether," Weber therefore suggests allotting parliamentary suffrage equivalent weight, "so as to counterbalance these other factors by making the ruled in society ... the equals of the privileged strata" (Weber 1994, 103–104).

The different religious logics to which he had traced social inequalities in the West and the Rest, respectively, turn out to be the structuring principles of the political organization in the (allegedly) secularized European city:

> Equal voting rights means in the first instance this: at this point of social life the individual, for once, is *not*, as he is everywhere else, considered in terms of the particular professional and family position he occupies, nor in relation to differences of material and social situation, but purely and simply *as a citizen*. This expresses the political unity of the nation (*Staatsvolk*) rather than the dividing lines separating the various spheres of life. (Weber 1994, 103; emphases in the original)

This idea would be central to the sociology of T. H. Marshall, who proposed the extension of citizenship as the principal political means for resolving, or at least containing, the contradictions between formal political equality and the persistence of social and economic inequality. Talcott Parsons later elaborated on the development of citizenship as a transition from societies based on ascriptive criteria to societies based on achievement criteria to include a shift from particularistic to universalistic values, such that the modern citizen emerges as a political subject no longer formally confined by the particularities of birth, ethnicity, or gender. Despite criticizing Weber for his Orientalist conception of citizenship, Bryan Turner further drew on Weber's analysis, arguing that citizenship is an essentially modern institution that "evolves through the establishment of autonomous cities, develops through the emergence of the nation-state in the eighteenth and the nineteenth centuries, and finds its full blossoming in the welfare states of the twentieth century" (Turner 1994).

## Global Inequalities and the Issue of Citizenship

However, both Weberian and neo-Weberian analyses have concentrated on the way the allotment of citizenship levels ethnic differences and appeases social conflict within nation-states, or on what Bryan Turner has referred to as "internalist accounts" of the emergence of citizenship (Turner 1990). While ethnic and racial allegiance are treated as traditional ascriptive criteria for social cohesion in national contexts, there is no awareness of the importance of race and ethnicity in the development of citizenship at the global level. Recent analyses of global inequalities, however, have focused on how birthright citizenship, whether under the jus soli or the jus sanguinis principle, functions as a kind of inherited property that restricts membership in well-off polities to a small part of the world population. Thus, according to legal scholar Ayelet Shachar, citizenship in both its gatekeeping (exclusionary) and opportunity-enhancing (inclusionary) functions bears striking similarities to the feudal entail, a legal means of restricting future succession of property to the descendants of a designated estate owner. In medieval England, the entail offered a tool to preserve land in the possession of dynastic families by entrenching birthright succession while tying the hands of future generations from altering the estates they inherited from their predecessors (Shachar 2009, 38). At the same time, studies of global income distribution have revealed national identity and citizenship to be the most important criteria shaping between-country inequalities (Korzeniewicz 2011; Korzeniewicz and Moran 2009), thus paradoxically making an ascribed characteristic of the type usually associated with the stratification order of feudal societies the main principle of global stratification of modernity. Citizenship is thus what Max Weber—had he taken the world-system as a unit of analysis—would have considered a clear instance of social closure. Switching back and forth between the nation-state perspective and the world as a whole, Korzeniewicz and Moran show how the institutionalization of birthright citizenship as pioneered in the Occidental city ensured the relative social and political inclusion of the populations of Western European nation-states, yet in doing so selectively excluded the colonized and non-European populations from the same rights throughout history. Although the low levels of income inequality in the West gradually came to be perceived as structured around achieved characteristics such as one's level of education or professional position, this is only half the story. The long-term stability of low-inequality contexts had in fact been safeguarded by restricting physical access to these regions on the basis of ascribed categories, especially national identity and citizenship, through the control of immigration flows. What appears as a pattern of *relative inclusion* of the population through redistributive state policies, demo-cratic participation, and widespread access to education in low-inequality contexts when taking the nation-state as a unit of analysis is thus revealed to entail the *selective exclusion* from the same rights of large sectors of the population located *outside* national borders once the analytical frame shifts to the world-economy (Korzeniewicz and Moran 2009, 78).

Against this background, the ascribed characteristics of nationhood and citizenship become as important for global stratification as class, usually con-sidered to depend on levels of achievement. Yet, while class membership has regulated the differential access to resources at the level of national populations, citizenship—i.e., nation-state membership—has restricted both the mobility and the access to resources of the poorest segments of the world population—especially the colonized, nonwhite, or non-European groups (Boatcă 2011, 21).

The double function of inclusion in the political community and exclusion of constructed aliens is easily illustrated by looking at the ambiguities and con-tradictions the granting of citizenship generated in continental France and the then-French colony of Saint-Domingue in the wake of the French revolution, or in Germany and its African colonies up to the first decades of the twentieth century. Tellingly, both arrangements resulted in defining the nonwhite population out of the political community of the nation.

In the wake of the French revolution, the granting of citizenship as the basis for the universal equality of political and social rights in a modern social order was understood not only as an expression of liberty (i.e., the opposite of slavery), but also as the mark of civilization. As such, citizenship was to be acquired as the result of a civilizing *process*—that is, gradually. Citizenship rights were therefore granted only to male property owners, whose ability to pay taxes and military tribute and thus contribute to the maintenance of social order qualified them as "active citi-zens." Women, foreigners, and children were in turn defined as "passive citizens" and denied political rights. The French constitution of 1793 extended active citi-zenship to all adult males, thus leaving women to derive their membership in the social community from their relationship to men. The institutionalization of the division between private and public spheres, habitually considered a characteristic of the specifically modern form of social organization, was therefore closely associated with the gendering of economic roles upon which the state-propagated, bourgeois family model was based. In turn, in the French colony of Saint-Domingue, where the revolution of the enslaved resulted in the abolition of slavery in 1794, skin color took precedence over property as a criterion for the granting of citizenship. Since not all whites were property owners, but relatively many free mulattos were, the colonial assembly gave *all* male whites the right to vote even before this was accomplished in continental France, but excluded both slaves and mulattos from franchise after a series of heated debates. By relegating women, children, former slaves, and foreigners to the part of the "civilizing process" that white men had supposedly completed, the implementation of universal principles was already creating its own particularisms.

Thus, if the gradual extension of citizenship rights from propertied white males to all white males and to white women accounted for the development of a relatively low income-inequality pattern within France as of the eighteenth century, the categorical exclusion of Saint-Domingue's black and mulatto population from French citizenship, irrespective of their property status, ensured the maintenance of a high inequality between France and Saint-Domingue/Haiti.

At the same time as citizenship rights were gradually extended to ever more groups within Europe, they were systematically used as a means for the selective exclusion of the colonized and nonwhite populations from the European political communities of citizens. Although France declared slavery illegal on its territory in 1716, leading to the freeing of slaves upon arrival, black Africans were increasingly singled out as exceptions to this rule. The immigration of "negroes" and "mulattoes" to France was finally prohibited in 1777 altogether. In England in 1772, a court ruled that slavery was "un-British"—i.e., incompatible with the liberties guaranteed in England, and that the influx of "negroes" should therefore be prevented. Similarly, in 1773, Portugal forbade the entry of blacks and Brazilian slaves on account of their being unfair competition to domestic labor (Davis, quoted in Buck-Morss 2009, 90ff.). State legislation restricting citizenship to white Europeans later came to include both partners in what were seen as "racially mixed" marriages. After the German colonial war in Southwest Africa, a heated debate among conservative groups aimed at imposing sanctions on mixed-race marriages by withdrawing citizenship and voting rights from both partners and their offspring in Germany's African colonies in 1908; in turn, informal sexual relationships between white male colonists and black women were encouraged as long as they did not produce offspring (Mamozai 1982, 129). Although the German parliament passed a measure forbidding marriage bans on racial grounds in 1912, both the secretary of colonial affairs and German colonial governors refused to put the decision into practice; as a result, marriage bans were enforced until Germany lost its colonies in World War I (El-Tayeb 1999). In the process, the notion of Germanness as whiteness was reinforced not only in relation to the colonies, but also in the context of the racialization of European Others along the lines of a particularly strict understanding of jus sanguinis enforced in the nationality law of 1913 (El-Tayeb 1999; Boatcă 2013).

The possession of the citizenship of the former metropole remains to this day a crucial factor deciding the timing and the destination of ex-colonial subjects' emigration as well as the pursuit of independence in the remaining colonial possessions: fear of losing Dutch citizenship and the privileges it incurs led to a dramatic increase in Surinamese emigration to the Netherlands in the years preceding Surinam's independence from the "motherland" (1974–1975) and until recently remained the main reason behind the lack of political pressure for independence in the Dutch Antilles and Aruba (van Amersfoort and van Niekerk 2006). Analogously, the extension of United States citizenship rights to the populations of all Caribbean colonies after World War II triggered a massive transfer of labor migrants from the Caribbean to the United States. Migrants from nonindependent territories such as Puerto Rico and the US Virgin Islands could thus enjoy both the welfare and the social rights that went with US citizenship, which constituted a strong incentive for migration across the lower social strata in their home countries. In turn, only the more educated, middle sectors of the working class from formally independent Caribbean states like Jamaica, Barbados, and St. Vincent, who therefore did not possess metropolitan citizenship, chose to migrate to the United States (Cervantes-Rodríguez, Grosfoguel, and Mielants 2009).

## Birthright Citizenship versus Citizenship by Investment

The character of inherited property that birthright citizenship acquired in modernity has been made particularly salient by the increasing commodification of citizenship rights across the world in recent years.

Although the legal notion of "birthright citizenship" has been associated with the US context, in which it first emerged, it should be neither reduced to nor mistaken for the right to citizenship of a child born on a particular territory. This arrangement, commonly known as the citizenship principle of jus soli—birthplace citizenship—has been characteristic of the Americas since colonization, with a few notable exceptions in Central America and the Caribbean (Schwarz 2013). In the United States, the phrase "birthright citizenship" was coined in the context of the Declaration of Independence and the 1787 Constitution by analogy with, yet in contradistinction from, the notion of "birthright subjectship" in the common law of medieval England. Birthright subjectship under English common law was a doctrine of perpetual allegiance to the king of England by all people born within his protection, something that the US Declaration of Independence explicitly rejected: in stating that "the good People of these Colonies ... are Absolved from all Allegiance to the British Crown, and that all political connection between them and the State of Great Britain, is and ought to be totally dissolved," the US Declaration of Independence replaced the feudal doctrine of birthright allegiance with the one of consent of the governed, seen as a necessary corollary to the principle of self-evident equality. Tellingly, this shift from subjectship to citizenship under the US Constitution is frequently conceptualized as "the movement from medieval ascription to modern consent" (Schuck and Smith 1985; Feere 2010, 6), although the new scheme still excluded slaves from US citizenship before the Civil War, and a series of legal measures at the state and federal levels prevented free blacks from acquiring citizenship and civil rights both before and after the abolition of slavery in 1865 (Feere 2010, 6). The Civil Rights Act of 1866 and the 1868 Citizenship Clause (Fourteenth Amendment) finally included all persons born within the United States and "subject to the jurisdiction thereof" in its citizenry, thereby effectively establishing jus soli—the right of soil—as a principle of allotment of US citizenship. At the same time, it excluded Native Americans on the assumption that they fell under the jurisdiction of tribal governments. Congress did not grant citizenship to Native Americans on reservations until 1924 (Indian Citizenship Act), yet in practice individual state laws barred Native Americans from voting in several states as late as 1957.

Independent of the history of the notion of "birthright citizenship" in the particular context of the United States, all states of the modern world currently limit access to their citizenship by virtue of an individual's birthright, typically by granting automatic—i.e., ascriptive—entitlement to political and social rights as well as welfare benefits only to a select group of individuals according to either birthplace (jus soli) or bloodline (jus sanguinis).

Birthright citizenship therefore encompasses all institutional arrangements that ascribe membership in a political community to an individual upon birth through either jus soli or jus sanguinis. Such arrangements thereby limit access to the community's resources to the heirs of membership titles as well as perpetuate unequal starting points through the intergenerational transfer of membership:

> By legally identifying birth, either in a certain territory, or to certain parents, as the decisive factor in the distribution of the precious property of membership, current citizenship principles render memberships in well-off polities beyond the reach of the vast majority of the world's population. It is in this way that citizenship may be thought of as the quintessential inherited entitlement of our time. (Shachar 2009, 11)

Equating the advantages offered on the basis of the different principles of allocating political membership under jus soli and jus sanguinis arrangements does not mean glossing over the differences between citizenship regimes as distinct as the US and the German ones, or between distinct moments in time. Rather, the analogies serve to show the extent to which the ascribed characteristic of citizenship as a principle of global stratification straddles national political traditions while functioning in all as a kind of inherited property usually associated with the stratification order of feudal societies, not liberal democratic ones. At the same time, if national identity, institutionalized as birthright citizenship, has been the main mechanism ensuring the long-term maintenance of high inequality between core and periphery, then migration to wealthy regions becomes the "single most immediate and effective means of global social mobility for populations in most countries of the world" (Korzeniewicz and Moran 2009, 107). Thus, international migration, which entails gaining access to at least the average income of the poorer strata of a much richer nation-state, represents not only a strategy of upward mobility for populations of ex-colonial countries possessing metropolitan citizenship, but also a means of eluding the ascribed position derived from the national citizenship of a poor state for populations able and willing to risk illegal, undocumented, or noncitizen status in a rich state.

## *Jus pecuniae* versus Premium Citizenship

Despite claims to modern, democratic, and egalitarian principles of inclusion in the political communities of nations, today's citizenship arrangements are based on ascriptive principles, as discussed previously. At the same time, we are increasingly facing a series of phenomena that do not seem to fit that picture. Two examples are particularly illustrative:

> In October 2012, headlines in several major newspapers announced that EU citizenship might be available for bond buyers: Hungary, looking to refinance billions of dollars in foreign debt that will mature in the next few years, had recently announced a plan to offer preferential immigration treatment and a fast track to citizenship to any foreigner who buys at least 250,000 euros of its government's bonds. The new legislation would grant investors residency and eventually a Hungarian passport, allowing the holder to live and work anywhere in the European Union. (*Daily Mail* 2012)

In September 2012, large billboards advertising the launch event of the Park Hyatt resort on the Caribbean island of St. Kitts linked it to the promise of benefits, including citizenship and visa-free travel to 139 countries, for investors or donors of US$400,000 to the island. Unlike Hungary's initiative, this program was far from new. St. Kitts and Nevis, a federation of two islands in the Caribbean, had established a "citizenship by investment" program in 1984, one year after the islands gained independence from the United Kingdom. Initially, investment was limited to a real-estate option of US$400,000. After the closing of the islands' sugar industry under pressure from the European Union and the World Trade Organization, a second option was introduced in the form of a donation to the Sugar Industry Diversification Foundation, a charity aimed at conducting research into the development of industries to replace the sugar industry (Dzankic 2012a).

Despite the similarities, there seems to be no obvious connection between these two examples. Not only are the two countries situated in (geographically, historically, and economically) very different regions of the world, but their citizenship-by-investment programs are actually far apart in time: While St. Kitts and Nevis's program was implemented in 1984, Hungary's was implemented in 2013. However, between 1984 and 2013, there was a steep increase in citizenship by investment around the world, especially in small semiperipheral countries. As one type of naturalization procedure, citizenship by investment has an economic rationale, according to which citizenship status is obtainable either with or without any residence requirement. Conferring citizenship by investment contingent upon residence in the country's territory is a common practice, including in the United Kingdom, the United States, Canada, Belgium, and Australia. The far less common but recently growing practice is to extend citizenship status to investors without a residence requirement. Firmly implemented in St. Kitts and Nevis and the Commonwealth of Dominica since 1984 and 1993, respectively, such programs are awaiting implementation in Antigua and Barbuda as well as Hungary in 2013, and have been planned, although on hold, in Montenegro since 2011 (Dzankic 2012a). Several other noncore European countries, including Ireland, Spain, and Portugal in Western Europe, alongside Bulgaria, Albania, and Macedonia in Eastern Europe, have recently implemented or are currently considering investor programs that facilitate access to citizenship with different degrees of residence requirements (Dzankic 2012b).

Visa-free travel to core countries, citizenship in a Schengen-zone state, or even the right to work in the European Union thereby become available for the (moderately or very) wealthy, consequently linking the inequality of income and property to the access to property commodified in the form of citizenship. Some authors have therefore introduced the term *jus pecuniae* (Dzankic 2012a; Stern 2011) as a new type of criterion for the allotment of citizenship alongside jus soli and jus sanguinis, as well as forms combining those two. However, the commodification of citizenship that *jus pecuniae* involves neither follows an alternative, nonascriptive logic, nor represents a viable option for most of the world's population. Instead, it either is an option purposely designed for a very select (wealthy) few or—more frequently—is scandalized, stigmatized, and, ultimately, criminalized when it threatens to become available to a wider number of people.

Thus, according to the *Daily Mail* (2012), British Tory MP Priti Patel referred to Hungary's plan to offer citizenship to bond buyers as "a shocking abuse of EU membership by the Hungarian Government" that "highlights one of many flaws in the EU and in the way it operates. This policy could pose significant challenges for the EU when it comes to immigration, social and economic policies and will do little to restore any trust and confidence in the EU with the British public."

Similar sharp criticism of strategies aimed at undermining the ascriptive logic of citizenship allotment has been instrumental in reasserting (EU) core countries' leverage on semiperipheral ones, as becomes clear from the austerity measures and other sanctions imposed on the latter during the 2008 financial crisis. In the context of the debate on EU economic aid to Cyprus, the head of the German Christian Social Union (CSU) in the EU Parliament, Markus Ferber, recently asked for a guarantee "that we are helping the citizens of Cyprus and not Russian oligarchs," who, according to him, probably deposited laundered money in the island state. Ferber went so far as to ask for reform of Cyprus's citizenship law, which allows foreigners to become Cypriot citizens upon investing or depositing at least ten million euros in Cyprus: "If Nikosia [Cyprus's capital] wants help, we have to see to it that not everyone who has a lot of money receives a Cypriot passport," Ferber added (quoted in Gammelin and Hulverscheidt 2013).

It was also the German CSU that criticized the Montenegrin government's decision to implement a citizenship-by-investment program in the country and announced that it might request the reinstatement of visas for the citizens of Montenegro, implying that this decision might affect the progress Montenegro had made in the area of border management and immigration control (Dzankic 2012a, 13). In the wake of such reactions, the Montenegrin government has put the implementation of its citizenship-by-investment program on hold.

Against this backdrop, it is important to note that, while any state's citizenship could theoretically be commodified by becoming the object of investor programs, it is only the citizenship of a few states that lends itself to being commodified by virtue of being a scarce good awarding (relatively) rare benefits. From this point of view, states whose citizenship includes the advantage of the aforementioned visa-free travel to core countries, or even the right to legal employment in them, offer what could be referred to as "premium citizenship" that could be attractive to investors. States that are not part of the core may, as in the case of St. Kitts and Nevis, use the residual benefits of having been British colonies and today being members of the Commonwealth of Nations—which share, among other things, a visa-free travel area. *Jus pecuniae*, therefore, is not only unavailable to the majority of the world's population, but would not prove a viable economic strategy in any but premium-citizenship states.

## From Political Sanctions to Racial Profiling: The Social Costs of Commodification

There is, however, a fine line between criticism and negative sanctioning of the commodification of citizenship-through-investment programs in noncore contexts and the ethnic and/or racial profiling of noncore citizens. As the real or perceived risk of more people gaining access to premium citizenship increases, so does the racial criminalization of migrants to core regions—most prominently, the European Union and the United States (Palidda 2011).

### Introducing New Crime: Forged Descent

Thus, according to French EU affairs minister Pierre Lellouche, one of the reasons France spoke out against Romanian efforts to join the European Union's border-free Schengen zone in 2010 was concern about the issuing of Romanian passports to Moldovans. The territory of Moldova was part of the Romanian Principality of Moldavia from the mid-fourteenth through the mid-nineteenth century and part of Greater Romania between 1918 and 1944. Formerly known as Bessarabia, the region was annexed by the Soviet Union during World War II and became an independent republic in 1991. Since many Moldovans are ethnically and linguistically Romanian and almost 95 percent are Romanian Orthodox Christians, as Moldova gained its independence Bucharest adopted a law granting foreign nationals of Romanian descent the right to become citizens of the country. Since then, Romania has processed an estimated 225,000 citizenship applications from Moldovans (Iordachi 2012). According to Romanian officials, many Moldovans regard the Romanian passport as the key to the European Union and try to acquire Romanian citizenship as quickly as possible using both official and unofficial channels (Călugăreanu and Mogos 2012). As illicit intermediaries can generate proof of Romanian ancestry where none exists,[2] thereby spurring illegal trade in Romanian passports, EU fears of "creeping expansion from the East" have fed on exaggerated prognoses of the "stream of Moldovan migration" into Western Europe. The widely read high-brow German magazine *Der Spiegel* illustrated the typical threat scenario mobilized in anti-immigration arguments with these words:

> The EU, which is already suffering from enlargement fatigue, is stealthily being expanded from the east—without a referendum or any agreements from Brussels, Berlin or Paris. The Moldovans are voting with their feet and marching into the EU's economic paradise—through the back door. (Bidder 2010)

The April 2012 report by the Soros Foundation in Romania argued that many of these fears were unfounded. While criticizing Bucharest for an apparent lack of transparency, the study said there was no evidence to support claims of Moldovan migrants surging unchecked into Europe, and that Romania's naturalization program—although disorderly—had created proportionately fewer citizens than similar efforts in countries such as the United Kingdom and France. The study also attributed the steep rise in citizenship awards after 2007, the year Romania joined the European Union, to the simplification of the process for awarding passports (Călugăreanu and Mogos 2012; Iordachi 2012). Nevertheless, France's concern with this very phenomenon in 2010 was the first in a line of Western European states' arguments against Romania (and Bulgaria) joining the Schengen zone, which since then has been postponed indefinitely several times. In March 2013, the then–German minister of the interior, Hans-Peter Friedrich, announced that "the attempt [to join] would fail because of a German veto" if Romania and Bulgaria insisted on a decision, and he urged both countries to take further steps "to prevent migrants abusing the system" (quoted in *Economist* 2013).

*Introducing New Crime, Continued: Forged Ascent*

If the ethnic profiling of Moldovans in the European Union is directed against immigrants suspected of having abused the right of blood in order to acquire citizenship, the ethnic and racial profiling of immigrants who come to the United States to give birth targets pregnant women accused of abusing the right of soil for the same purpose. In the latter case, immigration hard-liners describe a wave of migrants crossing the Mexican-US border in the advanced stages of pregnancy to have what are dismissively called "anchor babies" (Lacey 2011). The term refers to the automatic granting of US citizenship, by virtue of the Fourteenth Amendment, to children born on US soil, who can subsequently secure citizenship for their parents upon reaching the age of twenty-one. Although hospitals do report some immigrants arriving to give birth in the United States, many of those mothers are frequent border crossers with valid visas who travel legally to take advantage of better medical care. Moreover, although the total US immigrant population continues to grow, unauthorized immigration has slowed in the past decade (Pew Research Center 2013). Nevertheless, several Republican attempts at amending the US constitution since 2010 have mobilized terms like "anchor babies," "birth tourism," and "accidental citizens" to end the automatic granting of citizenship, arguing that the provision attracts high numbers of unauthorized migrants (Feere 2010; *Huffington Post* 2013). Migrants themselves, however, stress that it is access to medical care and the prospect of better-paying jobs, not a different passport for their children, that prompt them to take the risk of unauthorized migration upon themselves (Lacey 2011).

The increase in the commodification of citizenship in all of these instances not only reflects, but also reinforces the widening of the worldwide inequality gap. The emergence of official citizenship-by-investment programs as well as the illegal trade in EU passports in Eastern Europe and the Caribbean are similar strategies of eluding the ascription of citizenship through recourse to the market. Attempts to beat the ascriptive logic at its own game—i.e., by undermining the institution of birthright citizenship through illegal trade or illegal migration—meet with critique, sanctions, and criminalization from supra-state and financial institutions; legal countermeasures; and racially and ethnically based policing. The scandalization of "forged descent" in the case of Moldovan applications to Romanian citizenship and of "forged ascent" in the case of Mexican mothers' border crossing for medical purposes is a statement about the immutability of the ascription of citizenship for the wider population through bloodline and birthplace, respectively. Such scandalization ultimately represents a denial of equal opportunities for upward social mobility at the global level. Citizenship is thus not only a core mechanism for the maintenance of global inequalities, but also one on the basis of which the reproduction of these inequalities is being enacted in the postcolonial present.

# References

Bidder, Benjamin. 2010. "Romanian Passports for Moldovans: Entering the EU through the Back Door." *Spiegel,* July 13. www.spiegel.de/international/europe/romanian -passports-for-moldovansentering-the-eu-through-the-back-door-a-706338.html (accessed May 11, 2013).

Boatcă, Manuela. 2011. "Global Inequalities: Transnational Processes and Transregional Entanglements." desiguALdades.net Working Paper 11. www.desigualdades.net/bilder /Working_Paper/WP_Boatca_Online.pdf?1367229867 (accessed June 28, 2013).

————. 2013. "'From the Standpoint of Germanism': A Postcolonial Critique of Weber's Theory of Race and Ethnicity." *Political Power and Social Theory* 24: 55–80.

Buck-Morss, Susan. 2009. *Hegel, Haiti, and Universal History.* Pittsburgh: University of Pittsburgh Press.

Călugăreanu, Vitalie, and Adrian Mogos. 2012. "How to Buy an EU Citizenship." *Jurnalul National,* September 12. www.jurnalul.ro/anchete/how-to-buy-an-eu-citizenship -623530.htm (accessed May 17, 2013).

Cervantes-Rodríguez, Margarita, Ramón Grosfoguel, and Eric Mielants. 2009. "Introduction: Caribbean Migrations to Western Europe and the United States." In *Caribbean Migrations to Western Europe and the United States,* edited by Margarita Cervantes-Rodríguez, Ramón Grosfoguel, and Eric Mielants, 1–17. Philadelphia: Temple University Press.

*Daily Mail.* 2012. "Hungary 'Sells EU Passports' in Return for Bailout Funds." *Daily Mail,* October 2012.

Dzankic, Jelena. 2012a. "The Pros and Cons of Ius Pecuniae: Investor Citizenship in Comparative Perspective." European University Institute Working Papers, Robert Schuman Centre for Advanced Studies 2012/14: 1–18.

————. 2012b. "Investor Programs: Attempting to Cure the Struggling European Economies." *Citizenship in Southeast Europe.* http://citsee.eu/blog/investor-programs -attempting-cure-struggling-european-economies (accessed July 2, 2013).

*Economist.* 2013. "Romania and the EU: Not Ready for Schengen." *Economist,* March 17. www.economist.com/blogs/easternapproaches/2013/03/romania-and-eu (accessed July 2, 2013).

El-Tayeb, Fatima. 1999. "'Blood Is a Very Special Juice': Racialized Bodies and Citizenship in Twentieth-Century Germany." *International Review of Social History* 44: 149–169.

Erler, Edward J. 2008. "Birthright Citizenship and Dual Citizenship: Harbingers of Administrative Tyranny." *Imprimis* 7. www.hillsdale.edu/news/imprimis/archive/issue .asp?year=2008&month=07 (accessed June 30, 2013).

Feere, Jon. 2010. "Birthright Citizenship in the United States: A Global Comparison." *Center for Immigration Studies Backgrounder,* August 2010, 1–20. www.cis.org/sites/cis .org/files/articles/2010/birthright.pdf (accessed May 2, 2014).

Gammelin, Cerstin, and Claus Hulverscheidt. 2013. "SPD sträubt sich gegen Rettungspaket." *Süddeutsche Zeitung,* January 9. http://sz.de/1.1568342 (accessed May 11, 2013).

*Huffington Post.* 2013. "Steve King Introduces Bill to Stop 'Anchor Babies.'" January 4. www.huffingtonpost.com/2013/01/04/steve-king-anchor-babies_n_2411989.html (accessed July 5, 2013).

Iordachi, Constantin, ed. 2012. *Reacquiring the Romanian Citizenship: Historical, Comparative, and Applied Perspectives.* Bucharest: Curtea Veche.

Isin, Engin. 2002. "Citizenship after Orientalism." In *Handbook of Citizenship Studies*, edited by Engin F. Isin and Bryan S. Turner, 117–128. London: Sage.

Korzeniewicz, Roberto Patricio. 2011. "Inequality: On Some of the Implications of a World-Historical Perspective." desiguALdades.net Working Paper 3. www.desigualdades .net/bilder/Working_Paper/WP_Korzeniewicz_Online.pdf?1367229868.

Korzeniewicz, Roberto Patricio, and Timothy Patrick Moran. 2009. *Unveiling Inequality: A World-Historical Perspective*. New York: Russell Sage Foundation.

Lacey, Marc. 2011. "Birthright Citizenship Looms as Next Immigration Battle." *New York Times*, January 4.

Mamozai, Martha. 1982. *Herrenmenschen: Frauen im deutschen Kolonialismus*. Reinbek: Rowohlt.

Palidda, Salvatore. 2011. *Racial Criminalization of Migrants in the 21st Century*. Aldershot, UK: Ashgate.

Pew Research Center. 2013. "Unauthorized Immigrants: How Pew Research Counts Them and What We Know about Them." Pew Research Center. www.pewresearch.org /2013/04/17/unauthorized-immigrants-how-pew-research-counts-them-and-what-we -know-about-them (accessed July 5, 2013).

Schuck, Peter, and Rogers M. Smith. 1985. *Citizenship without Consent: Illegal Aliens in the American Polity*. New Haven, CT: Yale University Press.

Schwarz, Tobias. 2013. "Policies of Belonging: Nationale Mitgliedschaft und Zugehörigkeit in Lateinamerika." KLA Working Paper Series 2: 1–46.

Shachar, Ayelet. 2009. *The Birthright Lottery: Citizenship and Global Inequality*. Cambridge, MA: Harvard University Press.

Stern, Joachim. 2011. "*Ius Pecuniae*—Staatsbürgerschaft zwischen ausreichendem Lebensunterhalt, Mindestsicherung und Menschenwürde." In *Migration und Integration— wissenschaftliche Perspektiven aus Österreich Jahrbuch 1/2011*, edited by Julia Dahlvik, Heinz Fassmann, and Wiebke Sievers, 55–74. Wien/Göttingen: V&R Unipress.

Turner, Bryan. 1990. "Outline of a Theory of Citizenship." *Sociology* 24: 189–217.

———. 1994. "General Commentary." In *Citizenship: Critical Concepts*, edited by Bryan S. Turner and Peter Hamilton, np. London: Routledge.

van Amersfoort, Hans, and Mies van Niekerk. 2006. "Immigration as a Colonial Inheritance: Post-Colonial Immigrants in the Netherlands, 1945–2002." *Journal of Ethnic and Migration Studies* 32: 323–346.

Weber, Max. 1978. *Economy and Society: An Outline of Interpretive Sociology*. Vol. 1. Berkeley: University of California Press.

———. 1994. *Political Writings*. Cambridge: Cambridge University Press.

## Notes

1.  Previous versions of this chapter were presented at the Inter-American Studies (IAS) congress in Guadalajara, Mexico, in 2012 and at the Political Economy of the World-Systems (PEWS) Spring conference 2013 in Riverside, California. I owe special thanks to the session chairs, Julia Roth at the IAS congress and Chris Chase-Dunn at the PEWS conference, for providing me with the opportunity for rich interaction and constructive feedback on both occasions, as well as to Oliver Tewes at the Free University of Berlin for his valuable research assistance throughout the process.

2.  An investigation sponsored by the European Fund for Investigative Journalism and undertaken for the Romanian daily newspaper *Jurnalul National* in 2012 revealed that, despite official Romanian policy of expediting the acquisition of citizenship for Moldovan nationals, many Moldovans still prefer to acquire Romanian citizenship through unofficial channels and frequently pay hundreds of euros to brokers in the hope of expediting their applications. When the applicants' proof of Romanian ancestry is not genuine, unofficial channels prove especially efficient in that they are able to produce credible certificates of descent from state archives that result in the granting of Romanian nationality (Călugăreanu and Mogos 2012).

# 2

# THE POLITICAL ECONOMY OF LANGUAGE-EDUCATION POLICIES

**Gary Coyne**

## Abstract

The institutionalization of languages in the curricula of national school systems reflects inequalities between and within societies. The languages of a few current and former core powers are widely studied, and the interstate system and nationalism mean that many national languages are institutionalized in one country's curricula. The insertion of European languages into African schools, particularly when they are used as the media of instruction, is related to inequality within this group of societies; students who do not speak the European languages have trouble completing school and this, ultimately, serves elite interests by limiting competition for higher-status and higher-income jobs. Through the lens of language-education policies we see the interrelations of inequality within and between societies in the world-system.

## Introduction

This chapter takes on two interrelated issues. The first is how inequality between societies has influenced the institutionalization of languages in national school curricula. The 250 or so languages taught in primary and secondary schools world-wide are not a random sample of the 6,000 or so extant languages (Nettle 1999) and it is largely the dynamics associated with the expansion of the European-based world-systems from the fifteenth century that explain which languages were selected. Colonization has resulted in the widespread study of a few languages of European origin as first and second languages while the spread of the interstate system and the logic of nationalism have resulted in the study of a unique, national language as a first language in about half of all states.

The second issue is how the institutionalization of European languages in Africa has become part of national-level patterns of inequality. Elite groups—often with ties to former colonizers—are more likely to know these languages, and the use of these languages in school systems hinders educational attainment for students unable to master them. This reduces competition for high-paying (and high-status) jobs. Pooled time-series analysis of data from thirty-three African states indicates that the use of European languages as media of instruction in African schools has a significant positive relationship to economic inequality in the period 1980–2000.

Taken together, these two lines of analysis illustrate how the single world-system structures political and economic processes at multiple levels.

## Expansion of the European World-System and of European Languages

Languages associated with core powers are the most widely studied ones. The fact that English is so widely studied is clearly a result of British and American hege-mony in the nineteenth and twentieth centuries. Spanish, French, and Portuguese are also widely studied because of the historical central (or at least more central) place of these societies in the world-system. Indeed, these are most of a small hand-ful of languages that are studied in more than one or two countries;[1] where one language is studied in many countries, European colonization is generally the cause.

European contact with the New World in the fifteenth century meant dis-ease decimated indigenous populations, and European oceangoing vessels meant these areas could be integrated into the expanding Atlantic economy. In most of South America, Spanish became the dominant language because Spanish men married native women, producing Spanish-speaking families and increasing the Spanish-speaking population. Independence movements were largely led by men from these mixed families and once in power the revolutionaries tended to imitate the European elites who had controlled colonial governments. In Brazil, plantation slavery played a large part in the economy and this forced movement of populations from Africa eventually increased the number of Portuguese speakers (Burkholder and Johnson 1990). English is a first language in North America for some of the same reasons, although here the voluntary migration of large numbers of European immigrants in the nineteenth century added to the English-speaking population (Roberts 2006). The French also participated in colonization of the New World in the sixteenth and seventeenth centuries and there are French-speaking populations in several states, although France lost control of its American territories in the eighteenth and nineteenth centuries (Walter 1993). Dynamics in Australia and New Zealand were similar to those in British North America, although delayed by about a century and the populations, though involuntarily moved, were British convicts (Roberts 2006). In each of these cases more powerful societies in the core were able to eradicate and replace (or completely marginalize) the less powerful societies within the territories at the periphery of the expanding European world-system. Four centuries after the incorporation of the New World and the Antipodes, then, most of the 3,000–4,000 indigenous languages are completely extinct and many that remain are spoken by just a few people (Ostler 2005). This is directly related to the fact that school systems in the Americas, Australia, and New Zealand, by and large, teach just one of four European languages as a first language and are most likely to teach one of the others as a second.

The languages of other current or former core powers are still relatively widely studied. The hegemony of the Dutch in the sixteenth century meant they established a colonial empire; Dutch is still studied in a few Caribbean countries and (as Afrikaans) in South Africa (de Swaan 2001). Russian is the second language in several Central Asian and Eastern European countries because of Russian colonization, and the formation of the USSR meant territories were held until the early 1990s (Grant 1983).

The expansion of the European world-system also meant the spread of the interstate system and nationalism. On one hand, the concept of the nation-state and nationalism effectively reshaped existing polities (as in China and Japan); on the other hand, the creation of colonies—particularly in Africa—often set the boundaries for what would become nation-states in the mid-twentieth century when formal colonization was brought to an end (Chase-Dunn 1989). Nationalism suggests each nation-state should contain one culturally and linguistically homogeneous population (Anderson 1983). Where languages and states have been linked in this way the result is that one language receives high levels of institutional support and marginalizes other languages in the territory. This may happen in ways that are centrally planned, as when the French state mandated that the centralized school system built after the French Revolution not use regional dialects (Walter 1993). Or it may be unplanned, as in the mid-seventeenth century when regional variants of English began to emulate the version found in the capital (Crystal 2003). In many cases the linkage between nation and state is hard to miss: Nepali is the first language of Nepal, Thai of Thailand, and so on. However, those who do not speak the national language—and there are 121 languages spoken in Nepal and

76 in Thailand (Lewis, Simons, and Fennig 2013)—either have to learn it or be marginalized within their own state.

The dynamics of European world-system expansion explain much (although not all) of which languages have been incorporated into national school curricula.[2] Settler colonization and the movement of populations created almost fifty societies where just one of four European languages dominates and is studied as a first language. Administrative colonization introduced this same subset of languages to essentially every country outside of Europe, where they are often studied as second languages. Less directly, the logic of the nation-state suggested the selection of one language to represent the culture of the assembled population, and the majority of states—more than sixty—have chosen a unique national language as a first language.

At the same time, it is meaningful to talk about languages in this way only because of the existence of mass school systems with standardized curricula. The model for these curricula suggests the national language be a major subject of study and that some other language be a minor subject (Benavot 2004). This second language is generally thought of as providing access to information and cultures beyond one's own nation, and the subset of European languages mentioned previously is frequently studied because they meet this criterion (de Swaan 2001). At the same time, in the period since the end of formal colonization, core actors have promoted their languages—particularly in former African and Asian colonies where there are few native speakers—through cultural exchange programs, conditions of education aid, and the provision of educational materials and language teachers free of cost to less developed nations (Phillipson 1992). English is studied as a second language in more than half of the world's national school systems and French is a distant second, at just over 10 percent.

## European Languages and Inequality in Africa

The distribution of languages across national school systems is a result of inequalities between societies and it has been suggested that the study of European languages in Africa is related to inequality within these societies (Myers-Scotton 1993). With the colonial partition of Africa in the late nineteenth century, European languages were introduced to administer colonial states and were used in educational systems built along the lines of those found in Europe (Mazrui and Mazrui 1998). With the coming of independence, European languages were generally retained and decades after independence these languages are often official languages and still used in schools. This outcome is partly a result of institutional inertia, as there would have been considerable costs in translating legal codes, textbooks, and other curricular material into African languages (Simpson 2008). It is also the case that most of these societies have high levels of linguistic diversity, making it difficult to select one indigenous language to take on all official functions because most of the widely spoken languages have associations with particular regional, cultural, or religious groups (Laitin 1992). (To this we can add that peripheral states tend to be weak, which would make undertaking any project of this scope difficult even if core powers had no interest in the outcome.) The retention of European languages, particularly in schools, is also argued to be a result of elite groups acting to retain those languages. This group consists of the professional classes that acquired knowledge of these languages through education, families of European descent, or families that have a history of collaboration with colonial regimes and speak the language in the home. Like elites in other peripheral nations, they share interests with core elites (Chase-Dunn 1989), and in this case their interests are served by the continuing importance of European languages because knowledge of these languages is an advantage in securing certain kinds of jobs and accessing government services.

Where these European languages are official ones—as English and French are in about twenty countries each and Portuguese is in three—they are used by governments for internal and external communication (Brock-Utne 2001). This means they are required for employment in the government civil services that make up a large proportion of white-collar employment in Africa for most of the period under study here (Foster 1980).

European languages play a particularly important role in education. These languages are always a second, if not the first, language and are typically important on the exams that grant access to higher education. They are also used as the medium of instruction in some countries, in certain cases from early primary school. Some subjects (such as math and science) may be taught in European languages at earlier grade levels while others (namely, other languages, but also civics and history) may never be. European languages also dominate education at the postsecondary level as the medium of instruction, and it is not uncommon that textbooks and materials for some subjects are available only in these languages. Even in cases in which the European language does not dominate tertiary education, it may be more prevalent among higher-ranked institutions or in more prestigious fields of study (Altbach 1991; Kelly 1991).

Despite European languages being used in these ways, they are generally spoken by a small percentage of the population in most African nations. As examples, in Gabon and Kenya less than 5 percent of the population speaks a European language in the home, while in Botswana, Malawi, and the Central African Republic the corresponding figure is less than 1 percent (Lewis, Simons, and Fennig 2013). The use of these languages in schools may, then, constitute a significant barrier to education for most students.


## Data and Methods

Data were collected on language-education policies and inequality in thirty-three African states at five-year intervals from 1980 to 2000.[3] The data are modeled with pooled time-series techniques. (For a fuller discussion of the data, the methods used, and a more detailed discussion of European languages in Africa, see Coyne 2013.)

Inequality is measured with a Gini coefficient for net household income. The Gini coefficient (as measured here) ranges from 0, indicating perfect equality, to 100, indicating perfect inequality. Households are the appropriate unit to observe inequality because the effects of language on inequality play out in the home as parents attempt to pass advantages on to their children. These data come from the Standardized World Income Inequality Database (Solt 2009). Table 2.1 shows large standard deviations indicating variation across countries, but there is no clear trend over time for the sample as a whole.

Language-education policies were measured in two ways. First, the emphasis given to European languages as a subject of study was measured as the percent of instructional periods in the primary and secondary curriculum. Second, a dummy variable measures where European languages are the medium of instruction. This is coded "1" where instruction in a European language begins in the first or second grade and "0" otherwise. The variation in language of instruction already discussed notwithstanding, where European languages are introduced this early, school systems are attempting to build up skills in this language to use it as a medium of instruction (Alidou et al. 2006). The variables for language education are taken from the International Bureau of Education. As shown in Table 2.1, the percent of academic periods devoted to instruction in European languages increases from about 18 percent in 1980 to 23 percent in 2000. (Note, however, the relatively large standard deviations.) A little more than half of the countries use European languages as the medium of instruction.

*Colonial Variables*

I include a group of variables that test the effects of colonization. A dummy variable for identity of the colonizer is coded "1" if the country is a former British colony and "0" otherwise. A variable for independence is coded as the years between 1956 (when the first African colonies gained independence) and the year a given country gained independence. Data on colonization and decolonization are taken from Henige (1970) and other historical sources. These variables are time invariant for each country and reported only for all time points in Table 2.1.

Income inequality is widely studied and sector dualism, secondary enrollment, and population growth have been found to have robust effects on inequality, so they are included as a baseline model. Sector dualism is the extent to which a national economy is divided into a traditional, agricultural sector with low wages and a modern, industrial sector with higher wages (Alderson and Nielsen 2002); it is operationalized as the percentage of the labor force in agriculture minus agriculture's share of gross domestic product (Food and Agricultural Organization 2009). Expansion of education first increases inequality as individuals move out of low-wage sectors and, thereafter, decreases inequality as its continued expansion erodes the wage premium on skilled labor (Barro 1991); this is measured with gross secondary enrollments (World Bank 2011). Demographics also play a role

**Table 2.1  Descriptive Statistics for 33 African Countries (*N* = 119)**

| | All Time Points | 1980 | 1985 | 1990 | 1995 | 2000 |
|---|---|---|---|---|---|---|
| Gini (net household income) | 45.53 (8.13) | 45.55 (7.12) | 45.37 (8.78) | 46.74 (9.00) | 46.37 (8.66) | 45.45 (7.34) |
| Percent of Periods | 22.29 (11.40) | 17.69 (9.98) | 19.90 (11.96) | 24.32 (12.45) | 24.87 (10.06) | 23.21 (11.55) |
| European Medium | 0.56 (0.50) | 0.60 (0.45) | 0.56 (0.47) | 0.56 (0.46) | 0.56 (0.46) | 0.55 (0.47) |
| Dualism | 37.66 (17.34) | 42.12 (16.23) | 39.22 (15.78) | 38.93 (17.06) | 35.06 (17.84) | 33.38 (19.00) |
| Secondary Enrollment | 28.07 (21.29) | 20.39 (16.39) | 23.36 (17.27) | 23.45 (16.78) | 28.60 (20.13) | 35.03 (26.02) |
| Population Increase | 25.48 (6.30) | 29.11 (4.30) | 28.60 (4.81) | 26.77 (4.94) | 24.71 (5.62) | 23.53 (6.14) |
| British Colony | 0.35 (0.47) | | | | | |
| Later Independence | 5.43 (5.59) | | | | | |

in income inequality as the shift from high fertility and high mortality to low fertility and low mortality reduces inequality because countries with high birth rates have large numbers of young, nonworking individuals with no income (Williamson 1991). This is measured with natural population growth rate, or the crude birth rate minus the crude death rate; data come from the World Bank (2011). Table 2.1 shows a sizable increase in secondary enrollments while dualism and population growth rates decrease. All three categories show relatively large standard deviations.

*Estimation Procedure*

Individual observations are clustered by country, and this means that observations within clusters are likely to be more similar than observations from different clusters. Where this is the case, as it is here, heterogeneity bias arises and standard regression techniques are inefficient. A random-effects regression model is used and an autoregressive (AR[1]) correction is implemented (Baltagi and Wu 1999).

*Results*

Table 2.2 presents results. Model 1 is the baseline model, with only control variables. Dualism has a significant positive impact on inequality, as expected, which persists across all models. The baseline model performs somewhat poorly, however, because this group of less developed countries is moving through the uppermost part of Kuznets curve where the trend in inequality is relatively flat.

Model 2 adds the dummy for European language as medium of instruction to the baseline. This variable has a significant and positive impact on inequality, and the coefficient is large. If two countries had comparable values for dualism, secondary enrollments, and population growth, but one used a European medium of instruction and the other did not, this model would predict a Gini coefficient thirteen points higher in the former.

Model 3 adds only percent of periods devoted to European languages and finds it has no significant effect on inequality (nor does it in any model). Thus, the expectation that less time spent teaching these languages would be associated with higher inequality is not supported.

Model 4 adds both the percent of periods and dummy for medium of instruction to the baseline model. Percent of periods has no significant effect, while European medium significantly increases inequality. Although Model 2 shows

### Table 2.2 Random-Effects Regression Models with Income Inequality as Dependent Variable (*N* = 119)

|  | Model 1 | Model 2 | Model 3 | Model 4 | Model 5 | Model 6 | Model 7 |
|---|---|---|---|---|---|---|---|
| Dualism | .214**<br>(.091) | .195**<br>(.093) | .219**<br>(.092) | .199**<br>(.085) | .222**<br>(.091) | .182**<br>(.090) | .157**<br>(0.06) |
| Secondary Enrollments | .049<br>(.082) | .024<br>(.081) | .024<br>(.081) | .121<br>(.096) | .018<br>(.082) | .023<br>(.078) | .129<br>(.084) |
| Population Increase | .187<br>(.290) | .184<br>(.287) | .153<br>(.290) | .137<br>(.286) | .077<br>(.295) | .089<br>(.286) | .020<br>(.274) |
| European Medium |  | 13.237**<br>(5.851) |  | 13.107**<br>(3.064) |  |  | 13.515**<br>(3.335) |
| Percent of Periods |  |  | –.116<br>(.137) | –.179<br>(.118) | –.041<br>(.154) | –.131<br>(.130) | –.155<br>(.082) |
| British Colony |  |  |  |  | 3.656<br>(.509) |  | 1.572<br>(2.91) |
| Later Independence |  |  |  |  |  | .510*<br>(0.285) | .517**<br>(.262) |
| Constant | 30.223***<br>(9.593) | 27.548***<br>(10.475) | 34.068***<br>(10.576) | 33.005***<br>(8.938) | 33.055**<br>(10.662) | 35.137***<br>(10.282) | 33.875***<br>(9.201) |
| R² | 0.15 | 0.36 | .016 | 0.36 | 0.22 | 0.30 | 0.40 |
| Rho | 0.32 | 0.32 | 0.32 | 0.32 | 0.32 | 0.32 | 0.31 |

*Notes:* All two-tailed tests.
\* indicates significance at p < 0.10
\*\* indicates significance at p < 0.05
\*\*\* indicates significance at p < 0.01

that percent of instructional time is insignificant, there is a positive correlation between the two main independent variables (0.614, significant at the p < 0.05 level) because the medium of instruction is a subject to which considerable time is devoted. However, the effects of using the European language as a medium remain even when controlling for the percent of periods spent studying it. This suggests that even spending larger amounts of time teaching this subject does not make up for the impact of using it as a medium of instruction. Although an extended discussion of this follows, note that the coefficient for the European medium remains quite large in all models.

Model 5 tests for colonizer-specific effects and finds that former British colonies do not differ significantly in their rates of inequality compared to others. Whatever differences remain between school systems built by different colonizers, they do not seem to have an effect on inequality. This variable also captures, to a large extent, the effect of what language is taught; former British colonies in Africa all teach English (although not all countries that teach English are former British colonies). One might argue that because English is much more widely spoken globally than French or Portuguese, English language skills might have a different impact on wages, but this does not seem to be the case. (Analyses not shown use French colonies as the reference category and results remain insignificant.)

Model 6 adds a dummy for recent independence and finds a positive effect on inequality for countries that emerged from colonization later, although it is significant only at a relaxed level (p < 0.10). This will be touched on again shortly, but the cases that make up the late-independence group indicate that procolonial elites and settlers did delay independence.

Model 7 is a saturated model with all variables included. Dualism significantly increases inequality, as in other models. Again, percent of periods has no effect, but using European languages as a medium of instruction has a positive sign and a large coefficient; holding all the other variables in this model constant, the difference between using a European language as the medium of instruction is more than thirteen points on the Gini coefficient. Late independence again has a significant positive effect, and there is no effect of the colonizer here. Note that Model 7 has the largest r-square of any model in Table 2.2.

## Discussion

The use of European languages as the medium of instruction has a significant positive association with inequality in this group of African countries. Student achievement is lower where there is a mismatch between the language of instruction and the language spoken in the home; where students are unable to learn a language in the first few years of schooling, that language's continued use blocks further progress and diminishes prospects for social mobility (Alidou et al. 2006). Indeed, there is a negative and significant correlation between secondary-school enrollment and the use of European medium in the data here (–0.655, significant at the p < 0.05 level). Given the high levels of linguistic diversity in Africa, many individuals grow up speaking a language that is not widely spoken and this means they will likely have to learn at least one other African language and that the European language may be their third or possibly fourth (Laitin 1992).

This linguistic barrier to learning is distributed in terms of social characteristics that are already salient bases of inequality. Languages with fewer speakers are associated with ethnic groups that come from isolated and underdeveloped regions (Smits, Huisman, and Kruijff 2008) and there is variation in the extent to which different regional or ethnic groups have participated in modern schooling (Foster 1980). Variation also exists in the quality of education between schools, and the low end of the distribution in Africa is very low in absolute terms: these schools lack basic resources such as textbooks and have poorly trained teachers, and the quality of foreign-language teaching may be especially questionable (Fishman, Conrad, and Rubal-Lopez 1996). Students from rural areas or lower socioeconomic backgrounds are likely to attend such low-quality schools while students from urban areas or higher socioeconomic backgrounds are likely to attend better schools (Buchmann and Hannum 2001).

Children from elite groups and students who are successful in learning these languages get substantial exposure where such languages are used as media of instruction, further increasing the chances that they will be able to realize the benefits that come with knowing the language. The retention of European languages means these school systems not only serve the interests of some groups to the exclusion of others, but because school systems are run by the state these policies amount, in effect, to a transfer of resources from families whose children are unable to learn the languages and complete school to families of children that are. Moreover, there is evidence that elites actively support the use of European languages as media of instruction with the understanding that this will limit access to schooling for many students (Brock-Utne 2001; Watson 1994).

This line of argument links to the finding that late independence is associated with higher inequality, as it was argued that independence was delayed by procolonial elites. Looking at the history of decolonization in places such as Botswana, Lesotho, Malawi, and Uganda, indigenous groups allied with colonial administrations seem to have been important while in Algeria, Kenya, Zambia, and Zimbabwe, it appears that European settlers may have been more important in delaying independence (Springhill 2001). The last two cases are particularly noteworthy in that they had apartheid-like regimes in which European elites attempted to prevent independence as well as block access to the schools of white settlers where the quality of instruction in European languages was much higher. Although independence did eventually come, it was delayed until the mid-1960s, and for much of the population access to English was restricted for decades (Scarritt 1971).

## Conclusion

In a longer historical perspective, the expansion of the European world-system—both directly through colonization and indirectly through nationalism and the spread of other institutions—explains much (although not all) of which languages have been incorporated into national school curricula. At the global level, this same subset of European languages—English in particular—is most commonly used by international organizations. This means that actors in the periphery are likely to have to use a core language to communicate globally and this shifts much of the cost of the international communication order—teaching and learning one of these few languages—to school systems of states (mostly those in the periphery) where these languages are not widely spoken.

How these costs manifest themselves was taken up with a narrower investigation of European languages in Africa. The insertion of European languages into African school systems as the media of instruction becomes a barrier to continued schooling for a significant portion of the population. Students from lower socioeconomic groups, who are likely to attend lower-quality schools and be learning these languages as their third or fourth ones, will have trouble progressing through school. In this way peripheral elites are able to reproduce their own advantage at the national level by subsidizing the education of their children and limiting competition and social mobility. These education policies also, simultaneously, re-create the possibility for linkages to actors in the core. Indeed, the positive association between delayed independence and inequality suggests the machinations of just such a procolonial elite.

World-system processes mean that the languages of core states are widely studied in peripheral countries. These education policies, then, link global-level patterns of inequality to national patterns. Indeed, a fundamental insight that follows from taking the global system of interacting societies as the unit of analysis is that dynamics that appear to be internal to national societies are constituted, often to a large degree, by the dynamics of the world-system.

## References

Alderson, Arthur S., and Francois Nielsen. 2002. "Globalization and the Great U-Turn: Income Inequality Trends in 16 OECD Countries." *American Journal of Sociology* 107: 1244–1299.

Alidou, Hassan, Aliou Boly, Birgit Brock-Utne, Yaya Satina Diallo, Kathleen Heugh, and Ekkehard H. Wolff. 2006. *Optimizing Learning and Education in Africa: The Language Factor*. Libreville, GA: Association for the Development of Education in Africa.

Altbach, Philip G. 1991. "The Distribution of Knowledge in the Third World: A Case Study in Neocolonialism." In *Education and the Colonial Experience*, edited by Philip G. Altbach and Gail P. Kelly, 229–252. New York: Advent Books.

Anderson, Benedict. 1983. *Imagined Communities*. New York: Verso.

Baltagi, Badi H., and Ping X. Wu. 1999. "Unequally Spaced Panel Data Regression with AR(1) Disturbances." *Econometric Theory* 15, no. 6: 814–823.

Barro, Robert J. 1991. "Economic Growth in a Cross Section of Countries." *Quarterly Journal of Economics* 106, no. 2: 407–443.

Benavot, Aaron. 2004. *A Global Study of Intended Instructional Time and Official School Curricula, 1980–2000*. Background paper prepared for Education of All Global Monitoring Report 2005, UNESCO.

Brock-Utne, Birgit. 2001. "Education for All—in Whose Language?" *Oxford Review of Education* 27, no. 1: 115–134.

Buchmann, Claudia, and Emily Hannum. 2001. "Education and Stratification in Developing Countries: A Review of Theories and Research." *Annual Review of Sociology* 27: 77–102.

Burkholder, Mark A., and Lyman L. Johnson. 1990. *Colonial Latin America*. Oxford: Oxford University Press.

Chase-Dunn, Christopher. 1989. *Global Formation: Structures of the World-Economy*. Cambridge, MA: Blackwell.

Coyne, Gary. 2013. "Causes and Consequences of Second Language Education: A Global Analysis from 1980 to the Present." PhD diss., University of California, Riverside.

Crystal, David. 2003. *English as a Global Language*. Cambridge: Cambridge University Press.

de Swaan, Abram. 2001. *Words of the World*. Cambridge: Polity.

Fishman, Joshua A., Andrew W. Conrad, and Alma Rubal-Lopez. 1996. *Post-Imperial English: Status Change in Former British and American Colonies, 1940–1990*. Berlin: Mouton de Gruyter.

Food and Agricultural Organization of the United Nations (FAOUN). 2009. "FAOSTAT Online Statistical Service." FAOUN. http://faostat.fao.org.

Foster, Philip. 1980. "Education and Inequality in Sub-Saharan Africa." *Journal of Modern African Studies* 18, no. 2: 201–236.

Grant, Nigel. 1983. "Linguistic and Ethnic Minorities in the USSR: Educational Policies and Developments." In *Soviet Education in the 1980s*, edited by J. J. Tomiak, 24–49. New York: St. Martin's Press.

Henige, David. 1970. *Colonial Governors from the Fifteenth Century to the Present*. Madison: University of Wisconsin Press.

Kelly, Gail P. 1991. "Colonialism, Indigenous Society, and School Practices: French West Africa and Indochina, 1918–1938." In *Education and the Colonial Experience*, edited by Philip G. Altbach and Gail P. Kelly, 9–32. New York: Advent Books.

Laitin, David D. 1992. *Language Repertoires and State Construction in Africa*. Cambridge: Cambridge University Press.

Lewis, Paul M., Gary F. Simons, and Charles D. Fennig, eds. 2013. *Ethnologue: Languages of the World*. 17th ed. Dallas, TX: SIL International.

Mazrui, Ali A., and Alamin M. Mazrui. 1998. *The Power of Babel: Language and Governance in the African Experience*. Chicago: University of Chicago Press.

Myers-Scotton, Carol. 1993. "Elite Closure as a Powerful Language Strategy: The African Case." *International Journal of the Sociology of Language* 103, no. 1: 149–163.

Nettle, Daniel. 1999. *Linguistic Diversity*. Oxford: Oxford University Press.

Ostler, Nicholas. 2005. *Empires of the Word: A Language History of the World*. New York: Harper Perennial.

Phillipson, Robert. 1992. *Linguistic Imperialism.* Oxford: Oxford University Press.

Roberts, Andrew. 2006. *A History of the English Speaking Peoples since 1900.* New York: Harper Perennial.

Scarritt, James R. 1971. "Elite Values, Ideology, and Power in Post-Independence Zambia." *African Studies Review* 14, no. 1: 31–54.

Simpson, Andrew. 2008. "Introduction." In *Language and National Identity in Africa,* edited by Andrew Simpson, 1–25. Oxford: Oxford University Press.

Smits, Jeroen, Janine Huisman, and Karine Kruijff. 2008. "Home Language and Education in the Developing World." Background paper prepared for the Education for All Global Monitoring Report 2009. http://unesdoc.unesco.org/images/0017/001787/178702e .pdf.

Solt, Frederick. 2009. "Standardizing the World Income Inequality Database." *Social Science Quarterly* 90, no. 2: 231–242.

Springhill, John. 2001. *Decolonization since 1945.* New York: Palgrave.

Walter, Henriette. 1993. *French Inside Out: The Worldwide Development of the French Language in the Past, Present and the Future.* New York: Routledge.

Watson, Keith. 1994. "Caught between Scylla and Charybdis: Linguistic and Educational Dilemmas Facing Policy-Makers in Pluralist States." *International Journal of Educational Development* 14, no. 3: 321–337.

Williamson, Jeffrey G. 1991. *Inequality, Poverty, and History: The Kuznets Memorial Lectures.* Cambridge, MA: Basil Blackwell.

World Bank. 2011. *World Development Indicators.* Washington, DC: World Bank.

## Notes

1. Arabic, Chinese, Swahili, Malaysian, and German are among the few other languages studied in multiple countries; a number of others are studied to some extent in two adjacent countries. However, the vast majority of languages are not formally studied in schools anywhere.

2. There are two major counterexamples. First, there are languages like Arabic and Chinese that were not spread by the expansion of the European world-system, although these two were associated with the cores of other world-systems. Second, there are European colonizers—like the Germans and Italians—whose languages are not studied in their former colonies.

3. These states are Algeria, Angola, Benin, Botswana, Burkina Faso, Burundi, Cape Verde, Central African Republic, Egypt, Gabon, The Gambia, Ghana, Guinea, Kenya, Lesotho, Madagascar, Malawi, Mauritania, Morocco, Mozambique, Namibia, Niger, Rwanda, Senegal, Sierra Leone, Sudan, Swaziland, Tanzania, Togo, Tunisia, Uganda, Zambia, and Zimbabwe.

# 3

# POLITICAL PROMINENCE AND THE WORLD-SYSTEM

## CAN POLITICAL GLOBALIZATION COUNTER CORE HEGEMONY?

**Lindsay Marie Jacobs and Ronan Van Rossem**

**Abstract**

The ongoing globalization of political relations has raised the question of whether integration in the international political scene could enhance the power and influence of smaller and poorer nations. This chapter examines whether integration in the world polity constitutes a valid strategy for noncore states to gain economic prominence in the world-system. This question is subdivided into two research questions: (1) to what extent are political and economic prominence independent of each other, and (2) can political prominence contribute to gains in economic prominence? The structure of international import and export networks was compared to international networks of diplomatic relations and intergovernmental organization (IGO) membership between 1965 and 2005. Additionally, a multilevel growth curve model was estimated to analyze the impact of political prominence on economic mobility. Our results show that, though they are interrelated, considerable autonomy exists between the political and economic dimensions of the world-system. Moreover, political prominence can lead to increased economic prominence, especially for countries in the sub-top of the economic spectrum.

## Introduction

The rise of certain semiperipheral countries has induced an ever-increasing amount of academic attention focused on alleged changes in the world-system (e.g., Glosny 2010; Layne 2009). These countries, commonly referred to by a range of acronyms and nicknames—the BRICs (Brazil, Russia, India, and China), the MIST (Mexico, Indonesia, South Korea, and Turkey), the next eleven, or the outreach five—are expected to continue on a rise to power that could undermine the hegemony of the traditionally core countries, especially the United States (Layne 2009). The emergence of these "rising powers" has prompted questions concerning their ability to undermine stratification in the world-system, and thus to overcome structural inequalities and lead to a more equitable world in the long run. Evidence suggests that certain semiperipheral climbers, such as Brazil, India, and South Korea, relied heavily on political integration to facilitate their economic rise (Dent 2000; Harris 2005; Hart and Jones 2011). Likewise, research on the world polity has found a continued decline in inequality (Beckfield 2008; Boli, Loya, and Loftin 1999). World polity scholars emphasize the growing importance of international organizations and argue that "the structure of the world polity is progressing towards a relatively flat structure, as all states, especially those in poor countries, integrate into the world polity at a faster rate" (Beckfield 2008, 422). This political integration could constitute a source of power to noncore countries that is relatively autonomous from the economic mechanisms underlying the reproduction of the world-system, and could undermine its hierarchical structure in the long run. Hence, this chapter examines whether integration in the world polity constitutes a valid strategy for noncore states to gain economic prominence in the world-system. We thus question (1) to what extent political and economic prominence are independent of each other, and (2) whether political prominence can contribute to gains in economic prominence.

## Theoretical Framework

The world-system paradigm is characterized by its holistic nature, in which the world-system is defined as "all of the economic, political, social and cultural relations among the people of the earth" (Chase-Dunn and Grimes 1995, 389). Political, economic, and military relations are thus taken into account in explaining the structure and evolution of the world-system and are considered to be interrelated and interdependent (Chase-Dunn and Grimes 1995; Chase-Dunn and Hall 1993; Wallerstein 1974). Likewise, Chase-Dunn and Grimes (1995, 389) state that "the world-system is not just 'international relations' or the 'world market.' It is the whole interactive system, where the whole is greater than the sum of its parts." The hierarchical structure of the world-system is, however, fundamentally driven by the international division of labor (IDL) (Arrighi 1999; Chase-Dunn and Grimes 1995; Maoz 2011; Robinson 2011; Wallerstein 1974). A country's role in the IDL determines its position in the core, semiperiphery, or periphery. It is the systematic, institutionalized, and generalized nature of dependency that limits the opportunities of countries in the periphery, reproduces inequalities in the system, and is reflected in the structure of the relations among countries.

Upward mobility can be achieved by certain countries, but this does not undermine the stratified structure of the world-system. Rather, the logic inherent in the reproduction of the world-system and countries' position in the IDL enables mobility. As less profitable production processes are downgraded from the core to countries at lower positions in the IDL, certain countries (especially in the semiperiphery) may experience upward mobility. However, these benefits do not accrue equally to all countries in the world-system and core dominance is maintained by its ability to constantly shift to new and more innovative production processes. The presence of such mobility has been confirmed by several scholars, though debate remains regarding the magnitude of the phenomenon (Babones 2005; Clark 2010; Clark and Beckfield 2009; Kim and Shin 2002; Mahutga 2006; Mahutga and Smith 2011; Smith and White 1992). In sum, mobility is seen as "an important feature that sustains the capitalist world economy" (Clark and Beckfield 2009, 18) and thus aids the reproduction of old forms of structural inequality.

As the core dominates not only economic but also political and military relations in the world-system, these dimensions contribute to the reproduction of the exploitative processes of the semiperiphery by the core (Boswell and Chase-Dunn 2000; Chase-Dunn and Grimes 1995; Galtung 1971). Consequently, it will be very difficult for noncore countries to increase their political influence and power. Core countries can reinforce their political dominance by forming new IGOs, by dominating the existing ones, or even by excluding less powerful countries (Beckfield 2003). This prevents noncore countries from increasing their prominence in the world polity. Moreover, even if noncore countries succeed in attaining a more prominent position in the world polity, this does not necessarily provide them with influence or power gains. Political prominence may be ineffective when countries lack the economic clout to back it up. Integration into the world polity could therefore reinforce the exploitation of the noncore by rendering these countries even more exposed to policy scripts that benefit the core (Boswell and Chase-Dunn 2000). Additionally, as it is extremely difficult for noncore states to attain political-influence gains, political globalization will not lead to economic upward mobility. The political dominance of the core will reproduce and possibly reinforce the reproduction of inequality in the world-system.

Certain scholars studying the world-system elaborate on a multidimensional conceptualization of the core/periphery hierarchy (e.g., Chase-Dunn 1998; Kentor 2000; Kick and Davis 2001; Snyder and Kick 1979; Van Rossem 1996). Chase-Dunn (1998, 215) argues that the core/periphery hierarchy may be multidimensional and calls for more research on the relationships between the economic and political (and military) power/dependence relations. Babones (2005, 35) distinguishes between the division of the world-economy into discrete zones and status in the world-system, or "a state's ability to project its will in the global arena." He follows Chase-Dunn in stating that the latter is a more continuous and multidimensional phenomenon. Others acknowledge that noneconomic networks may be relevant in predicting a variety of (more noneconomic) outcomes in the world-system (Clark and Beckfield 2009). Some states will thus rely more on economic power for global "status" or prominence, while others rely more on political and/or military power (Babones 2005; Clark and Beckfield 2009; Kick and Davis 2001; Snyder and Kick 1979; Van Rossem 1996). It follows from this that a country's degree of power in the "global arena" can flow forth from its combined position in these various power networks, and countries' positions in these networks can vary substantially. This argument does not contradict the fact that a country's position in the IDL is an important determinant of power in the world-system, nor does it refute that core countries have a considerable impact on the world polity. However, certain noncore countries could be able to draw on political resources to project their will in the world-system, despite their lower level of economic might. In this case, countries will be able to attain a more prominent political position than would be expected based on their degree of economic dominance. These power networks must, then, be relatively autonomous and follow their own logic to a certain extent, though this does not imply that they are completely independent. This raises questions regarding the fungibility of the power-conversion process and the degree to which economic power can stem from other power sources. The use of political resources to attain a more prominent position in the economic hierarchy may undercut the economic mechanisms that reproduce the stratified structure of the world-system, thereby challenging the persistence of inequalities in the system in the long run.

This could happen in various ways. Some authors stress the increased political integration of countries in the world polity and the more equal distribution of political power (e.g., Boli, Loya, and Loftin 1999; Meyer et al. 1997). Research shows that though the core dominates the interstate networks of IGOs and that their polity scripts subsequently serve core interests, this dominance is declining (Beckfield 2003; 2008). Beckfield (2003, 404) found that the core dominance of IGOs has decreased over time. His "conflict model" sees (multilateral) integration into the world polity as a means for noncore states to expand their influence on global policy and decisions, including the economic, with the aim of securing and improving their "symbolic and material interests." This is backed up by findings that substantial trade benefits were reaped between states sharing joint membership in both economic and sociocultural IGOs (Ingram, Robinson, and Busch 2005). Evidence from global events also suggests that certain noncore countries have been able to increase their weight in the world polity (Harris 2005; Hart and Jones 2011). Brazil and India, for instance, the least economically prominent of the BRIC countries, rely heavily on their political integration to promote opportunities for developing nations. They pursue this through a combination of regional and south-south cooperation, and cooperation among the BRIC nations. This has allowed them to gain considerable influence in regional organizations and they have been able in some cases to significantly restructure existing ones or even create new ones, such as UNASUR (the Union of South American Nations) (Harris 2005; Hart and Jones 2011). An equally important strategy has been to form political power blocks of developing nations within multilateral institutions. Both Brazil and India played a leading role in the creation of the G-20. These strategies also provide them with considerable power and influence within smaller and developing nations (Hart and Jones 2011). The enhanced weight of certain noncore countries in the world polity could be seen in Brazil's World Trade Organization victory over the United States concerning the latter's subsidies to cotton farmers, and over the European Union concerning sugar subsidies, both of which were harmful to poorer and developing nations (Harris 2005).

Integration could also impact countries' economic prominence through more bilateral mechanisms. Network studies of the world-system have highlighted how diplomatic relations are opportunities to influence domestic (economic) policy and may facilitate (preferential) trade agreements and constitute an important form of information flow (Kick and Davis 2001; Snyder and Kick 1979). South Korea, for instance, has long relied on the United States' relational and systemic support for its economic rise, as a result of the Cold War geography (Dent 2000; Wallerstein 1997). Though debate exists concerning the effects of this South Korean strategy (Dent 2000), it serves here as an example of how regional-strategic considerations and economic diplomacy can impact countries' domestic economic policy and sustain trade relations.

Finally, we expect the impact of political integration on economic prominence to differ according to a country's role in the world-system. As discussed, upward mobility has especially been found for countries in the semiperiphery, these being particularly flexible in adapting to global economic downturn (e.g., Kick and Davis 2001; Terlouw 1993; Wallerstein 1976). Previous research (Jacobs and Van Rossem 2014) showed that political globalization was strongest for the core, but that the semiperiphery was far more politically globalized than the periphery, and that countries in the semiperiphery shared a significant degree of political ties to each other. As the core presently dominates both political and economic relations, we expect its need and ability to employ political integration as a means of increasing economic prominence to be smaller than they are for the semiperiphery. Peripheral countries often lack both the basic potential to induce economic mobility and the resources to forge political relations with a large number of other countries. Therefore, they tend to establish representation in countries that are politically most important to them, most often core countries that use these political relations to their own benefit (Van Rossem 1996). Accordingly, economic exploitation will be reproduced and their ability to increase their economic position through political integration will be small. The semiperiphery, however, "possesses the strong motive and related potential for upward mobility in the world-system" (Arrighi and Drangel 1986; Chase-Dunn 1998; Kick and Davis 2001; Wallerstein 1976). We therefore expect the impact of political prominence on economic role in the world-system to be largest for countries in the semiperiphery.

## Methods and Operationalization

*Dependency Relations*

To capture the relations among countries, we compiled network data representing economic, political, and military dependencies between countries. The data were collected for all years 1965–2005. A tie from country A to country B implies that A is dependent on B, and thus that B has some power over A. The rationale for conceptualizing dependency relations was taken from Van Rossem (1996). Dependent and overseas territories and colonies were considered dependent on their mother country for diplomatic relations.

Economic relations were operationalized using import and export dependency. Country A is considered import or export dependent on country B when the respective flow exceeds one percent of A's gross domestic product (GDP). The rationale is that the importance of a trade flow depends on the overall size of a country's economy and the trade flow must be substantial for it to constitute a dependency relation. For instance, Panama will be much more dependent on a country it exports one million dollars of goods to than the United States will be for the same sum. The data are based on both the International Monetary Fund's *Direction of Trade Statistics* (IMF 2010a) and the Correlates of War "International Trade" dataset (Barbieri and Keshk 2012). The GDP data were obtained from the World Bank's World Development Indicators (World Bank 2011). Missing data were supplemented by the United Nations *Statistical Yearbook* (United Nations 2010) and the IMF's *International Financial Statistics* (IMF 2010b). Missing export flows were imputed from the corresponding import flow, and vice versa.

For political relations, we included data on diplomatic representation and joint memberships of IGOs. These are the most often included indicators of political prominence in the world polity (Snyder and Kick 1979; Van Rossem 1996), data for which are hard to come by. Though these relations cannot be said to measure political power in its entirety, they do approximate important dominance relations (or prominence) in the world polity. Diplomatic representation refers to the presence of an embassy of one country in another (Europa Publications 2011). These relations can influence power relations directly but they also constitute a proxy for a country's perceived importance in the world polity. Small or poor countries lack the resources to establish embassies in all countries with which they have diplomatic relations and will restrict themselves to establishing representation in countries that are politically most important to them. The presence of a diplomatic mission means a possibility of influencing policy in the host country. Whether it represents an outcome of other dependencies, a mechanism of dominance, or an attempt to avoid dependency or domination, the number of embassies in a country indicates the importance of that country in the global political system. Joint membership of intergovernmental organizations was operationalized as the number of joint IGO memberships of two countries divided by the number of IGO memberships of the sending country (Pevehouse, Nordstrom, and Warnke 2004).

*Hierarchy and World-System Structure*

**World-system position.** A country's position in the world-system was obtained from Jacobs and Van Rossem (2014). We used Hummell and Sodeur's (1987) triad-census based blockmodeling approach to derive a six-block solution—primary core, secondary core, primary semiperiphery, secondary semiperiphery, primary periphery, and secondary periphery—to which each country could be allocated for every year 1965–2005.

   **The continuous prominence measures** can be interpreted as proxies for dominance on the political and economic networks, covering important—though not all—aspects of political and economic power. The measures are also based on the triad censuses generated for the blockmodels, and were created as the first principal component of the relative triad censuses for all networks involved. Separate prominence indicators were generated for the economic and the political networks. Both indicators are standardized over the entire period studied. Economic mobility was operationalized as the change in economic prominence between t–1 and t. To make the tables more legible, the scores were multiplied by 1,000.

*Analyses*

The degree of autonomy between the economic and political hierarchies in the world-system was analyzed by running quadratic assignment procedure (QAP) correlations between the various economic and political networks. Pearson's correlations were run between the measures of economic and political prominence for each year.

   **Multilevel analyses.** A multilevel growth curve model was estimated to analyze the impact of political prominence on the change in economic prominence. Included in the analysis are time (both linear and quadratic), a country's political prominence the year before (t–1), and economic prominence in t–1 as a control variable. Moreover, interaction effects between political and economic prominence (linear and quadratic) in t–1 were included to capture the nonlinear benefits of political prominence at various levels of economic prominence.

# Results

## Hierarchy and Autonomy of Dimensions in the World-System

The question whether noncore countries can attain a structurally higher—or more prominent—position on the international power networks carries within it the debate as to whether the power dimensions of the world-system are relatively autonomous. The core dominance of political networks entails that newly developed political ties will mainly be between countries in the core and the semiperiphery, but not among countries within the semiperiphery. These ties will largely remain asymmetric from countries in the periphery to those in the core, focusing exclusively on a single or a few of the latter. The structure of the political networks will thus closely mirror that of the economic. Conversely, if noncore countries are able to attain a structurally higher position on the political networks, structural overlap between these dimensions will be lower and political and economic prominence will represent autonomous dimensions of the world-system. As a first step in comparing the structure of the political and economic networks, a blockmodel was created representing the hierarchically stratified nature of the world-system over time.

Figure 3.1 depicts the overall structure of the world-system, consisting of six blocks and remaining constant during 1965–2005. The thickness of the lines refers to the number of ties for which the interblock density is above average. The interblock densities confirm a hierarchically stratified three-tiered structure: core, semiperiphery, and periphery. Within each of the strata, however, a stronger and weaker group can be distinguished. These results confirm Galtung's (1971) notion of the feudal interaction structure. Periphery-periphery (P1 and P2) relations are largely absent, and periphery-core (C1 and C2) relations tend to be vertical, with countries in the periphery being dependent on those in the core. This is even more so for countries in the semiperiphery (SP1 and SP2), but they also have more relationships among themselves. As the political relations are more symmetrical, however, the political and economic relations do not perfectly mirror each other, suggesting that political relations can be established independently from the economic. Where there is little economic dependency within the semiperiphery, there is a certain amount of political dependency among them. Countries in the semiperipheries share membership in IGOs and diplomatic relations exist between countries within the first semiperiphery (SP1). Moreover, diplomatic relations are directed from the core blocks to the first and second periphery.

This certain degree of autonomy between the structure of the political and the economic networks is confirmed by the results of our QAP-correlation analysis in Table 3.1. Correlations between the economic and political networks are low in 1965 as well as in 2005, varying between 0.145 and 0.266 as minimum and maximum correlations.

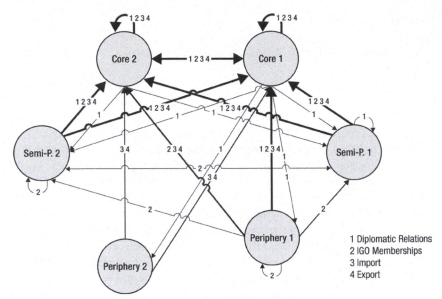

**Figure 3.1  Dependency Relations between the
Blocks by Network, Pooled 1965–2005**

World-systems analysis assumes a strong association between a country's economic and political prominence. The relative autonomy of the political and economic dimensions, however, implies that it is possible for countries to possess divergent degrees of prominence in both dimensions. As the structure of the political networks does not mirror that of the economic, a country's political prominence is not identical to its prominence in the economic network. Therefore, noncore countries should be able to integrate and attain a prominent position in the political networks while remaining economically dependent on the core. The correlation coefficient between political and economic prominence varies little over time (between 0.38 and 0.46), further backing up these findings of relative autonomy.

**Table 3.1  QAP Correlations between Political and
Economic Networks**

|  |  | *Diplomatic Relations* | *IGO Membership* |
|---|---|---|---|
| Export | 1965 | 0.213 *** | 0.145 *** |
|  | 2005 | 0.239 *** | 0.147 *** |
| Import | 1965 | 0.234 *** | 0.154 *** |
|  | 2005 | 0.266 *** | 0.175 *** |

*** $p \leq 0.001$.

The scatterplots in Figure 3.2 depict countries' prominence in the political and economic dimensions in 1965 and 2005. In both years, considerably more inequality exists in the economic than the political dimension. As world-systems analysis would expect, the primary core dominates both political and economic dimensions. However, countries assigned to the secondary core and—to some extent—the primary semiperiphery tend to have more political prominence than expected based on their economic prominence. This proves that it is possible for noncore countries to attain political prominence. Between 1965 and 2005, a group of countries, including Belgium, Sweden, South Korea, Thailand, and Turkey, increased their degree of both economic and political prominence.

*Political Prominence and Upward Economic Mobility*

As the cases of India and Brazil illustrate, certain countries have employed political leverage to realize economic growth. In this section we analyze whether this strategy can be generalized and thus whether a prominent position in international political networks can effectuate upward mobility in the world-economy. Our findings indicate a certain degree of autonomy between the dimensions of the world-system. However, the possibility remains that this structurally prominent position for noncore countries might be rendered void, as integration in political networks does not guarantee influence or power gains (Boswell and Chase-Dunn 2000). One could argue that though countries in a structurally more prominent position enjoy a higher degree of integration in the political networks, they are incapable of provoking change, due to their lack of economic clout to back up their demands. Accordingly, we must analyze whether political prominence could cause—and not only result from—economic prominence, substantiating political prominence's capability to provoke change in the world-system.

To analyze the impact of a country's degree of political prominence in t–1 on the change in economic prominence (or economic mobility) in t, we applied a multilevel growth curve model (Shek and Ma 2011), represented in Table 3.2. The negative linear effect of "time," in combination with its positive quadratic effect, indicates that overall changes in economic mobility have been curvilinear. Economic mobility decreased and was lowest in the middle of the period studied. Then, after 1983 the rate of economic mobility gradually accelerated again. The positive parameter for economic prominence in t–1 indicates that, on the average, more prominent countries experience more economic mobility than less prominent ones.

We then analyzed whether political prominence in t–1 can have a positive effect on a country's economic mobility between t–1 and t, controlling for its economic prominence in t–1 (Model 2). The positive parameter indicates that a country's prominence position in the political networks significantly predicted its change in economic prominence: on average, politically more prominent countries experienced higher increases in economic prominence than politically less prominent ones, even after controlling for economic prominence. To take into account the possibility of reversed causality, we ran additional models that analyzed the impact of economic prominence in t–1 on the change in political prominence between t–1 and t. Neither economic nor political prominence in t–1 were found to have a significant impact on a country's change in political prominence between t–1 and t.

To test the hypothesis that the impact of political prominence on economic mobility will be larger for countries in the semiperiphery, an interaction between political and economic prominence in t–1 was added in Model 3. As we expected the interaction to be curvilinear, both a linear and quadratic interaction term were included in the model. Both interaction terms are significant, confirming that the impact of political prominence varies by a country's degree of economic prominence, and that this effect is curvilinear (see Figure 3.3).

Our hypothesis that the impact of political prominence on economic upward mobility is largest for countries in the middle of the economic hierarchy is thus confirmed. As the core is already strongly politically and economically integrated, it follows that political prominence has a smaller impact on economic upward mobility for these core countries. Moreover, countries lowest on the spectrum occupy such low positions in the economic hierarchy that political integration is insufficient to gain upward economic mobility. As expected, the upper semiperiphery and the lower core have the most potential regarding economic prominence, and political integration is most beneficial for these countries.

## Conclusion

Our results confirm the world-systems argument that the political and economic dimensions are interrelated and that the core occupies a dominant position in each.

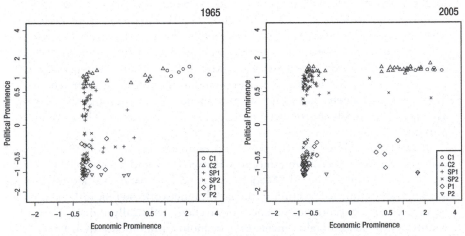

**Figure 3.2 Dispersion of Countries by Political and Economic Prominence, 1965–2005**

Table 3.2   The Impact of Political Prominence on Changes in Economic Prominence

| | Model 1 | | Model 2 | | Model 3 | |
|---|---|---|---|---|---|---|
| | Estimate | Std. Error | Estimate | Std. Error | Estimate | Std. Error |
| Intercept | 21.40 *** | 4.87 | 22.82 *** | 4.88 | 21.16 *** | 4.90 |
| Time | −2.28 *** | 0.54 | −2.37 *** | 0.54 | −2.35 *** | 0.54 |
| Time$^2$ | 0.06 *** | 0.01 | 0.06 *** | 0.01 | 0.06 *** | 0.01 |
| Economic Prom. in t–1 | 22.17 *** | 1.52 | 19.39 *** | 1.67 | 25.72 *** | 3.35 |
| Political Prom. in t–1 | | | 6.46 *** | 1.65 | 7.88 *** | 1.71 |
| Interaction Political & Economic Prom. in t–1 | | | | | 15.95 *** | 3.11 |
| Interaction Political Prom. in t–1 & (Economic Prom in t–1)$^2$ | | | | | −4.50 *** | 0.63 |
| Akaike's Information Criterion (AIC) | 97781.55 | | 97763.39 | | 97708.17 | |
| Schwarz's Bayesian Criterion (BIC) | 97795.44 | | 97777.28 | | 97722.06 | |

Dependent var.: Change in economic prominence between t and t–1. Significance (p ≤ 0.001).

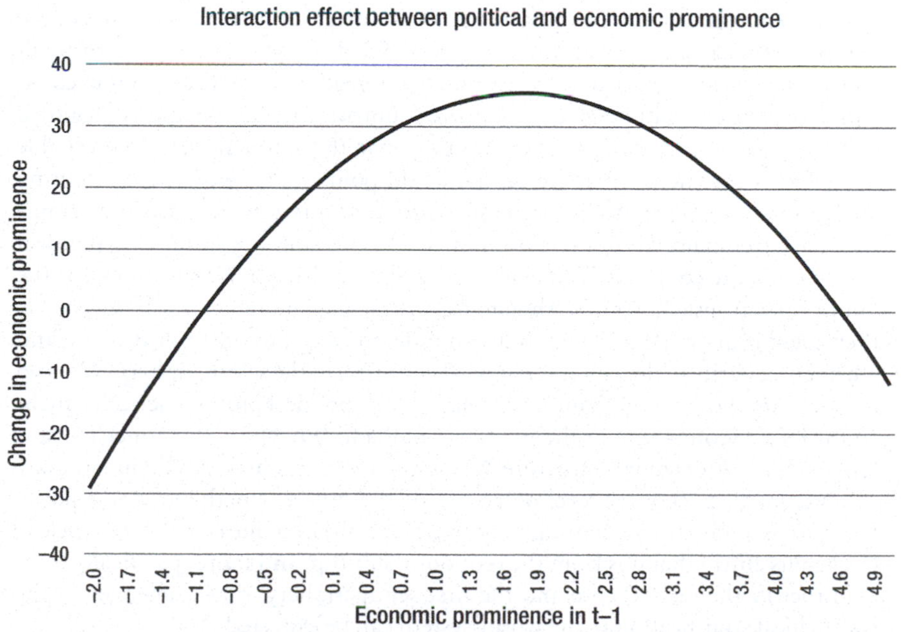

Interaction effect between political and economic prominence

Figure 3.3  The Impact of Political Prominence (in t–1) on Change in Economic Prominence (in t), by Degree of Economic Prominence in t–1

Both the political and economic dimensions of the world-system are hierarchically stratified and dominated by the core. However, the structure of these dimensions does not overlap entirely and considerable autonomy exists between them. Our findings provide evidence in favor of a multidimensional conceptualization of the world-system (Chase-Dunn 1998; Kentor 2000; Kick and Davis 2001; Snyder and Kick 1979; Van Rossem 1996). We argue that inequalities within the world-system are created and reproduced by a country's position in international political and economic networks and that hierarchy in the world-system flows forth from unequal, multidimensional power relations between countries. Noncore countries are able to attain a more prominent political position than forecast based on their level of economic prominence. Moreover, political prominence can be converted into higher economic prominence and especially countries in the sub-top of the economic spectrum are able to benefit from political integration. This suggests that integration into the world polity can indeed lead to influence and power gains for noncore countries. Political relations back up and reproduce the process of exploitation by the core, and can also serve as an instrument to improve noncore countries' roles in the world-system.

Attaining a more prominent position in global political networks can be a viable strategy for countries to improve their economic position in the world-system. In an ideal scenario, this would undermine the economic mechanisms underlying the reproduction stratification and inequality in the world-system. However, countries can follow various paths to integration in the world polity and it remains to be seen how profound the impact of political integration on the structure of the world-system can and will be in the long run. We discussed various ways through which bilateral and multilateral integration in international political networks could enhance economic prominence for noncore countries. The combination of regional and south-south cooperation between countries in the semiperiphery could enable them to increase their influence on the world polity and contribute to securing and maintaining policy scripts that safeguard their interests. Alternatively, countries pursue enhanced economic prominence by forming and improving political relations to core countries (bilaterally and within multilateral institutions), as the South Korean case illustrates. Though these strategies are not mutually exclusive, they could impact economic mobility in different ways, to different degrees, and are not necessarily in the best interest of all countries in the semiperiphery. We need research into the exact mechanisms through which political prominence can benefit countries' economic role in the world-system, and the effects these mechanisms have on the world-system's structure. Moreover, future research should incorporate the intermediary country-level outcomes of the different paths to world polity integration, such as democratization or trade-liberalization measures. Nevertheless, our results affirm that it is from the economic sub-top, and more specifically from countries in the second core and the first semiperiphery, that challenges to the hierarchical stratification in the world-system can be expected.

# References

Arrighi, Giovanni. 1999. "The Global Market." *Journal of World-Systems Research* 5, no. 2: 217–251.

Arrighi, Giovanni, and Jessica Drangel. 1986. "The Stratification of the World-Economy: An Exploration of the Semiperipheral Zone." *Review* (Fernand Braudel Center) 10, no. 1: 9–74.

Babones, Salvatore J. 2005. "The Country-Level Income Structure of the World-Economy." *Journal of World-Systems Research* 11, no. 1: 29–55.

Barbieri, Katherine, and Omar Keshk. 2012. "Correlates of War Project Trade Data Set Codebook: Version 2.01." Correlates of War. http://correlatesofwar.org (accessed April 13, 2012).

Beckfield, Jason. 2003. "Inequality in the World Polity: The Structure of International Organization." *American Sociological Review* 68, no. 3: 401–424.

———. 2008. "The Dual World Polity: Fragmentation and Integration in the Network of Intergovernmental Organizations." *Social Problems* 55, no. 3: 419–442.

Boli, John, Thomas A. Loya, and Teresa Loftin. 1999. "National Participation in World Polity Organization." In *Constructing World Culture: International Nongovernmental Organizations since 1875*, edited by John Boli and George M. Thomas, 50–78. Stanford, CA: Stanford University Press.

Boswell, Terry, and Christopher Chase-Dunn. 2000. *The Spiral of Capitalism and Socialism: Toward Global Democracy*. Boulder, CO: Lynne Rienner.

Chase-Dunn, Christopher. 1998. *Global Formation: Structures of the World-Economy*. Cambridge, MA: Blackwell.

Chase-Dunn, Christopher, and Peter Grimes. 1995. "World-Systems Analysis." *Annual Review of Sociology* 21, no. 1: 387–417.

Chase-Dunn, Christopher, and Thomas D. Hall. 1993. "Comparing World-Systems: Concepts and Working Hypotheses." *Social Forces* 71, no. 4: 851–886.

Clark, Rob. 2010. "World-System Mobility and Economic Growth." *Social Forces* 88, no. 3: 1123–1152.

Clark, Rob, and Jason Beckfield. 2009. "A New Trichotomous Measure of World-System Position Using the International Trade Network." *International Journal of Comparative Sociology* 50, no. 1: 5–38.

Dent, Christopher M. 2000. "What Difference a Crisis? Continuity and Change in South Korea's Foreign Economic Policy." *Journal of the Asia Pacific Economy* 5, no. 3: 275–302.

Europa Publications. 1965–2011. *The Europa World Yearbook*. London: Routledge.

Galtung, Johan. 1971. "A Structural Theory of Imperialism." *Journal of Peace Research* 8, no. 2: 81–117.

Glosny, Michael A. 2010. "China and the BRICs: A Real (but Limited) Partnership in a Unipolar World." *Polity* 42, no. 1: 100–129.

Hanneman, Robert A., and Mark Riddle. 2005. *Introduction to Social Network Methods*. University of California, Riverside. http://faculty.ucr.edu/~hanneman (accessed March 15, 2013).

Harris, Jeffrey. 2005. "Emerging Third World Powers: China, India and Brazil." *Race and Class* 46, no. 3: 7–27.

Hart, Andrew F., and Bruce D. Jones. 2011. "How Do Rising Powers Rise?" *Survival* 52, no. 6: 63–88.

Hummell, Hans J., and Wolfgang Sodeur. 1987. "Strukturbeschreibung von positionen in sozialen beziehungsnetzen [Description of the structure of positions in social networks]." In *Techniken der empirischen Sozialforschung. Band 1. Methoden der Netzwerkanalyse*, edited by Franz Urban Pappi, 280. München: R. Oldenbourg Verlag.

Ingram, Paul, Jeffrey Robinson, and Marc L. Busch. 2005. "The Intergovernmental Network of World Trade: IGO Connectedness, Governance, and Embeddedness." *American Journal of Sociology* 111, no. 3: 824–858.

International Monetary Fund (IMF). 2010a. *Direction of Trade Statistics (DOTS)*. Washington, DC: IMF.

———. 2010b. *International Financial Statistics (IFS)*. Washington, DC: IMF.

Jacobs, Lindsay M., and Ronan Van Rossem. 2014. "Globalization, Inequality and Development: Structural Changes in the World-System between 1965 and 2005." Working paper, Research Group POS+, Department of Sociology, Ghent University.

Kentor, Jeffrey. 2000. *Capital and Coercion: The Economic and Military Processes That Have Shaped the World Economy, 1800–1990*. New York: Garland Publishing.

Kick, Edward L., and Byron L. Davis. 2001. "World-System Structure and Change." *American Behavioral Scientist* 44, no. 10: 1561–1548.

Kim, Sangmoon, and Eui-Hang Shin. 2002. "A Longitudinal Analysis of Globalization and Regionalization in International Trade: A Social Network Approach." *Social Forces* 81, no. 2: 445–471.

Layne, Christopher. 2009. "The Waning of U.S. Hegemony—Myth or Reality? A Review Essay." *International Security* 34, no. 1: 147–172.

Mahutga, Matthew C. 2006. "The Persistence of Structural Inequality? A Network Analysis of International Trade, 1965–2000." *Social Forces* 84, no. 4: 1863–1889.

Mahutga, Matthew C., and David A. Smith. 2011. "Globalization, the Structure of the World Economy and Economic Development." *Social Science Research* 40: 257–272.

Maoz, Zeev. 2011. *Networks of Nations: The Evolution, Structure and Impact of International Networks, 1816–2001*. New York: Cambridge University Press.

Meyer, John W., John Boli, George M. Thomas, and Francisco O. Ramirez. 1997. "World Society and the Nation State." *American Journal of Sociology* 103, no. 1: 144–181.

Pevehouse, John C., Timothy Nordstrom, and Kevin Warnke. 2004. "The COW-2 International Organizations, Dataset Version 2.3." *Conflict Management and Peace Science* 21, no. 2: 101–119.

Robinson, William I. 2011. "Globalization and the Sociology of Immanuel Wallerstein: A Critical Appraisal." *International Sociology* 26, no. 6: 723–745.

Shek, Daniel T. L., and Cecilia M. S. Ma. 2011. "Longitudinal Data Analyses Using Linear Mixed Models in SPSS: Concepts, Procedures and Illustrations." *Scientific World Journal* 11: 42–76.

Smith, David A., and Douglas R. White. 1992. "Structure and Dynamics of the Global Economy: Network Analysis of International Trade, 1965–1980." *Social Forces* 70, no. 4: 857–893.

Snyder, David, and Edward L. Kick. 1979. "Structural Position in the World System and Economic Growth, 1955–1970: Multiple-Network Analysis of Transnational Interactions." *American Journal of Sociology* 84, no. 5: 1096–1126.

Terlouw, Cornelius P. 1993. "The Elusive Semiperiphery: A Critical Examination of the Concept Semiperiphery." *International Journal of Comparative Sociology* 34, no. 12: 87–102.

United Nations. 1965–2010. *Statistical Yearbook.* New York: United Nations Statistics Division.

Van Rossem, Ronan. 1996. "The World System Paradigm as General Theory of Development: A Cross-National Test." *American Sociological Review* 61, no. 3: 508–527.

Wallerstein, Immanuel. [1974] 2011. *The Modern World-System.* Vol. 1. New York: Academic Press.

———. 1976. "Semiperipheral Countries and the Contemporary World Crisis." *Theory and Society* 3, no. 4: 461–483.

———. 1997. "The Rise of East Asia, or the World-System in the Twenty-First Century." Keynote address at the symposium "Perspective of the Capitalist World-System in the Beginning of the Twenty-First Century," January 23–24, Meiji Gakuin University, Japan.

World Bank. 2011. "World Development Indicators." Washington, DC: International Bank for Reconstruction and Development. http://data.worldbank.org/data-catalog/world-development-indicators/wdi-2011 (accessed December 23, 2011).

# 4

# FOREIGN INVESTMENT, POLITICAL CORRUPTION, AND INTERNAL VIOLENCE

## A STRUCTURAL ANALYSIS, 1970–1995

**Jeffrey Kentor and Matthew R. Sanderson**

### Abstract

Internal violence remains a significant impediment to development prospects in less developed countries. This chapter refines previous research on the relationship between economic globalization and internal conflict (see Kentor and Mielants 2007) by providing a more nuanced assessment of the role of foreign investment: specifically the impact of two related aspects of foreign investment—foreign investment concentration and foreign subsidiary concentration, both relatively new concepts of economic globalization. We empirically identify the causal paths linking these aspects of foreign investment to internal conflict over a long-term time horizon using a structural equation model that includes the mediating effect of political corruption. The results indicate that a high geographic concentration of ownership of foreign subsidiaries, referred to as foreign subsidiary concentration, raises internal violence through various causal pathways. First, foreign subsidiary concentration in 1970 increases levels of internal violence in 1985. This effect is magnified at high levels of foreign investment concentration, as indicated by a significant interaction of these two variables. Second, high levels of political corruption in 1985 increase internal violence in 1995. Third, foreign subsidiary concentration in 1970 has a direct positive impact on internal violence in 1995.

## Introduction

Internal political violence remains the predominant form of conflict in the world today (Wallensteen and Sollenberg 2001) and it continues to impede development prospects in less developed countries. Globally, the prevalence of internal conflicts has remained persistently above pre-1960 levels (Gurr 1989). Internal conflicts continue to exceed their pre-1960 levels in most regions of the world, including West Africa, North Africa, Central America, and South America, while East Africa, the Middle East, and South Central Asia continue to experience rising levels of internal conflict.

Scholars have long debated the consequences of globalization for development outcomes in less developed countries. Yet the implications of globalization for internal conflict within less developed countries have received much less attention (for exceptions see Barbieri and Reuveny 2005; Hegre, Gissinger, and Gleditsch 2003; Kentor and Mielants 2007). Where this relationship has been investigated, research provides only mixed results.

The purpose of this chapter is to empirically examine the relationship between foreign investment and internal conflict. It extends previous research in several respects. First, we develop and test more refined measures of foreign investment: foreign investment concentration and foreign subsidiary concentration. Second, we empirically identify the causal paths through which these aspects of foreign investment affect conflict, focusing on the role of political corruption. Third, compared to previous studies, we model the relationships over a long-term time period, which allows for any unintended consequences of integration to become more apparent. Finally, we contextualize our findings within a new theoretical framework that is broader than previous studies in this area.

## Background

Globalization is a form of economic interdependence among states that has been achieved through a series of market liberalizations across the world. As domestic markets have been liberalized, states have become much more tightly integrated into a global economy. The effects of global economic integration on internal political and economic outcomes have been the subject of a large and expanding research literature. We focus specifically on the relationship between foreign investment and internal political stability in less developed countries.

In general, the debate over whether global financial integration is on balance beneficial or detrimental to internal political outcomes in less developed countries has been pursued through two lines of inquiry. Proponents of financial integration contend that openness reduces internal conflict through several mechanisms (Fearon and Laitin 2003; Hegre, Gissinger, and Gleditsch 2003; Mason 2003; Sachs and Warner 1995). From this perspective, foreign investment provides the capital, knowledge, and access to modern technologies that are crucial for development. The liberalization of capital flows increases efficiency, which promotes aggregate increases in living standards in a virtuous cycle that reduces internal conflict and instability.

Critics of financial integration contend that liberalization increases internal conflict in less developed countries. From this perspective, financial integration further extends developed countries' control or influence in less developed countries. As foreign investment assumes a larger proportion of the domestic economy, it furthers uneven development within the economy (Bornschier and Chase-Dunn 1985; Dixon and Boswell 1996). The outcome is often a dual-sector (Nielsen and Alderson 1995) or disarticulated economy (Amin 1974) composed of an advanced modern sector oriented toward export markets and a relatively underdeveloped traditional agricultural-oriented sector—and lack of domestic linkages between them. By promoting uneven development, foreign investment dominance undermines development and promotes political instability (Boswell and Dixon 1990).

The mixed results of previous studies may be the result of a conceptualization problem. Both perspectives tend to operationalize financial integration as either foreign investment inflows or accumulated stocks of foreign investment capital. These measures are argued to represent the degree of financial openness in a country. However, the concept of openness may not adequately capture the impacts of financial integration on internal conflict. That is, it may not be openness to foreign investment per se, but the type or structure of openness to foreign investment that affects internal conflict. We utilize the concepts of foreign investment concentration and foreign subsidiary concentration in an attempt to refine and extend previous research on the question of how global financial integration affects political stability in less developed countries.

## The Structure of Foreign Investment

The impact of foreign investment on various aspects of development (i.e., economic growth, health, inequality) has been debated for more than forty years (Chase-Dunn 1975), with little consensus. This lack of agreement begins with the question of how to measure foreign investment. Scholars working within a modernization framework typically use inflows of foreign capital. They argue that these inflows provide capital and reflect a transfer of technology necessary for economic growth. Researchers from a dependency perspective argue that foreign capital dominance—the ratio of foreign capital to domestic (or total) capital (Dixon and Boswell 1996)—is a meaningful dynamic. They argue that foreign dominance of capital "disarticulates" the host economy, with a variety of negative consequences.

Kentor and Boswell (2003) argue that the reason for this four-decade-long impasse is that the question investigators were asking—"Is foreign investment good or bad?"—was an unanswerable one. They introduced a new aspect of foreign investment, foreign investment concentration, defined as the percentage of foreign investment stocks owned by firms headquartered in the largest single investing country. Their findings indicated that high levels of foreign investment concentration inhibited economic growth in less developed countries, while overall foreign capital dominance had little impact.

A second, related aspect of foreign investment is foreign subsidiary concentration, which refers to the percentage of foreign subsidiaries owned by corporations located in the same country. An example may be helpful. If, hypothetically, 75 of 100 foreign subsidiaries in Peru in 1970 were owned by corporations located in the United States, Peru would have a foreign subsidiary concentration of 75 percent. Foreign subsidiary concentration addresses the impact of the physical presence of foreign subsidiaries of multinational firms. This concept, first identified by Kentor (2005) is in some ways a more tangible aspect of foreign investment than foreign investment flows or stocks, given the physical location of foreign corporate executives who can interact at various levels with domestic corporate and government interests. Kentor and Jorgenson (2010) found that the number of foreign subsidiaries is positively related to economic growth in less developed countries, while high levels of foreign subsidiary concentration slow economic growth in these countries.

The concepts of foreign investment and subsidiary concentrations draw upon previous theorizing about the impact of trade dependency on development in less developed countries. Less developed countries with higher degrees of export-commodity concentration, where the largest proportions of exports were directed to a single importing country, were hypothesized to suffer lower levels of development (Galtung 1971; Hirschmann 1981). Higher levels of export-commodity concentration increased a less developed country's vulnerability to international market forces and facilitated uneven terms of trade with more powerful developed countries.

Foreign investment and subsidiary concentrations reflect the structure, or quality, of foreign investment in a host country. Compared to foreign capital penetration—an indicator of overall foreign capital—the concepts of foreign investment and subsidiary concentrations more explicitly specify the mechanisms through which foreign economic interests can influence the host country. We argue that countries with higher levels of foreign investment and/or subsidiary concentration confront a relatively integrated set of interests with ties to a single originating country. In these contexts, state actors are weakened vis-à-vis foreign capital and state autonomy is reduced, constraining the state's ability to implement policies that reflect the collective public will.

Using the concepts of foreign investment and subsidiary concentrations, it is possible to integrate insights from neoclassical and dependency theories into a coherent explanation of how financial integration impacts internal conflict. Neoclassical economic theory suggests that liberalization has distributional effects; some will benefit from opening and others will lose. With respect to trade, the Heckscher-Ohlin theory suggests that support for liberalization policies is associated with the relative distribution of the factors of production in the domestic economy. Specifically, more abundant factors of production will favor trade liberalization while more scarce factors will favor protectionist measures. When applied to foreign economic liberalization, the theory suggests that, in less developed countries, labor would favor foreign economic liberalization and domestic capital would promote policies that limit foreign economic liberalization, as capital is more scarce than labor. Domestic owners of capital oppose liberalization because in relatively closed economies, they can extract rents. Moreover, states use the revenue from trade barriers to support domestic industry. Foreign economic liberalization, however, reduces the ability of protectionists to extract rents. From this perspective, then, foreign economic liberalization may generate political instability because it redistributes the benefits of economic activity away from owners of relatively scarce factors toward owners of relatively abundant factors.

This tendency is further exacerbated by the existing power disparity between winners and losers. That is, the benefits of foreign economic liberalization for any particular individual will be relatively few because the group that stands to benefit is so large, but the costs will be distributed among a small group of elites. Thus, neoclassical economic theory suggests that foreign economic liberalization provides incentives for owners of domestic capital to prevent, or at least mitigate, the redistributive effects of foreign economic liberalization. One of the possible outcomes of foreign economic liberalization, then, is an increase in the level of corruption and collusion in the society as domestic capital owners and other elites whose power is threatened by liberalization act to limit its effects on their relative position. In this sense, owners of domestic capital are incentivized to *constrain* the openness of the domestic economy in an attempt to preserve their relative position in the domestic economy.

At this point, the structure of foreign economic liberalization becomes important. Although foreign economic liberalization theoretically is detrimental to domestic owners of capital, it also strengthens the power of domestic actors with connections to international capital and increases the influence of foreign capital in the domestic economy: "Increasing interdependence increases the weight of domestic actors with foreign ties, expands the array of interests likely to benefit from and demand greater openness of financial markets, and thus tilts the balance of power in a more internationalist direction" (Haggard and Maxfield 1996, 37). Here, the interests of domestic and foreign capital become more closely aligned. Where domestic capital owners confront a relatively concentrated foreign-investment structure, there is a greater opportunity to undertake collusion and corruption in an attempt to mitigate the deleterious effects of liberalization. The incentives work both ways: domestic capital has an incentive to constrain the degree of openness and foreign capital has an incentive to limit competition for resources within the domestic sphere. Both parties have an incentive to maintain high profit levels after liberalization. This context promotes corruption and other forms of collusion, which likely increases the potential for internal conflict and violence.

Neoclassical economic theory therefore provides a theoretical framework for understanding the relationship between foreign economic liberalization and internal conflict. However, incorporating the concept of foreign investment concentration from dependency theory enriches the explanatory framework. Foreign investment and subsidiary concentration variables provide a potential way out of the conundrum of why foreign economic liberalization is sometimes associated with positive development outcomes and other times is associated with less desirable outcomes, including internal conflict.

## Corruption and Internal Conflict

Corruption is the use of public resources for private gain (Jain 2001). It is associated with an array of deleterious social and economic outcomes (for reviews, see Montinola and Jackman 2002; Rose-Ackerman 1999), but among the most important is its destabilizing effects on social structures.

State legitimacy is fundamental to maintaining internal stability (Lipset 1994). Corruption, however, undermines state legitimacy; erodes confidence in democratic principles of accountability, transparency, and equality (Anderson and Tverdova 2003); and generates feelings of alienation and exclusion (Warren 2004). Higher levels of corruption indicate to citizens that the state is not a neutral party that serves the interest of the broader public, but is rather an institution to be used for private gain by those with power. As corruption becomes more pervasive, normative structures are altered to the extent to which corruption becomes commonly accepted as "the way things are done" (You and Khagram 2005, 154). In this context, impartial and rule-based principles of modern bureaucracy are violated, reducing the prospects for procedural and distributive fairness. Corruption therefore has the effect of undermining civil-society relations by reducing the level of interpersonal trust (Seligson 2006) and decreasing the level of satisfaction with the state (Tavits 2008).

The detrimental political effects of corruption can be compounded by its economic effects, which further promote instability and internal conflict. Corruption has been shown to reduce investment and slow the rate of economic growth (Mauro 1995; 1998), two factors that increase instability. Corruption creates a drag on growth by reducing economic efficiency (Ades and Di Tella 1996), undermining the state's capacity to promote growth by lowering the general level of economic activity with tax consequences, and reorienting the use of public revenues toward sectors represented by private interests (Ades and Di Tella 1996; Mauro 1995; Warren 2004). By reducing state capacity and undermining state legitimacy, corruption promotes political instability and internal conflict.

Kentor and Mielants (2007) provide the only previous empirical work exploring the impact of structural aspects of foreign investment on corruption and violence. They found, in a cross-national, lagged, dependent-variable regression model, that foreign subsidiary concentration increased both political corruption and violence in a sample of less developed countries.

## Methods, Data, and Model

We expand the previous work by Kentor and Mielants by including in the analyses an additional structural aspect of foreign investment, foreign investment concentration, along with interaction terms. Our basic hypothesis is that foreign investment and subsidiary concentrations will exacerbate political corruption, as detailed in the preceding discussion. Countries with high levels of both investment and subsidiary concentrations will experience higher levels of corruption and violence than countries high on only one concentration variable.

### Method

A structural equation model, shown in Figure 4.1, was estimated to identify the causal pathways by which our measures of foreign investment may impact internal violence in 1970–1995 for a sample of sixty-six less developed countries. A fully saturated model was estimated, and all exogenous variables were allowed to covary.

### Data

Exogenous variables include three aspects of foreign investment: foreign investment concentration, foreign subsidiary concentration, and total number of foreign subsidiaries, all around 1970. Data are taken from Kentor and Boswell (2003) and Kentor (2005). Other exogenous variables measured in 1970 include GDP per capita (logged) and total population. These data are taken from the World Bank (various years). Also included is Polity 2, a measure of democracy (Gurr 1989). Two multiplicative interaction terms are also included: foreign investment concentration × foreign subsidiary concentration and foreign subsidiary concentration × total foreign subsidiaries.

The two endogenous variables, political corruption and internal violence, are taken from the *International Country Risk Guide* (ICRG 2005). The ICRG defines political corruption as follows:

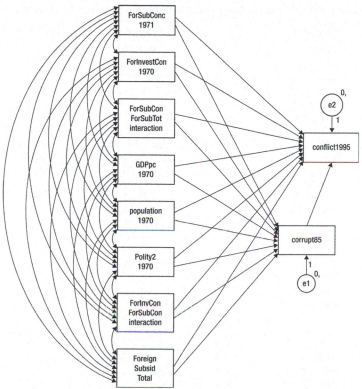

**Figure 4.1  Structural Equation Model of the Effect of Foreign Investment and Foreign Subsidiary Concentrations in 1970 on Political Corruption in 1985 and Internal Violence in 1995**

This indicator measures financial corruption, including demands for bribes and special payments associated with trade licensing, tax assessments, loans, and state protection. It also takes into account real or potential corruption such as patronage, nepotism, and other "questionable" relationships between business organizations and the state apparatus. (ICRG 2005)

Internal violence is defined as follows:

This is a measure of the level of political violence in the country. Countries with no armed opposition to [their] government and without arbitrary violence on the part of the government receive the highest score, while countries experiencing civil war receive the lowest score. (ICRG 2005)

It is important to note that higher scores on these two variables reflect lower levels of corruption and violence. Bivariate correlations are given in Table 4.1.

**Table 4.1  Correlations of Exogenous Variables in Structural Equation Model**

| Variable | | Variable | Correlation |
|---|:---:|---|---|
| GNPpc 70 | ↔ | POP 70 | –.167 |
| GNPpc 70 | ↔ | FSC 70 | .297 |
| POP 70 | ↔ | Polity 70 | –.039 |
| GNPpc 70 | ↔ | Polity 70 | .056 |
| POP 70 | ↔ | Polity 70 | .059 |
| Polity 70 | ↔ | FSC × FIC 70 | –.036 |
| POP 70 | ↔ | FSC × FIC 70 | .100 |
| GNPpc 70 | ↔ | FSC × FIC 70 | .006 |
| FSC × FIC 70 | ↔ | TFS 70 | .028 |
| Polity 70 | ↔ | TFS 70 | .092 |
| POP 70 | ↔ | TFS 70 | .372 |
| GNPpc 70 | ↔ | TFS 70 | .467 |
| FSC 70 | ↔ | TFS 70 | .145 |
| FSC 70 | ↔ | FIC 70 | .084 |
| GNPpc 70 | ↔ | FIC 70 | –.054 |
| POP 70 | ↔ | FIC 70 | –.251 |
| Polity 70 | ↔ | FIC 70 | .231 |
| FSC × FIC 70 | ↔ | FIC 70 | –.125 |
| TFS 70 | ↔ | FIC 70 | .024 |
| FIC 70 | ↔ | FSC × TFS 70 | –.039 |
| FSC 70 | ↔ | FSC × TFS 70 | –.364 |
| GNPpc 70 | ↔ | FSC × TFS 70 | .211 |
| POP 70 | ↔ | FSC × TFS 70 | .102 |
| Polity 70 | ↔ | FSC × TFS 70 | .084 |
| FSC × FIC 70 | ↔ | FSC × TFS 70 | .140 |
| TFS 70 | ↔ | FSC × TFS 70 | .487 |
| POP 70 | ↔ | FSC 70 | –.215 |
| FSC 70 | ↔ | FSC × FIC 70 | –.159 |

*Notes:* FIC 70 = foreign investment concentration 1970
FSC 70 = foreign subsidiary concentration 1970
GNPpc 70 = gross national product per capita 1970
Polity 70 = Polity 2 dataset 1970
POP 70 = total population 1970
TFS 70 = total number of foreign subsidiaries 1970

*Model*

In this fully saturated model, the two theoretically significant foreign investment variables—foreign investment and foreign subsidiary concentrations (along with control variables)—measured in 1970 impact the two endogenous variables: political corruption in 1985 and internal violence in 1995. Political corruption in 1985 affects internal violence in 1995.

**Table 4.2  Maximum Likelihood Estimates for the Structural Equation Model Presented in Figure 4.1**

|  |  |  | Unstd. Estimate | Std. Error | Critical Ratio | Std. Estimate |
|---|---|---|---|---|---|---|
| POP 70 | → | Corruption 1985 | −.008 | .114 | −.070 | −.011 |
| GNPpc 70 | → | Corruption 1985 | .510 | .197 | 2.591 | .421 |
| FSC 70 | → | Corruption 1985 | .016 | .009 | 1.847 | .303 |
| Polity 70 | → | Corruption 1985 | −.021 | .019 | −1.096 | −.133 |
| FSC × FIC 1970 | → | Corruption 1985 | .279 | .135 | 2.068 | .282 |
| TFS 70 | → | Corruption 1985 | .006 | .020 | .324 | .067 |
| FIC 70 | → | Corruption 1985 | .006 | .008 | .761 | .104 |
| FSC × TFS 70 | → | Corruption 1985 | .419 | .582 | .721 | .132 |
| FSC 70 | → | Violence 1995 | .060 | .018 | 3.348 | .525 |
| FIC 70 | → | Violence 1995 | .015 | .016 | .904 | .118 |
| FSC × FIC 1970 | → | Violence 1995 | .047 | 1.150 | .041 | .007 |
| GNPpc 1970 | → | Violence 1995 | 1.343 | .420 | 3.194 | .522 |
| POP 1970 | → | Violence 1995 | −.061 | .227 | −.271 | −.041 |
| Polity 70 | → | Violence 1995 | −.018 | .039 | −.452 | −.053 |
| FSC × FIC 70 | → | Violence 1995 | .537 | .284 | 1.890 | .255 |
| TFS 70 | → | Violence 1995 | .010 | .039 | .261 | −.050 |
| Corruption 1985 | → | Violence 1995 | .585 | .280 | 2.091 | .275 |
| $R^2$ |  |  |  |  |  |  |
| Corruption 1985 | .256 |  |  |  |  |  |
| Violence | .354 |  |  |  |  |  |

*Notes:* FIC 70 = foreign investment concentration 1970
FSC 70 = foreign subsidiary concentration 1970
GNPpc 70 = gross national product per capita 1970
Polity 70 = Polity 2 dataset 1970
POP 70 = total population 1970
TFS 70 = total number of foreign subsidiaries 1970

## Results

Several key findings emerge from the analysis, and are presented in Table 4.2. Foreign subsidiary concentration in 1970 increased political corruption in 1985, while foreign investment concentration and total foreign subsidiaries had no significant effect. The interaction of foreign investment and subsidiary concentrations in 1970 also increased corruption in 1985. The other interaction term of foreign subsidiary concentration × total foreign subsidiaries had no effect. Foreign subsidiary concentration also had a significant direct positive effect on internal violence in 1995. The interaction of foreign investment and foreign subsidiary concentrations in 1970 increased internal violence in 1995. As expected, political corruption in 1985 increased internal violence in 1995. The only other significant variable in the model is gross national product (GNP) per capita, which reduces both political corruption in 1985 and internal violence in 1995.

## Conclusion

This chapter examined the impact of two structural aspects of foreign investment—foreign subsidiary concentration and foreign investment concentration—on political corruption and internal violence in less developed countries. We argued that high levels of these variables exacerbate political violence, which in turn increases internal violence. Our hypotheses were partly supported by our empirical analyses. Results from our structural equation model indicated that foreign subsidiary concentration had direct positive effects on both political corruption and internal violence, as did the interaction of these two variables. We theorize that the interests of domestic and foreign capital in countries with relatively high levels of foreign economic concentration may coincide to limit both openness and competition in order to maintain high profits. It is also worth noting that countries high in economic concentration are likely to be weak states that lack the ability to restrain political corruption. The dominance of foreign corporations becomes a visible symbol of this corruption to the local population, increasing the likelihood of violence. Weak, oil-rich countries such as Nigeria are prime examples of these dynamics.

## References

Ades, Alberto, and Rafael Di Tella. 1996. "The Causes and Consequences of Corruption: A Review of Recent Empirical Contributions." *IDS Bulletin* 27, no. 2: 6–11.

Amin, Samir. 1974. "Accumulation and Development: A Theoretical Model." *Review of African Political Economy* 1, no. 1: 9–26.

Anderson, Christopher J., and Yuliya V. Tverdova. 2003. "Corruption, Political Allegiances, and Attitudes toward Government Corruption in Contemporary Democracies." *American Journal of Political Science* 47, no. 1: 91–109.

Barbieri, Katherine, and Rafael Reuveny. 2005. "Economic Globalization and War." *Journal of Politics* 67, no. 4: 1228–1247.

Bornschier, Volker, and Christopher Chase-Dunn. 1985. *Transnational Corporations and Underdevelopment.* New York: Praeger.

Boswell, Terry, and William J. Dixon. 1990. "Dependency and Rebellion: A Cross-National Analysis." *American Sociological Review* 55, no. 4: 540–559.

Chase-Dunn, Christopher. 1975. "The Effects of International Economic Dependence on Development and Inequality: A Cross National Study." *American Sociological Review* 40: 720–738.

Dixon, William, and Terry Boswell. 1996. "Dependency, Disarticulation, and Denominator Effects: Another Look at Foreign Capital Penetration." *American Journal of Sociology* 102, no. 2: 543–562.

Fearon, James D., and David D. Laitin. 2003. "Ethnicity, Insurgency, and Civil War." *American Political Science Review* 97, no. 1: 75–90.

Galtung, Johan. 1971. "A Structural Theory of Imperialism." *Journal of Peace Research* 8, no. 2: 81–117.

Gurr, Ted R. 1989. *POLITY II: Political Structures and Regime Change, 1800–1986*. Boulder, CO: Center for Comparative Politics (producer); Ann Arbor, MI: Inter-university Consortium for Political and Social Research (distributor).

Haggard, Stephan, and Sylvia Maxfield. 1996. "The Political Economy of Financial Internationalization in the Developing World." *International Organization* 50, no. 1: 35–68.

Hegre, Havard, Ranveig Gissinger, and Nils Petter Gleditsch. 2003. "Globalization and Internal Conflict." In *Globalization and Armed Conflict*, edited by Gerald Schneider, Katherine Barbieri, and Nils Petter Gleditsch, 251–276. Lanham, MD: Rowman and Littlefield.

Hirschmann, Albert O. 1981. *National Power and the Structure of Foreign Trade*. Berkeley: University of California Press.

*International Country Risk Guide* (ICRG). 2005. East Syracuse, NY: PRS Group.

Jain, Arvind K. 2001. "Corruption: A Review." *Journal of Economic Surveys* 15: 71–121.

Kentor, Jeffrey. 2005. "Transnational Corporate Power: Expansion, Spatial Distribution, and Concentration, 1962–1998." In *The Future of World Society*, edited by Mark Herkenrath, Claudia Konig, Hanno Scholtz, and Thomas Volken. Zurich: Intelligent.

Kentor, Jeffrey, and Terry Boswell. 2003. "Foreign Capital Dependence and Development: A New Direction." *American Sociological Review* 68, no. 2: 301–313.

Kentor, Jeffrey, and Andrew Jorgenson. 2010. "Foreign Investment and Development: An Organizational Perspective." *International Sociology* 25, no. 3: 419–441.

Kentor, Jeffrey, and Eric Mielants. 2007. "Connecting the Global and Local: The Impact of Globalization on Civil Society from 1990 to the Present." In *Civil Society, Local and Regional Responses to Global Challenges*, edited by Mark Herkenrath, 27–47. Münster: LIT Verlag.

Lipset, Seymour M. 1994. "The Social Requisites of Democracy Revisited." *American Sociological Review* 59: 1–22.

Mason, T. David. 2003. "Globalization, Democratization, and the Prospects for Civil War in the New Millennium." *International Studies Review* 5, no. 4: 19–35.

Mauro, Paolo. 1995. "Corruption and Growth." *Quarterly Journal of Economics* 110: 681–712.

———. 1998. "Corruption and the Composition of Government Expenditure." *Journal of Public Economics* 69: 263–279.

Montinola, Gabriella R., and Robert W. Jackman. 2002. "Sources of Corruption: A Cross-Country Review." *British Journal of Political Science* 32: 147–170.

Nielsen, Francois, and Arthur S. Alderson. 1995. "Income Inequality, Development, and Dualism: Results from an Unbalanced Cross-National Panel." *American Sociological Review* 60, no. 5: 674–701.

Rose-Ackerman, Susan. 1999. *Corruption and Government: Causes, Consequences, and Reform*. Cambridge: Cambridge University Press.

Sachs, Jeffrey D., and A. M. Warner. 1995. "Economic Reform and the Process of Global Integration." *Brookings Papers on Economic Activity* 1, no. 1: 1–118.

Seligson, Mitchell A. 2006. "The Measurement and Impact of Corruption Victimization: Survey Evidence from Latin America." *World Development* 34, no. 2: 381–404.

Tavits, Margit. 2008. "Representation, Corruption, and Subjective Well-Being." *Comparative Political Studies* 41, no. 12: 1607–1630.

Wallensteen, Peter, and Margareta Sollenberg. 2001. "Armed Conflict, 1980–2000." *Journal of Peace Research* 38, no. 5: 629–644.

Warren, Mark E. 2004. "What Does Corruption Mean in a Democracy?" *American Journal of Political Science* 48, no. 2: 328–343.

You, Jong-Sung, and Sanjeev Khagram. 2005. "A Comparative Study of Inequality and Corruption." *American Sociological Review* 70: 136–157.

## Appendix: Countries Included in Our Analysis

| | | |
|---|---|---|
| Algeria | Guinea | Papua New Guinea |
| Angola | Guyana | Paraguay |
| Argentina | Hungary | Peru |
| Bahrain | India | Philippines |
| Bangladesh | Indonesia | Poland |
| Bolivia | Iran | Portugal |
| Botswana | Israel | Saudi Arabia |
| Brazil | Jamaica | Senegal |
| Bulgaria | Kenya | Sierra Leone |
| Cameroon | Malawi | Syria |
| Chile | Malaysia | Tanzania |
| Colombia | Mali | Thailand |
| Congo, Republic | Malta | Togo |
| Costa Rica | Mexico | Trinidad and Tobago |
| Cote d'Ivoire | Morocco | Tunisia |
| Ecuador | Namibia | Turkey |
| Egypt | Nicaragua | Uganda |
| El Salvador | Niger | Uruguay |
| Ethiopia | Nigeria | Venezuela |
| The Gambia | Oman | Vietnam |
| Ghana | Pakistan | Zambia |
| Greece | Panama | Zimbabwe |

# 5

## TRANSNATIONALLY IMPLICATED LABOR PROCESSES AS TRANSNATIONAL SOCIAL RELATIONS

### WORKPLACES AND GLOBAL CLASS FORMATION

**Jason Struna**

**Abstract**

Globalization in the contemporary period is marked by the proliferation of transnational corporations using global commodity chains largely made possible by information technology and the standardized shipping container. Good scholarship on transnational class formation and the existence of a transnational capitalist class emerging on the basis of such firms and processes is manifold in broad literatures, but the impacts of these institutions and technologies on particular workers implicated in global commodity chains needs explication. To contribute to that effort, this chapter considers evidence gathered from the analysis of warehouses and distribution centers in Southern California. In particular, it considers the types of relationships that exist among firms in the sector, workers' understanding of the command and control of the labor process, and what these kinds of evidence mean for class theorization relative to contemporary capitalist globalization.

## Introduction

Globalization is an essentially "contested concept" (Gallie 1956; Robinson 1996). On one hand it refers to a broadly conceived trajectory of worldwide social formation "as part of a much older process of capitalist development and expansion in which there are important continuities as well as changes" (Chase-Dunn 1999, 188), and on the other it connotes an epochal shift marked by "the centralization of command and control of the global economy in transnational capital" (Robinson 2004, 15). While there are certainly many other perspectives (Arrighi 2001; Carroll 2010; Dicken 2007; Hutton and Giddens 2000; Sklair 2001; Wallerstein 2004), this chapter considers globalization from the perspective of the latter—"centralization of command and control" of global circuits of production in the contemporary period roughly spanning the 1970s to the present (Dicken 2007; Laibman 2005; Robinson 2004).

There have long been commodity chains in the world-system that functioned across vast geographies (Gereffi 1994; Hopkins and Wallerstein [1986] 2000; Mahutga 2012), but the rise of transnational corporations in the contemporary period (Bornschier and Chase-Dunn 1985; Dicken 2007; Robinson 2012a) marks a departure from previous iterations of capitalist practice insofar as there is an "increased geographical spread" of transnational circuits of production on the basis of "'revolutions' in transportation and communications technologies" (Dicken 2007, 17). Specifically, the rise of standardized shipping containers and the shift away from break bulk cargo stowed in the holds of oceangoing ships has led to significantly increased efficiency, far lower rates of loss associated with broken or damaged goods, shorter shipping times, refined customs processes, and intermodal—ship-railroad-road—transport (Bonacich and Wilson 2007; Levinson 2006; Rodrigue, Comtois, and Slack 2006). The transport revolution combined with communication technology has led to commodity chains in which a product's design can be transmitted electronically "to a factory in Thailand, [using] local labor to combine Chinese fabric made from American cotton" picked by Mexican migrant farm workers, "Malaysian buttons made from Taiwanese plastics, Japanese zippers, and decorations embroidered in Indonesia. The finished order, loaded into a 40-foot container, would be delivered in less than a month to [an inland

US] distribution center … or a *hyper-marché* in France" (Levinson 2006). The shipping container and information technology are thus the core innovations of the epoch, and make the just-in-time production and delivery of goods possible in commodity circuits that have inputs from a vast array of geographies.

But what does the emergence of vertically disintegrated and globally dispersed production networks of intermediate and semifinished commodities mean for *work*? What do *workers* know about globalization and their role in the handling of transnationally sourced commodities? How does the structure of the firms for which they work and the process of command and control in specific workplaces condition workers' understanding of transnational class relations?

I contribute partial answers to these questions by analyzing warehouses and distribution centers in Southern California. After a brief discussion of methods, I describe the sector and region, the basic nature of employment relations and demographics, types of warehouses and distribution centers, and the primary institutional actors in the industry. I further explore the specific means of command and control on the shop floor, the shape of labor-capital relations in a globalized workplace, and evidence concerning workers' perception of the objective social relations experienced in warehouses and distribution centers. Finally, I discuss the implications of these and similarly situated labor-capital relations for class theorization in the global epoch.

## Methods

The following analysis is based on evidence collected from twenty-one semi-structured interviews with warehouse workers and managerial or support staff in the Riverside–San Bernardino–Ontario metropolitan statistical area—home to one of the largest "logistics clusters" in the world (Sheffi 2012). Additionally, several worker-informants have contributed to the data-collection process by providing background information, diagrams, written materials from workplaces, and assistance with interview transcription and translation. Many hours of participant observation via Warehouse Workers United contributed data from informal conversations at strike actions and rallies, worker health and safety training meetings, and many other events (2011–2013).[1] Finally, demographic information was obtained from surveys collected with the assistance of University of California Riverside undergraduate researchers.[2]

## The Sector

A massive agglomeration of warehouses and distribution centers in Southern California covers one-billion-plus square feet in the Riverside–San Bernardino–Ontario area (Bonacich and Wilson 2007). The region's proximity to the ports of

LA/Long Beach (handling roughly 25 percent of imports to the United States), with its access to global and regional markets and the relatively cheap real estate and low-wage labor force, have made it a prime destination for warehouses and distribution centers. An innumerable variety of goods sourced from transnational and local commodity chains is handled in these facilities prior to retailing in contexts including conventional brick-and-mortar stores, online outlets, and other modes of marketing.

The industry employs roughly 114,000 warehouse workers in the region (California Employment Development Department 2011), with a large proportion of workers being employed by temporary employment agencies. While the number of temporary workers is difficult to estimate—neither the state of California nor the US Bureau of Labor Statistics consistently collects data on specific job titles for workers employed by temporary agencies—temporary agencies as employer of record (contrasted with direct hires by a warehouse firm) range from estimates of 40 to 61 percent (Allison, Reese, and Struna 2013). Given that, the number of temporary workers in the industry is *substantially* higher than the state average of 2 percent estimated by Dietz (2012). However, as Bonacich and de Lara (2009) report, the higher location quotient of temporary agencies incorporated in the region may account for this divergence—especially insofar as the spatial relationships of the sector's primary institutional actors, discussed later, apply. Regardless, there is a prevalence of contingent and precarious work (Kalleberg 2000; Peck, Theodore, and Ward 2005) in the industry, as documented by various studies and journalistic and government-agency accounts (Bonacich and Wilson 2007; *Cal-OSHA Reporter* 2012; California Department of Industrial Relations 2011; Luo, Mann, and Holden 2010; Lydersen 2011; McClelland 2012; Meyerson 2009; Struna et al. 2012).

In terms of the work itself, a great deal of occupational variety exists in warehouses and distribution centers. Loading and unloading the ubiquitous shipping containers by hand, forklift, or other machines represents one type of material-handling occupation, but other specific tasks include picking and packing individual commodities from racks or bins to be shipped to retail outlets or directly to end users (see McClelland 2012). Another common task is product aggregation or disaggregation: creating individual salable packages from a multitude of differently sourced products brought together in a distribution center to be finished prior to shipping. The components of a new Dell or Apple computer—cables, power adapters, software packages, accessories, and the machine itself—often enter a warehouse or distribution center in separate containers, from many different suppliers in many different geographies. Logistics firms that run these facilities assign workers to create the final packages to the suppliers' and retailers' specifications. Product labeling often occurs in warehouses and distribution centers as well; workers in these facilities often put on goods the final physical touches that distinguish between the brand name and the supposed knockoff. Finally, as commodity chains elongate and diversify, warehouse workers increasingly participate in activities more accurately considered light manufacturing, and blur the lines between material handling and commodity production. In all, warehouse and distribution center workers finish a great deal of the goods we consume—from electronics to pens and from food to sporting goods their labor is present in commodities from many, many sources.

## Demographics

According to the Allison, Reese, and Struna (2013) survey, 85.2 percent of warehouse and distribution-center workers identify as Latino/a, while 7.4 percent identify as African American, 4.4 percent identify as white, and 3 percent identify as belonging to some other ethnic, racial, or national group. Although Allison, Reese, and Struna find a gender distribution of 68.9 percent male and 31.1 percent female, anecdotal reports from workers and my own observation-based findings suggest the distribution of men and women is closer to 60 percent male and 40 percent female. Tasks tend to be gendered in the industry, and a more balanced distribution is more likely. The average age of workers in the Allison, Reese, and Struna study was twenty-eight (range of eighteen to sixty-one), with more than half falling between the ages of eighteen and twenty-five. Nearly 50 percent of workers in the survey had a secondary education, with 35 percent of respondents reporting at least some college education. Contrary to ideologically centered assumptions about the ignorance of low-wage workers, workers in the sector are relatively well educated—albeit from traditionally marginalized populations.

Allison, Reese, and Struna also find 23 percent of warehouse and distribution-center workers to be foreign born—yet owing to the political and social complexities of immigration status and its self-reporting in the United States, the number of immigrant workers in the industry could be substantially higher, as suggested by Allen (2010). Thus, the demographic composition of the labor force in warehouses and distribution centers in the region contributes to the transnational milieu in which the sector is situated. The facilities are often bilingual or multilingual environments where workers may prefer to communicate in Spanish over English, and Spanish is often predominantly heard. However, the hiring process for both temporary and direct-hire employment often includes English-proficiency exams in addition to math and numeracy tests that can make or break a worker's employability.

## Warehouse and Distribution-Center Structure

Previous research (Struna 2012) indicates that warehouses and distribution centers fall into two categories in terms of the structuring of the labor process: labor-intensive facilities that maximize output through human inputs, and capital-intensive facilities that minimize human inputs through varying degrees of automation. Labor-intensive facilities appear to remain more common than highly capital-intensive systems, but new construction in the area and competition in the industry suggest that larger capital-intensive systems are on the rise locally and globally (Bonacich and Wilson 2007; Hompel and Schmidt 2007; Sheffi 2012). Of course, the categories presented here represent two extremes on a continuum, and the empirical distribution of capital- or labor-intensive facilities represents a mix of both in most cases.

Conventional labor-intensive facilities can be roughly 600,000 square feet, and employ as many as 1,000 workers for three shifts. The capital-intensive systems (although size varies) can be more than one million square feet, and employ as few as 600 workers for three shifts. To put the scale of the larger facilities into perspective, one million square feet is equivalent to approximately seventeen American football fields or thirteen football (soccer) pitches. In both types of systems, flexible workforces can increase or decrease the number of workers employed on the basis of demand and season—i.e., "back-to-school" season in the United States, Christmastime shopping and consumption, and minor holidays like Valentine's Day can significantly increase the number of workers needed to execute logistics operations.

*Firm Structure and Relationships*

There are four primary institutional actors in warehouses and distribution centers: third-party logistics firms contracted by retailers or suppliers to manage inventory (Bonacich and Wilson 2007), temporary employment agencies (Kalleberg 2000), global retailers (Gereffi and Christian 2009), and commodity suppliers and manufacturers (Gereffi 1994).[3] All often are transnational firms or their subsidiaries—transnational corporations like the shipper Maersk, temporary-employment firms like Manpower, global retailers like Walmart, and manufacturers like Sony, to name a few examples. Any one of the firm types can own warehouses and distribution centers (although this is probably less likely for temporary agencies) and operate them for proprietary systems, contracted services, or some combination thereof.

In warehouses and distribution centers operated by third-party logistics contractors, relationships among all four types of institutional actors are common. While the actors are technically and often legally distinct in terms of firm boundaries, the functional integration of their operations makes it difficult for both observers and workers to determine where one entity ends and the other begins, and for whom a worker labors. In particular, shared information across boundaries, especially digital communication through electronic data interchanges, serves as the primary mechanism by which labor is manipulated. Digital communications as well as algorithms directing specific behavior "structure possible forms of work performances" (Aneesh 2009) in commodity chains that are closely orchestrated—from the retail register's barcode scanner tracking inventory as it is purchased, backward through the warehouse and distribution center, including the temporary agencies used to "flex" labor on demand, and finally to the supplier preparing to replenish the commodity stock as it communicates with each of the other actors.

Beyond the "algocratic" relationships (Aneesh 2009) that pertain in such systems, the firms often share space in the warehouse and distribution center: any and all may have offices and staff permanently present on the shop floor. Although the example is external to the Southern California case, the following quote from a trade journal sums up the structure well: "The carriers' representatives have offices in the Prague [distribution center] alongside those of Lego's and DHL's employees. 'In our corporation, one day a year we negotiate. The rest of the year we work together'"(Cooke 2009). The industry by nature requires collaboration and the manipulation of labor across firm boundaries.

Thus, the command and control over work happens in closely coordinated networks, and ideally functions smoothly despite institutional and geographic borders that often formally separate actors. What workers do, when they do it, and where (in the warehouse) they do it can be known and influenced by any and all parties in the network. As one high-level manager in charge of logistics at a distribution firm contracting with multiple global retailers and temporary agencies and operating in North America, Asia, Africa, Europe, and Latin America stated in an interview, "We have a proprietary [warehouse-management system] that's extremely sophisticated. . . . It has interfaces into our material handling systems, our ERP [enterprise resource planning systems that communicate with supplier firms and retail customers]. We also have a . . . labor management system on top of that, so that we can manage our labor, . . ." including communication internally and with temporary agencies. These "systems . . . allow us to manage both the workforce [size], the flow, the stocking, the pick-rate, where we put things, the positioning and movement [in the warehouse and geographically across locations in the system]—all of those types of activities" (Struna 2012).

Relationships among capitals' agents and workers are constituted through electronic data interchanges, the commodities handled and transshipped via containers and aggregated/disaggregated prior to sale, and the shared space of the shop floor. Yet whether or not labor-capital relations exist because of copresence, it is important to keep in mind the ability to manipulate labor across vast distances and complex institutional boundaries. With speed and relative precision, transnational corporations extract labor throughout their commodity chains. Observing warehouses and distribution centers allows us to zoom in on a particular moment of the transnational process.

## Globalization on the Shop Floor

The question is, how do these processes and relations transform work and the experience of it? Do they? Do they alter labor-capital relations (or the experience of class relations created in the labor process)? While I can only partially answer these questions here, the key is to begin with more questions. Specifically, to what degree is transnational command and control over the labor process *observed* by workers through their use of physical capital linked to other geographies by information technology and containerization? Second, to what degree are workers aware of the transnational ownership and management of the facilities in which they work? Finally, insofar as we can develop answers to these questions, how do these two factors—labor's use of systems that are transnationally commanded and controlled in the production process, and workers' cognizance of transnational labor-capital relations—affect class theorization under conditions of contemporary capitalist globalization?

*Workers' Observation of Globalized Labor Processes*

Evidence about the degree to which workers observe the transnational command and control of the labor process—gained through interviews, Warehouse Workers United observations, informal conversations, long-term informants, and observation of hiring practices—presents a mixed picture. Workers talk about physical evidence of transnational links, and awareness of workers at different geographic points of production in the commodity circuits through a material record: a fallen cigarette lighter found among frozen shrimp from Asia, Chinese newspapers wrapping chrome products unloaded from shipping containers, an old pair of worn sandals found in a carton of brand-new running shoes. There is an ethereal and mysterious presence of others and otherness in the goods and incidental objects found among them.

Further, workers present knowledge of branding and firm/contractor complexity insofar as they see retail client and supplier logos on the commodities and capital they interact with in the production process. While they are hired by temporary agencies managing their payroll, they know they work in a facility owned or leased by a third-party logistics firm contracted to mediate between the suppliers and the retailers. Their forklifts and hand scanners may have inventory tags from both the contract firm and the retailer for which they work. Thus, there is awareness that the end user of the workers' labor power is often the big-box store they hope to shop at when the shift ends—assuming they will be given enough hours that day, and that they will be called back by the temp agency tomorrow.

However, beyond branding and the nascent knowledge of connections between people at different but vaguely conceived points of production in different geographies, worker knowledge of transnational command and control processes used on the shop floor is nominal. Although many do understand that the digital scanners and computer displays or the electronically transmitted bills of lading managers print out and distribute to workers guide their labor—sometimes measured in steps and seconds between directives—workers are not markedly aware that the instructions may be generated in Great Britain, Norway, Japan, or the United States. Evidence regarding awareness of process-generated observations of transnational links by workers is limited at best at this stage of research—especially in terms of specificity about the processes from point to point in the commodity chain.

## Workers' Knowledge of Transnational Ownership and Management

Workers do tend to exhibit knowledge about transnational ownership and management a bit less emergently than evidence from labor-process-oriented observations. Branding present on memos and other official communications, including manuals, training materials like videos and safety instructions, paychecks, and explanations of benefits indicates to workers the range of firms implicated in their working lives.[4] The presence of a retailer's imprimatur alongside the temporary agency's logo on a new company policy memo drafted on a European third-party logistics firm's letterhead offers workers evidence of organizational complexity and transnational ownership or management. Further, workers tend to see merger and acquisition activity through the same types of symbols and communication. The logos may change, the personnel directing and observing the work may or may not be altered, and the specific commodities handled could differ from one shift to the next with little fanfare or official announcement, but workers often observe changes in the global or local composition of the institutional actors.

Workers on the shop floor often observe the presence of supplier or retailer managerial agents with or without firm name badges. There may be direct daily interaction, or little to no contact with the engineers and quality-control managers sent by suppliers and retailers to observe and alter the labor process in their contract facilities. Whether or not the firm's agents preside over specific offices, workers understand that the individuals represent the interests of specific (transnational) corporations, and that their decisions impact quotas, relative rates of mechanization, product placement, and workflow, etc. Workers also know that the often-nameless agents can have their particular tasks assigned to other workers without notice. Therefore, workers seem in general to be attuned to the ownership and management presence of transnational corporations even if the specific digital and productive links remain obscured in the labor process itself.

Finally, it is worth mentioning worker-education initiatives by Warehouse Workers United directed at exposing transnational corporations' participation in labor processes detrimental to workers' health and safety both locally and globally. Worker-organizers have a highly developed understanding of global political economy as a result of their participation in Warehouse Workers United's campaign focusing on the interconnections among warehouses, temporary agencies, and retailers (see also Bonacich 2003; Bonacich and Wilson 2005; Gereffi and Christian 2009). The organization's emphasis on the notion that all of the firms implicated on the shop floor hold joint responsibility for working conditions throughout the global commodity chains resonates with workers. In addition to developing in workers an understanding of ownership and management relations among firms,

Warehouse Workers United fosters active links among workers throughout the global supply chains in which they labor—having strategic contact with workers and labor organizations in El Salvador, Chile, China, South Korea, Bangladesh, and Australia, among other locales.

## Class Theorization under Conditions of Contemporary Capitalist Globalization

Objective transnational links exist between labor and capital via algocratic modes of organization (Aneesh 2009), containerization, and global circuits of production (Robinson 2004). And objective links among workers throughout the commodity chains exist on the same bases, whether consciously understood or not by the workers who participate in the production process. In some cases, workers and labor organizations are forming conscious connections within the most egregious supply chains, and are leveraging firms to homogenize working conditions throughout the circuits. At the same time as transnational firms are pushing the logic of a race to the bottom throughout the global system, some workers are advocating global standards for contractor and supplier codes of conduct. Thus the objective and subjective conditions are convergent in at least a few well-publicized instances. Regardless of the perceived efficacy of the Black Friday Walmart strikes that take place at stores in the United States; the strikes and lawsuits targeting warehouses, temporary agencies, and retailers in Southern California;[5] or the outcry over tragic fires at Walmart suppliers in Bangladesh, the concerted effort to organize at each phase of the Walmart supply chain is more than coincidental. Although it is only one example of "transnational class formation from below" (Carroll 2013), it is an important example of "newly emerging working classes that are successively made and strengthened as an unintended outcome of historical capitalism" (Silver 2003) and capital's efforts to more effectively exploit labor across geographic contexts.

### A Globalized Proletariat; a Transnational Working Class

To be clear, theorizing the transnationality of labor must not be limited to considerations of worker mobility alone, nor to subjective or conscious links among workers across transnational commodity chains. The global expansion of the ranks of the proletariat through formal or informal wage-labor markets has created conditions where more than half of the planet's inhabitants sell—or hope to sell—their labor power in an effort to support their daily existence (Freeman 2008; International Labor Office 2012). Of course, the movement of labor to points of production across borders occurs with varying degrees of freedom or constraint (Kennedy 2010; Levitt and Jaworsky 2007; Nowicka 2007; Sassen 2005), but it is important to remember that points of production often move to laborers (Arrighi 1994; Ietto-Gillies 2002; Mahutga 2012), and that extensive and intensive enlargement of the capitalist project (Robinson 2004) impacts specific populations in a multitude of ways. In so doing, connections between people are forged, destroyed, or renewed both within the workplace and within markets.

It is worth reiterating some of the key points already made: commodity production occurs across varying geographic contexts for many if not most of the goods we consume or hope to consume (Sklair 2001)—especially in terms of finished and semifinished consumables available through global retailers. The actual command and control of such production—and thus the labor-capital relation that pertains in workplaces implicated in these processes—operates via logics that enable nearly seamless, instantaneous coordination across zones of development, and despite political and institutional (firm) boundaries. If we take seriously the notion that a commodity is a relation between people expressed as a relation between things (Marx [1867] 1906), we cannot fail to note that transnational commodity production constitutes transnational social relations by definition. Our task is to explicate those relations, point out strategic opportunities for mobilization (Bonacich 2003), and develop frameworks for understanding the contours of the transnational class relations observed (Chase-Dunn 1998; Robinson 2012b; Struna 2009; Wallerstein 2000).

## Conclusion

We must not stop with the theorization and explication of the transnational capitalist class, nascent transnational state apparatuses, or other global social formations constituted on the basis of elite action (Carroll 2010; Carroll 2013; Chase-Dunn 1998; Robinson 2004; Sklair 2010). The globalization of one side of relations of domination and subordination suggests the concomitant globalization of the other side. That is, there can be no transnational capitalist class in the absence of a proletariat that to some degree has been transnationalized. Even if one rejects the claims of the global capitalism perspective regarding the novelty of the contemporary period of capitalist development, the empirical analysis of specific modes of exploitation employed in world-systemic structures of production and distribution must include the observation of particular moments of social interaction between dominant and subordinate groups if such analysis is to explain ways to transcend, overcome, or ameliorate unequal relations.

In particular, I argue that the contours of labor-capital relation must be assessed from the shop floor upward. Despite the power of markets to overdetermine status differentials and reinforce perceptions of social inequalities, relationships between labor and capital that occur within the "hidden abode" of production (Marx [1867] 1906) still have a great deal of power in the correlation of forces that condition who is exploiter and who is exploited, or who lives among the haves and the have-nots.[6] The idea that transnational corporations are the correct locations to initiate an analysis of global capitalism is absolutely correct, but we must extend our analyses from the bottom up (Burawoy 1998; Edwards 1979; Parreñas 2001; Salzinger 2003) as well as from the top down (Carroll 2010; Robinson 2013; Sklair 2001).

Work under conditions of capitalist globalization is still controlled by specific people in specific places despite the geographic dispersion of production, the computerized rationalization of decision making, and the removal of the face of the capitalist from the presence of labor. Theoretical and empirical perspectives on class formation need to reflect these modalities, and account for time and space when we try to unpack the creation of things better understood as relations among people.

# References

Allen, Nicholas. 2010. "Exploring the Inland Empire: Life, Work, and Injustice in Southern California's Retail Fortress." *New Labor Forum* 19: 36–43.

Allison, Juliann, Ellen Reese, and Jason Struna. 2013. "Under-Paid and Temporary: Key Survey Findings on Warehouse Workers in the Inland Valley." Working Paper 13-04, Center for Sustainable Suburban Development. http://cssd.ucr.edu/Papers/PDFs /UnderpaidTempWorkers.pdf.

Aneesh, A. 2009. "Global Labor: Algocratic Modes of Organization." *Sociological Theory* 27: 347–370.

Arrighi, Giovanni. 1994. *The Long Twentieth Century.* New York: Verso.

———. 2001. "Global Capitalism and the Persistence of the North-South Divide." *Science and Society* 65: 469.

Bonacich, Edna. 2003. "Pulling the Plug: Labor and the Global Supply Chain." *New Labor Forum* 12: 41–48.

Bonacich, Edna, and Juan David de Lara. 2009. "Economic Crisis and the Logistics Industry: Financial Insecurity for Warehouse Workers in the Inland Empire." Los Angeles: Institute for Research on Labor and Employment, University of California, Los Angeles.

Bonacich, Edna, and Jake B. Wilson. 2005. "Hoisted by Its Own Petard: Organizing Wal-Mart's Logistics Workers." *New Labor Forum* 14: 67–75.

———. 2007. *Getting the Goods: Ports, Labor, and the Logistics Revolution.* Ithaca, NY: Cornell University Press.

Bornschier, Volker, and Christopher Chase-Dunn. 1985. *Transnational Corporations and Underdevelopment.* New York: Praeger.

Burawoy, Michael. 1998. "The Extended Case Method." *Sociological Theory* 16: 4–33.

*Cal-OSHA Reporter.* 2012. "Cal/OSHA Blitzes Inland Empire Warehouse Chain, Staffing Agency, with Citations." www.cal-osha.com/Cal-OSHA-Hits-SoCal-Warehouses -with-Citations2.aspx (accessed January 30, 2012).

California Department of Industrial Relations. 2011. "California Labor Commissioner Issues Additional $616,250 Citation in Riverside County Warehouse Case." California Department of Industrial Relations. www.dir.ca.gov/DIRNews/2011/IR2011-24 .html (accessed May 13, 2014).

California Employment Development Department. 2011. "Industry Employment and Labor Force Annual Average: Riverside–San Bernardino–Ontario MSA." Sacramento, CA: California Employment Development Department.

Carroll, William K. 2010. *The Making of a Transnational Capitalist Class: Corporate Power in the 21st Century.* New York: Zed Books.

———. 2013. "Networks of Cognitive Praxis: Transnational Class Formation from Below?" *Globalizations* 10, no. 5: 691–710.

Chase-Dunn, Christopher. 1998. *Global Formation: Structures in the World-Economy.* Lanham, MD: Rowman and Littlefield.

———. 1999. "Globalization: A World-Systems Perspective." *Journal of World-Systems Research* 2: 187–215.

Cooke, James A. 2009. "Lego's Game-Changing Move." *Supply Chain Quarterly,* vol. 3. www.supplychainquarterly.com/topics/Logistics/scq200903lego/ (accessed June 24, 2014).

Dicken, Peter. 2007. *Global Shift: Mapping the Changing Contours of the World Economy.* New York: Guilford Press.

Dietz, Miranda. 2012. "Temporary Workers in California Are Twice as Likely as Non-Temps to Live in Poverty: Problems with Temporary and Subcontracted Work in California." University of California, Berkeley, Center for Labor Research and Education.

Edwards, Richard. 1979. *Contested Terrain: The Transformation of the Workplace in the Twentieth Century.* New York: Basic Books.

Freeman, Richard B. 2008. "The New Global Labor Market." *Focus* 26: 1–6.

Gallie, W. B. 1956. "Essentially Contested Concepts." *Aristotelian Society* 56: 167–198.

Gereffi, Gary. 1994. "The Organization of Buyer-Driven Global Commodity Chains: How U.S. Retailers Shape Overseas Production Networks." In *Commodity Chains and Global Capitalism,* edited by G. Gereffi and M. Korzeniewicz, 95–122. Westport, CT: Praeger.

Gereffi, Gary, and Michelle Christian. 2009. "The Impacts of Wal-Mart: The Rise and Consequences of the World's Dominant Retailer." *Annual Review of Sociology* 35: 573–591.

Hompel, Michael, and Thorsten Schmidt. 2007. *Warehouse Management: Automation and Organization of Warehouse and Order Picking Systems.* Berlin: Springer.

Hopkins, Terence K., and Immanuel Wallerstein. [1986] 2000. "Commodity Chains in the World-Economy Prior to 1800." In *The Essential Wallerstein.* New York: New Press.

Hutton, Will, and Anthony Giddens. 2000. *Global Capitalism.* New York: New Press.

Ietto-Gillies, Grazia. 2002. *Transnational Corporations: Fragmentation amidst Integration.* London: Routledge.

International Labor Office (ILO). 2012. "Global Employment Trends 2012: Preventing a Deeper Jobs Crisis." Geneva: ILO.

Kalleberg, Arne L. 2000. "Nonstandard Employment Relations: Part-Time, Temporary and Contract Work." *Annual Review of Sociology* 26: 341–365.

Kennedy, Paul. 2010. *Local Lives and Global Transformations: Towards World Society.* New York: Palgrave.

Laibman, David. 2005. "Theory and Necessity: The Stadial Foundations of the Present." *Science and Society* 69: 285–315.

Levinson, Marc. 2006. *The Box: How the Shipping Container Made the World Smaller and the World Economy Bigger.* Princeton, NJ: Princeton University Press.

Levitt, Peggy, and B. Nadya Jaworsky. 2007. "Transnational Migration Studies: Past Developments and Future Trends." *Annual Review of Sociology* 33: 129–156.

Luo, Tian, Amar Mann, and Richard Holden. 2010. "The Expanding Role of Temporary Help Services from 1990 to 2008." *Monthly Labor Review* 133: 3–16.

Lydersen, Kari. 2011. "California Workers Take Walmart's Warehouses to Court." *In These Times*, October 21.

Mahutga, Matthew C. 2012. "When Do Value Chains Go Global? A Theory of the Spatialization of Global Value Chains." *Global Networks* 12: 1–21.

Marx, Karl. [1867] 1906. *Capital: A Critique of Political Economy*. New York: Modern Library.

McClelland, Mac. 2012. "I Was a Warehouse Wage Slave: My Brief, Back-Breaking, Rage-Inducing, Dildo-Packing Time inside the Online-Shipping Machine." *Mother Jones* (March/April). www.motherjones.com/politics/2012/02/mac-mcclelland-free-online-shipping-warehouses-labor (accessed May 13, 2014).

Meyerson, Harold. 2009. "L.A.'s Warehouse Workers: Invisible and Exploited." *Los Angeles Times*, September 7. http://articles.latimes.com/2009/sep/07/opinion/oe-meyerson7 (accessed May 13, 2014).

Nowicka, Magdalena. 2007. "Mobile Locations: Construction of Home in a Group of Mobile Transnational Professionals." *Global Networks* 7: 69–86.

Parreñas, Rhacel Salazar. 2001. *Servants of Globalization: Women, Migration, and Domestic Work*. Stanford, CA: Stanford University Press.

Peck, Jamie, N. I. K. Theodore, and Kevin Ward. 2005. "Constructing Markets for Temporary Labour: Employment Liberalization and the Internationalization of the Staffing Industry." *Global Networks* 5: 3–26.

Robinson, William I. 1996. *Promoting Polyarchy: Globalization, US Intervention, and Hegemony*. Cambridge: Cambridge University Press.

———. 2004. *A Theory of Global Capitalism: Production, Class, and State in a Transnational World*. Baltimore: Johns Hopkins University Press.

———. 2012a. "Capitalist Globalization as World-Historic Context." *Critical Sociology* 38: 349–363.

———. 2012b. "Global Capitalism Theory and the Emergence of Transnational Elites." *Critical Sociology* 38, no. 3.

———. 2013. "Global Capitalism and Its Anti-'Human Face': Organic Intellectuals and Interpretations of the Crisis." *Globalizations* 10, no. 5. www.tandfonline.com/doi/abs/10.1080/14747731.2013.828966 (accessed May 13, 2014).

Rodrigue, Jean-Paul, Claude Comtois, and Brian Slack. 2006. *The Geography of Transport Systems*. New York: Routledge.

Salzinger, Leslie. 2003. *Genders in Production: Making Workers in Mexico's Global Factories*. Berkeley: University of California Press.

Sassen, Saskia. 2005. "When National Territory Is Home to the Global: Old Borders to Novel Borderings." *New Political Economy* 10: 523–541.

Sheffi, Yossi. 2012. *Logistics Clusters: Delivering Value and Driving Growth*. Cambridge, MA: MIT Press.

Silver, Beverly. 2003. *Forces of Labor: Workers' Movements and Globalization since 1870*. New York: Cambridge University Press.

Sklair, Leslie. 2001. *The Transnational Capitalist Class*. Oxford: Blackwell.

———. 2010. "From International Relations to Alternative Globalizations." *Journal of Critical Globalization Studies* 3: 114–126.

Struna, Jason. 2009. "Toward a Theory of Global Proletarian Fractions." *Perspectives on Global Development and Technology* 8: 230–260.

———. 2012. "Global Chains, Global Workers: Warehouse Workers' Experience of Globalized Labor Processes and Transnational Class Relations." Examination paper thesis, University of California, Riverside.

Struna, Jason, Kevin Curwin, Edwin Elias, Ellen Reese, Tony Roberts, and Elizabeth Bingle. 2012. "Unsafe and Unfair: Labor Conditions in the Warehouse Industry." *Policy Matters: A Quarterly Publication of the University of California, Riverside* 5: 1–11.

Wallerstein, Immanuel. 2000. "Class Formation in the Capitalist World-Economy." In *The Essential Wallerstein*. New York: New Press.

———. 2004. *World-Systems Analysis: An Introduction*. Durham, NC: Duke University Press.

## Notes

1. For additional methodological and data information see Struna (2012). Warehouse Workers United is a worker and community organization seeking transformations in working conditions in the industry. It is sponsored by the Change to Win labor federation.

2. Preliminary findings are available in Allison, Reese, and Struna (2013). A University of California Humanities Research Institute grant provided funding for the survey.

3. Citations provide examples from the literature on each individual actor, not necessarily their specific interaction or participation in warehousing and distribution.

4. Where present, the Allison, Reese, and Struna (2013) survey shows only 36 percent of warehouse and distribution-center workers have health benefits.

5. See *Evarardo Carrillo et al. v. Schneider Logistics Inc. et al.* 2013. In *Minutes of US District Court Central District of California.*

6. For a discussion of market-based or production-based perspectives on class and power see Robinson (2004).

# PART II

Geopolitics and Warfare as Arenas of Struggle

# 6

# TERRITORIAL ALLIANCES AND EMERGING-MARKET DEVELOPMENT BANKING

## A VIEW FROM SUBIMPERIAL SOUTH AFRICA

**Patrick Bond**

## Abstract

A new "seat at the world table" is demanded by major emerging market powers, especially the BRICS (Brazil, Russia, India, China, and South Africa) bloc. The idea of establishing both a US$50 billion BRICS Bank headquartered in Shanghai and a $100 billion Contingent Reserve Arrangement was articulated and endorsed at the March 2012 New Delhi and 2013 Durban summits of BRICS leaders, as well as at the September 2013 G20 meeting in St. Petersburg. At the latter, BRICS finance ministers expressed dissatisfaction about the International Monetary Fund's (IMF's) governance, notwithstanding having collectively spent $75 billion in the IMF's recapitalization the year before. Yet flaws in the global financial architecture remain vividly apparent and another world crisis is looming. The BRICS strategy—especially in relation to the expedited extraction of Africa's minerals, petroleum, gas, and cash crops—raises questions about how different the BRICS' procorporate economic growth model is from the West's, and whether those nations' role in world capitalism is limited to assimilation rather than what is needed: a rupture with existing orthodox models, such as a radically new approach to development finance.

## Introduction

The need for dramatic changes to global financial governance is more than obvious, yet the gumption to make these changes has not been generated either from above or below. From the vantage point of South Africa, leader of the "fragile five" emerging markets that began suffering massive currency crashes in mid-2013, the tragedy of ongoing financial turbulence is obvious. Yet in its most recent world public-opinion survey, the Pew Research Global Attitudes ProjectCenter (2013) found that only one-third of South Africans identified "international financial instability" as a major threat (third highest, after climate change and Chinese economic competition) compared to 52 percent of those polled across the world (for whom it was a close second, after climate change at 54 percent). Our relative ignorance is a shame, for since South African freedom was won in 1994, the rand has collapsed seven times by more than 15 percent within a few weeks. During the crash from late 2012 to early 2014, it lost more than a third against the US dollar.

In part, South African society's rather blasé attitude is a result of soothing messages coming from the financial industry and its government allies, a problem typical across the world. For example, in late August 2013 as the rand started to tank, finance minister Pravin Gordhan assured, "We have a floating exchange rate, which will be able to absorb some of the shocks emerging from events that we have little control over at this time" (Reuters 2013). But the rand "floats" (or better, zigzags) without the kinds of flotation-type protection we had in earlier years, especially local exchange controls (the "finrand" from 1985–1995). In the United States financial regulations that protected the entire system were destroyed during the late 1990s by the Clinton administration so New York bankers could earn higher profits (Palast 2013). Deregulation reflected the rise of financialization within imperialism, as well as in South Africa, and made the world currency order—and with it the rand—extremely volatile. The "float" will get far more turbulent once the vast balance-of-payments deficit—caused by flight of profits and dividends to former South African companies now mainly listed on overseas stock markets—pushes South Africa's total foreign debt above US$150 billion. That leaves us the same ratio of debt to gross domestic product (GDP) that P. W. Botha encountered thirty years earlier, after which nothing could stay the same—he defaulted and from then on the demise of apartheid via financial-sanctions pressure was inexorable.

Gordhan sometimes shows a panicky side. In a *Financial Times* interview during a US monetary policy conference in August 2013, he complained of his peers' "inability to find coherent and cohesive responses across the globe to ensure that we reduce the volatility in currencies in particular, but also in sentiment" (England and Harding 2013). The following week, at the St. Petersburg G20 meeting, Gordhan joined others in the BRICS network to congratulate themselves about a forthcoming BRICS New Development Bank and Contingent Reserve Arrangement, or CRA (Republic of South Africa, the Presidency 2013). Might these two infants challenge the Bretton Woods Institutions in the coming years' chaotic world financial environment? Nearly seven decades after the World Bank and International Monetary Fund (IMF) were established to restore Western interstate banking following the Depression and World War II, the BRICS nations stand at the verge of replacing Washington and its neoliberal ideology with South-centered, state-aided capital accumulation.

That is the rhetoric, at any rate. But especially in mid-2013, the question arose of whether BRICS strategies are profoundly different from—or instead reinforcing of—the global financial architecture's self-destruction. After all, one of the CRA's objectives, according to South African Treasury officials, is to "complement existing international arrangements" (Republic of South Africa, Department of National Treasury 2012). The Chiang Mai Initiative and Asian Monetary Fund are similarly accommodationist, notwithstanding the extreme anger in Asia in 1997–1998 when they were first promoted by elites insulted by whole-scale takeover of their macroeconomic policies by IMF officials.

As for the BRICS Development Bank, critical details regarding institutional leadership and location were promised initially at the Durban summit in March 2013 and then in Russia prior to the G20 finance ministers meeting and heads-of-state summit. Details did not materialize at either meeting, but there are sufficient indications of what might be expected. A $50 billion BRICS bank capitalization wouldn't initially challenge the World Bank (which lends or invests almost that much every year). And a $100 billion CRA would quickly be exhausted in the event of a more serious financial meltdown. Perhaps those sums can be increased in coming years since they are pitiable amounts to face off against emerging-market financial melting of the sort witnessed since the mid-1990s, when numerous countries have needed a $50 billion package overnight so as to halt financial disinvestment in the form of herd-instinct runs, including Russia's record mid-1998 $57 billion bailout. The Russian crisis in turn directly catalyzed one of South Africa's most severe post-apartheid currency crashes, and South African Reserve Bank governor Chris Stals controversially raised interest rates 8 percent over a two-week period to attract capital back, thus pushing the economy into a brief recession (Bond 2003).

Fifteen years later, the dangers worsen because South Africa still fails to learn from its prior vulnerabilities. In mid-2013, trillions of dollars' worth of paper assets shifted around, driving intense currency crashes in most BRICS. The proximate cause was an announced change in US Federal Reserve policy in which a bit less artificial stimulation ("Quantitative Easing") would be provided to banks thanks to Fed "tapering"; interest rates more than doubled over a few weeks. This then caused dramatic outflows from emerging markets and the crash of the South African rand, the Brazilian real, the Russian rouble, and especially the Indian rupee.

Many concluded that, as the *Economist* (2013) put it, "booming emerging economies will no longer make up for weakness in rich countries." Influential Swedish economist Anders Aslund (2013) of the Peterson Institute for International Economics was scathing in a *Financial Times* article: "The BRICS party is over. Their ability to get going again rests on their ability to carry through reforms in grim times for which they lacked the courage in a boom." Added former South African opposition party leader Tony Leon (2013), "The investor community's love affair with developing-market economies has soured. The romance has been replaced by recrimination." Goldman Sachs banker Jim O'Neill, when asked by the *Wall Street Journal* about the BRICS acronym he had created a dozen years earlier, said this: "If I were to change it, I would just leave the 'C'" (Magalhaes 2013).

Tempting as it is to write off the more *schadenfreude*-suffused and neoliberal of BRICS-pessimist commentators, their confidence grows from several countries' deep-seated problems, not just momentary financial fluctuations. As Tsinghua University economist Li Dokui argued in September 2013, the inevitable winding down of the US Fed's Quantitative Easing printing press is "good news for the renminbi" which need no longer rise in value (Tian 2013). But in the process, he went on, "the concept of the BRICS may vanish, leaving just China versus other emerging economies." According to Merrill Lynch economist Lu Ting, "China will be largely immune to the impact due to its sustained current-account surplus, low foreign debt, huge exchange reserves, high savings and capital controls" (Tian 2013). Offering official multilateral acknowledgment of severe danger, deputy IMF managing director Zhu Min warned that if China opens its capital account by liberalizing the currency, it would exacerbate the global crisis—which is typically an observation an IMF man would repress (Tian 2013).

There are, however, some who believe in eco-social justice and think that not only can BRICS help fix problems caused by the end of the commodity cycle, fiscal austerity, and credit constraint, but that they also have the potential to *change* the structures of global power and potentially the world capitalist system at the same time. These commentators' arguments are not addressed through specific rebuttals, but the reader is encouraged to consult more optimistic recent BRICS analyses by Radhika Desai (2013), Pepe Escobar (2013), Glen Ford (2013), Dot Keet (2013), William Martin (2013), William Pesek (2013), Vladimir Shubin (2013), and Third World Network (2013).

However, even sympathetic commentators must concede that aside from halting the bombing of Syria in September 2013 and promoting Russia's geostrategic interests in relation to Crimea, the strategies advocated by BRICS leaders have so far had no discernible effect on the world's economic and ecological crises. Within the IMF, for example, Chinese voting power has risen substantially but left no genuine change in the institution's agenda. As for the World Bank, its presidency was grabbed by Barack Obama's nominee Jim Yong Kim in 2012 without a united response from the BRICS nations (Fry 2012). The Brazilians nominated a progressive economist, Jose Antonio Ocampo; the South Africans nominated neoliberal Nigerian finance minister Ngozi Okonjo-Iweala; and the Russians supported Kim. As for China, the reward for not putting up a fight was getting leadership of the bank's International Finance Corporation for Jin-Yong Cai. An Indian, Kaushik Basu, was made World Bank chief economist. And reflecting assimilation, not antagonism, in 2012 the BRICS countries contributed $75 billion to the recapitalization of the IMF, which meant that while China's voting share increased, Africa's decreased. In early 2014, however, the Republicans in the US Congress refused to codify the full set of adjustments to IMF voting power, leaving BRICS financial leaders furious but impotent.

Thus it was reasonable to ask whether the BRICS leaders were really serious about challenging the Bretton Woods system and other structures of global power. After all, for revolutionizing development finance, there was an alternative already in place that they could have supported: Banco del Sur (Bank of the South). Founded by the late Venezuelan president Hugo Chavez in 2007 and supported by Argentina, Bolivia, Brazil, Ecuador, Paraguay, and Uruguay, Banco del Sur already had $7 billion in capital by 2013. It offered a more profound development finance challenge to the Washington Consensus, especially after Ecuadoran radical economists led by Pedro Paez improved the design. Instead, the BRICS members appear to favor the stabilization of the world financial status quo rather than radically changing the most unfair and intrinsically destabilizing components.

The main evidence is China's ongoing financing of Washington's massive trade deficit by continuing to hold more than $1.3 trillion of US Treasury bills. Although in mid-2013 the Chinese sold around $40 billion net of T-bills, this would not genuinely weaken Washington's power, much less serve to catalyze a new currency that the world could more democratically manage instead of the Fed with its bias to the interests of the world's largest banks. Indeed, at this very time the Fed's monetary policy signaling was helping to tear apart the BRICS grouping. Notwithstanding rhetoric about increasing use of BRICS currencies or barter trade, not much more is being done to end the destructive system in which the US dollar has world seigniorage—i.e., it is the world's reserve currency, no matter how badly Washington officials abuse that power. If China really wants the renminbi to one day take its place, the pace at which this is happening is agonizingly slow, with only a 2014 energy deal between Russia and China hinting at future postdollar trade. In the meantime, as mid-2013 financial chaos showed, the other BRICS nations paid the price.

The BRICS experiment won't stand or fall on narrow grounds of development finance. But the most critical aspects of the world-economy operate through finance, for financiers still pull the strings in most national contexts, including in South Africa. Given the context of such extreme need for change, it is worth examining South Africa's particular stance, given its own record of having so dramatically moved from one kind of subimperialist power—a rogue regime hated by all civilized people—to another kind, one with enormous legitimacy in 1994.

## South Africa's "Seat at the Table"

In the immediate wake of apartheid, the global responsibilities that South Africa accepted under the leadership of Nelson Mandela (1994–1999) and his successor Thabo Mbeki's first four years as president were indeed impressive. In the first decade of democracy, Pretoria's representatives had hosted, chaired, initiated, or played leading roles in the following:

- Board of governors of the IMF and World Bank
- Non-Aligned Movement and G77 group of poor and middle-income countries
- United Nations (UN) Conference on Trade and Development
- The Commonwealth of Britain and its former colonies
- Organization of African Unity and later the African Union launch
- Southern African Development Community
- 2000 International AIDS Conference
- World Commission on Dams
- World Conference against Racism
- New Partnership for Africa's Development
- World Trade Organization (WTO) ministerial summits
- UN Financing for Development Monterrey Summit
- G8 Summits
- World Summit on Sustainable Development
- Davos World Economic Forums

Mbeki was subsequently occupied trying to hold onto power in South Africa, with a distracting three-year period (2005–2008) dominated by the unsuccessful campaign to keep Jacob Zuma at bay. After Mbeki was fired by his party's leadership collective in September 2008 and as the world-economy simultaneously melted down (thus requiring a new global configuration of power to arbitrate an urgent global financial bailout), caretaker president Kgalema Motlanthe sat quietly in two G20 summits: Washington in 2008 and London in 2009. At the latter (on

April 1), then finance minister Trevor Manuel played a crucial role in legitimating the recapitalization of the IMF.

Later in 2009, the newly installed President Zuma's first major international role was to join four other signatories to the Copenhagen Accord during the UN fifteenth session of the Conference of the Parties (COP 15) climate summit. By mid-2010 he could claim the hosting of both the soccer World Cup and a Chinese invitation to join the BRIC club with Brazil, India, and Russia. The following year, Zuma personally stepped onto the world stage by cochairing Ban Ki-moon's UN High-Level Panel on Global Sustainability. In December 2011, he and foreign minister Maite Nkoana-Mashabane hosted the UN COP 17 climate summit and by 2012 Zuma's ex-wife, former foreign minister Nkosazana Dlamini-Zuma, was installed in the African Union chair after a controversial election against Francophone Africa's incumbent candidate.[1] In 2013 Zuma hosted BRICS so as to present a "gateway" role for these fast-growing economies to more favorably invest on the African continent.

In these respects, Pretoria's in-house South African International Marketing Council (2013) was pleased that "evidence of South Africa's ability to punch above its weight includes the success of the BRICS summit in March in Durban. Outcomes from this meeting, including the idea of an international development bank for the developing world, seemed to set the BRICS club on a course of action after almost a decade of scheming and dreaming. Now Goldman Sachs bank official Jim O'Neill said, the time had come for the newest member of the group to get on with proving it deserved that seat at the table."

A year before, as a *New York Times* report argued, the BRICS members could "agitate for a seat at the table" of the global economy, through "signing new financial cooperation agreements ... [and] signaling discontent at their lack of influence over decision-making within the world's existing financial institutions, and exploring steps to do something about it" (Tatlow 2012).

What, however, was actually accomplished through these extraordinary opportunities? As I have spelled out elsewhere (Bond 2003; 2006a; 2006b; 2009; 2012a),

- The IMF and World Bank made only trivial changes to their operations, such as a slight shifting of their voting power to accommodate China, mainly at the expense of Africa, even when the South African finance minister was in the chair and ran the institutions' development committee.
- The Non-Aligned Movement and G77 faded into obscurity, unable to wrestle the potentially vast power of China ("G77 + China") into a unified stance.
- The UN Conference on Trade and Development was pulled toward the neoliberal Washington Consensus during South African trade minister Alec Erwin's presidency.
- In its single major challenge, the Commonwealth failed to shift Zimbabwe to democracy (Robert Mugabe withdrew Zimbabwe's membership).

- The African Union first fell under Muammar Ghaddafi's influence (and then in 2011 chided Pretoria for officially supporting the NATO bombing of Libya instead of pursuing the African Union peace strategy), and in 2012 suffered a severe Anglophone/Francophone split over Dlamini-Zuma's leadership candidacy, in view of the prior agreement that the continent's most powerful countries (South Africa, Nigeria, and Egypt) would not propose their citizens for such central posts.
- The Southern African Development Community proved incapable not only of achieving economic coherence (the Southern African Customs Union nearly breaking apart over a European Union trade deal in 2012–2013) given South Africa's domination, but also of defending even liberal rights (e.g., white farmers' property rights against Mugabe's 2000s land redistribution), much less liberal democracy (Mugabe's various infringements of the 2008 Global Political Agreement power-sharing).
- The 2000 International AIDS Conference was the scene of the opening rounds in the battle between the Treatment Action Campaign and Pretoria's genocidal AIDS-denialist policy makers led by Mbeki.
- The World Commission on Dams report discouraging mega-hydro projects was subsequently rejected not only by the World Bank and prolific dam-building nations like China and India, but even by South Africa, whose water minister Ronnie Kasrils, following commission chair Kader Asmal, downgraded Asmal's work.
- At the World Conference against Racism Mbeki shot down nongovernmental organizations (NGOs) and African leaders who were demanding slavery/colonialism/apartheid reparations, as well as the reasonable Palestine-solidarity demand that Zionism be considered a form of racism.
- The New Partnership for Africa's Development provided merely a "home-grown" Washington Consensus, was rejected even by one of the four cosponsors (Senegal's Abdoulaye Wade), and failed to generate even the anticipated Western neoliberal countries' support (in part because its African Peer Review Mechanism (APRM) was ultimately farcical).
- The World Trade Organization ministerial summits were, at their worst (especially Doha in 2001), an opportunity for Erwin to split African delegations so as to prevent consensus denial by trade ministers (nevertheless, WTO critics prevailed by paralyzing the summits in Seattle in 1999 and Cancun four years later).
- At the UN Financing for Development Monterrey Summit, Manuel was summit cochair and legitimized ongoing IMF/World Bank strategies, including debt bondage, yet the proposed new international financial architecture proved incapable of addressing systemic risk and contagion with the resulting world financial chaos in 2008–2013.
- The G8 Summits provided Africa only patronizing rhetoric.

- At the World Summit on Sustainable Development, Mbeki undermined UN democratic procedure, facilitated the privatization of nature, and did nothing to address the plight of the world's poor majority.
- At the Davos World Economic Forums, Africa was largely ignored.
- At G20 meetings, including in London in 2009 (where Manuel presented his IMF committee's plan for a $750 billion recapitalization of the IMF and hence the world-economy), the only accomplishment was to delay and dis- place—not *resolve*—the world crisis by shifting the burden from private-sector overindebtedness to public-sector bailout/austerity.
- The Copenhagen Accord boiled down to the United States–Brazil–China– India–South African destruction of the Kyoto Protocol in favor of Washing- ton's preferred avoidance of binding emissions cuts, and in terms of process the five leaders "blew up the United Nations," as climate activist Bill McKibben (2009) accurately observed.

In all of this, as commentator Xolela Mangcu (2013) correctly observes, Pretoria politicians and their Johannesburg corporate allies were simply "competing for global resources alongside many others." But, Mangcu claims, in none of the afore- mentioned mishaps do South Africa's ruling elites genuinely "have a foreign policy dispute with the US." This may be an exaggeration, since Syria and Libya—and later, Russia's expansionism—were cases in which Pretoria took a position opposed to the United States. But more general Washington-Pretoria collaboration meant, as Mangcu put it, "We do not have prisoners in Guantanamo and face no threat of drone strikes."

Reflecting how closely Washington and Pretoria worked when the stakes were seen to be high, South African officials connived in unconstitutional "rendition"—i.e., involuntary deportation for the purpose of torture—of supposed foreign terrorists (Ross 2010). Ironically, "terrorist" was the very description that Washington officially gave Nelson Mandela from the time the CIA helped put him in jail in 1962 until a Congressional vote removed the label in 2008. Former South African housing minister and mining tycoon Tokyo Sexwale learned in late 2013 that he remains on terrorist watch lists.

Cooperation with neocolonial Western powers apparently requires the latter's courtesy, for according to Khadija Patel (2013b), the visit by Francois Hollande in October 2013 confirmed a spirit of collaboration, not hostility, when it came to sharing military duties up-continent:

Zuma was more receptive to French intervention in Mali than he was of French intervention in Cote d'Ivoire. Deputy Minister of International Relations and Co-Operation, Ebrahim Ebrahim, in reconciling the difference in South Africa's stance on French intervention in Cote d'Ivoire and Mali in January, said one key difference between Mali and Cote d'Ivoire was that Hollande had telephoned

Zuma to ask his opinion and inform him about the French plans in Mali. "Sarkozy did not ring our president to inform him."

Is Pretoria therefore a "subimperialist" ally of the West? If you choose to use that term, the risk is of being chided—by no less than Nkoana-Mashabane (2013)—for "a dogmatic application of classical notions of imperialism and Immanuel Wallerstein's core-periphery model to a situation that is fundamentally different from what these theories were trying to comprehend and explain.... The tragic mishap in this case is that such intellectuals will be left behind and rendered irrelevant by history." But by way of rebuttal, is a prerequisite for being "relevant"—and getting the desired seat at the table—to follow the logic of neoliberalism, financialization, and extreme uneven and combined development, especially in intensifying the looting of Africa? The adjective "subimperial" is one way to describe that form of "relevance."

## Subimperial or Anti-Imperial BRICS?

In 1965, Ruy Mauro Marini (1965, 22) defined subimperialism as "collaborating actively with imperialist expansion, assuming in this expansion the position of a key nation." Nearly half a century later, such insights appear prescient in the wake of the rise of BRICS as an active alliance. By 2013 these five key nations encircling the traditional triad (the United States, European Union, and Japan) were decisive collaborators with imperialism. They advanced the cause of neoliberalism by reaffirming and recapitalizing its global institutional power structures. They colluded in its core logic by driving overproductive and overconsumptive maldevelopment. And they hastened the destruction of the world environment through unprecedented contributions to climate change. Further, they assisted in sabotaging any potentially workable global-scale ecological regulation. Overall, their role in the "new imperialism"—as David Harvey (2003) describes the recent burst of super-exploitative eco-social relations—was *accommodating*, not *oppositional*.

Confusingly to some, BRICS regimes carried out this agenda at the same time they offered radical, even occasionally "anti-imperialist," rhetoric and mainly diplomatic actions—e.g., at the United Nations Security Council, mainly for the sake of their internal nationalist political needs. In two cases in mid-2013, the diplomatic strategy served to put Washington on its back foot. First, in the case of Syria, Russian leader Vladimir Putin organized strong opposition—and then an alternative strategy to facilitate the Assad regime's chemical-weapon disarmament—at the G20 meeting in St. Petersburg, supported by the other BRICS members. Obama was forced to retreat on his bombing threat.

Second, there were objections made especially powerfully by Brazilian president Dilma Rousseff regarding Edward Snowden's whistleblower revelations about US National Security Agency hacking into a large proportion of the world's emails, text messages, and phone conversations. She even canceled a state visit to Washington in October 2013 to protest, as she was one of thirty-five world leaders—including many US allies—whose personal phone was tapped. The Brazilian state oil company Petrobras was another victim of NSA hacking, confirming US economic espionage on an unprecedented scale. Snowden, meanwhile, enjoyed well-earned respite from US persecution in Russia as a refugee, although he waited several weeks in Moscow's international airport departure lounge after fleeing Hong Kong because China could not offer him safety. Ironically, at the same time Snowden was evading the fate of fellow US whistleblower Chelsea Manning, the Russian government arrested thirty Greenpeace activists for protesting Arctic oil drilling; they faced fifteen-year jail terms but because of Putin's need for global political credibility prior to the 2014 Winter Olympics, they and Pussy Riot band members were given amnesty.

Aside from these two 2013 episodes and the 2014 Russian invasion of Crimea (supported by the BRICS nations, especially after Russia was temporarily expelled from the G8 and threatened with suspension from the G20's November 2014 Australian summit), there was active BRICS collaboration with imperialist expansion in many other ways, extending far deeper into geopolitics and processes of accumulation. One was the regional geopolitical relationship of imperial and subimperial agendas in Africa. Another was Pretoria's relegitimization of neoliberalism, which reinforces US power, especially dollar hegemony. Neoliberalism is a project that most explicitly benefits each BRICS country's financial and commercial fractions of capital. In South Africa, although some of the longstanding (apartheid-era) critique of subimperial regional domination still applies, in part because of South African corporate self-interests, what is new comes mainly from the economy's "financialization." Indeed, financial deregulation was a prerequisite for the country's "elite transition" from racial to class apartheid during the 1990s, and this process also has a subimperial dimension (Bond 2005).

Seen from Africa, how does subimperialism relate to imperialism? In the recent era, the main military conflicts associated with US-centered imperialism have been in the Middle East, Central Asia, and North Africa; there, Israel, Saudi Arabia, Turkey, and Egypt have long been cited as Washington's subimperial allies. But from the 1960s through late 1980s, southern Africa was the site of numerous wars featuring anticolonial liberation struggles and Cold War rivalries. Apartheid South Africa was such a strong and comforting deputy to Washington that the latter regularly assisted the former in material and ideological terms, at least through the Reagan administration, which ended in 1989.

Over two subsequent decades in this region, however, we have witnessed mainly state-civil tensions. These are typically associated with conflict-resource battles (e.g., in the Great Lakes region, where southern Africa meets central Africa and where millions have been killed by minerals-oriented warlords), neoliberalism (e.g., South Africa and Zambia), an occasional coup (e.g., Madagascar), dictatorial rule (e.g., Zimbabwe, Swaziland, and Malawi), and in many cases a combination.

The civil wars engineered by apartheid and the CIA in Mozambique and Angola had ceased by 1991 and 2001, respectively, with millions dead but with both Lusophone countries subsequently recording high GDP growth rates, albeit with extreme inequality. (In late 2013 the Mozambican National Resistance, RENAMO, revived armed hostilities against a far stronger FRELIMO, the Mozambique Liberation Front, and with no obvious external support.)

Obama's visit to South Africa in mid-2013, celebrated by some (Mangcu 2013) but protested by thousands, coincided with 350 US soldiers training South African Defense Force (SANDF) troops in Port Elizabeth. As the *New York Times* reported, "The soldiers worked together to analyze an enemy and how it would react, and in the end seized a rebel base. For the South Africans, it was a chance to learn tactics and techniques that American troops refined in Iraq and Afghanistan. For the Americans, it offered an opportunity to gain new insights on African counterinsurgency" (Schmitt 2013).

Less than six months later, 1,350 South African troops and 1,700 Tanzanian and Malawian allies helped Congolese forces destroy the guerrilla group M23 (a breakaway from the Democratic Republic of the Congo, army backed by Rwanda and Uganda) in the minerals-rich eastern part of the country. At the time of writing, several dozen similar—although less equipped—groups remain as localist warlords there, in a site where over the last two decades *six million* people have died as "resource curse" victims.

With fewer direct military conflicts in Africa but more subtle forms of imperial control, and with "Africa Rising" rhetoric abundant since the early 2000s' commodity price boom, the continent and specifically the southern Africa region appear as attractive sites for investment, in no small measure because of South Africa's "gateway" function, with Johannesburg as a regional branch-plant base for a variety of multinational corporations.

According to a National Union of Metalworkers of South Africa (2013) policy analysis,

> Over the past 20 years, *the neo-liberal petit bourgeois leadership of the ANC* has ensured that imperialism not only retains its interest in South Africa, but imperialism consolidated and restructured its operations through de-listing and dual listing of South African monopolies. The imperialist grip on South Africa has been consolidated through the rapid increase in foreign monopoly ownership of key sectors in the South African economy. Having consolidated its interests in South Africa as its springboard, imperialism further benefits by using South Africa as a gateway to the rest of the continent.

Yet thanks to South African politicians' anti-imperialist rhetorical twitch, one of the most confusing features of the post-apartheid era has been foreign policy. This is especially true in light of conflicting traditions of internationalism from which the African National Congress (ANC), operating mainly in exile from 1963 to 1990, during the period Mandela was imprisoned, launched its bid for power.

Material and ideological supporters of the ANC ranged from the United Nations, the Soviet Union, and Sweden to black consciousness, Third Worldist, and international progressive movements and institutions in civil society. Hence it was not out of character, given the ANC's hot political traditions, to hear Nelson Mandela declare, just prior to the invasion of Iraq in 2003, that George W. Bush, "who cannot think properly, is now wanting to plunge the world into a holocaust. If there is a country which has committed unspeakable atrocities, it is the United States of America" (Murphy 2003).

But reality reasserted, and within weeks three Iraq-bound US warships docked and refueled in Africa's largest harbor, in Durban. South Africa's state-owned weapons manufacturer sold $160 million worth of artillery propellants and 326 handheld laser range-finders to the British army, and 125 laser-guidance sights to the US Marines. Bush visited Mandela's successor, Mbeki, in Pretoria in July 2003 and left the impression, according to Johannesburg's *Business Day* newspaper, "of a growing, if not intimate trust between himself and Mbeki. The amount of public touching, hugging and backpatting they went through was well beyond the call of even friendly diplomatic duty" (*Business Day* 2003). By May 2004, Mandela had withdrawn his criticism: "The United States is the most powerful state in the world and it is not good to remain in tension with the most powerful state" (Associated Press 2004). Mandela's outburst was one of many confusing signals from South Africa's leaders: occasionally talking left while mainly walking right, indeed sometimes talking left *so as to walk right.*

Throughout this period, there was a restrained yet increasingly important Washington geopolitical agenda for Africa, which Bush's first secretary of state, Colin Powell endorsed in a commissioned document entitled *Rising US Stakes in Africa*: political stabilization of Sudan (whose oil was craved by Washington); support for Africa's decrepit capital markets, which could allegedly "jump-start" Washington's Millennium Challenge Account; more attention to energy, especially the "massive future earnings by Nigeria and Angola, among other key West African oil producers"; promotion of wildlife conservation; increased "counterterrorism" efforts, which included "a Muslim-outreach initiative"; expanded peace operations transferred to tens of thousands of African troops thanks to new G8 funding; and more attention to AIDS (Morrison and Kansteiner 2004). On all but Sudan, South African cooperation was crucial for the US imperial agenda. However, after the US military's humiliating 1993 Black Hawk Down episode in Somalia, there was insufficient appetite at the Pentagon for direct troop deployment in Africa, and as a result President Bill Clinton was compelled to apologize for standing idly by during the 1994 Rwandan genocide.

In the future, as Africa Command (Africom) head Carter Ham explained in 2011, Washington "would eventually need an Africom that could undertake more traditional military operations ... [although] not conducting operations—that's for the Africans to do" (Africom Public Affairs 2012). Likewise, the US Air University's *Strategic Studies Quarterly* cited a US military advisor to the African Union: "We don't want to see our guys going in and getting whacked.... We want Africans to go in" (Cochran 2010). In late 2006, for example, when Bush wanted to invade Somalia to rid the country of its nascent Islamic Courts government, he called in Mbeki to assist with legitimating the idea, though it was ultimately carried out by Meles Zenawi's Ethiopian army three weeks later (White House Press Office 2006). When in 2011 Obama wanted to invade Libya to rid the country of Muammar Ghaddafi, South Africa voted affirmatively for NATO bombing within the UN Security Council (where it held a temporary seat), in spite of enormous opposition within the African Union (Bond 2012b).

## Subimperial Commercial Processes

The broader economic context for South African subimperialism is crucial because South African expansion into African markets was a logical aspect of geopolitics. Put simply but accurately by the Texas intelligence firm Stratfor (2009) in an internal memo (as revealed by WikiLeaks in 2013),

> South Africa's history is driven by the interplay of competition and cohabitation between domestic and foreign interests exploiting the country's mineral resources. Despite being led by a democratically-elected government, the core imperatives of South Africa remain the maintenance of a liberal regime that permits the free flow of labor and capital to and from the southern Africa region, as well as the maintenance of a superior security capability able to project into south-central Africa.

Concretely, Stratfor (2009) argues,

> Angola and the Democratic Republic of the Congo (DRC) are prime areas of interest. South Africa has long held an interest in those two countries' diamond mines, but it has been unable to develop lasting control over them. South Africa has had a little more success with mining operations in the DRC, which it accesses through Zambia's Copperbelt province. Angola and the DRC are anxious to develop diamond concessions in the remote interior of their respective countries, where mining operations so far remain largely artisanal. South African technical and financial know-how can be used to develop the largely untapped diamond riches in those two countries, and the ANC government knows that it can bring its influence to bear to present South African companies favorably to gain mining concessions.

In other words, according to Nairobi-based journalist Charles Onyango-Obbo (2013),

> South Africa put on its suit, picked up its fat briefcase, and stepped out into the continent. Imperial expeditions have not changed over the ages. They always require that the generals, princelings, and businessmen earn some silver and gold from it, if they are to continue cultivating elite and ruling class support for it back home. Places like the DRC, where there is plenty of silver and gold will therefore always be the logical and rational destination—whether the imperialist is Asian, European, American, or African.

With capital pushed and pulled to and from the region the "silver and gold" earned were increasingly important to shore up South African firms' balance sheets. The earlier opening of South Africa to the world-economy was a vital prerequisite, however, introducing its own intense contradictions. In late 1993 as apartheid walls tumbled, Mandela authorized agreements binding on the first democratic government to repay apartheid-era debt, to give the South African Reserve Bank insulation from democracy and to take up an IMF loan with standard structural-adjustment conditions. In 1994 South Africa acceded to what became the World Trade Organization, at great cost to its uncompetitive manufacturing industries and their workers, and in 1995 the financial rand-exchange-control system was entirely lifted, thus allowing wealthy South Africans permission to export a much greater share of their apartheid-era wealth (Bond 2005).

Repeated exchange-control relaxation by the South African Reserve Bank subsequently prioritized South African corporate investment in the Africa region. But by 2000 the financial headquarters of what were formerly Johannesburg- and Cape Town–based corporations—Anglo American Corporation, DeBeers, Gencor (later BHP Billiton), Old Mutual and Liberty Life insurance, South African Breweries (later merged with Miller), Investec bank, Dimension Data ITMondi paper, etc.—escaped the continent entirely. These largest of South African firms are now primarily listed in London, New York, and Melbourne. The resulting outflows of profits, dividends, and interest after 2000 are the main reason South Africa was ranked by the *Economist* (2009) as the riskiest among seventeen emerging markets in early 2009. And as mentioned earlier, in order to cover the hard currency required to facilitate the vast capital flight, which apparently peaked at 23.4 percent of GDP in 2007 (Mohammed 2010), vast new foreign-debt obligations were taken on.

During this period of increasing economic desperation, the regional hinterland was shifting, especially because of the commodity super-cycle that rose especially quickly from 2002 to 2008. The African continent expanded its rate of trading with the major emerging economies—especially China—from around 5 to 20 percent of all commerce in the post-apartheid era (1994–2012). By 2009, China had overtaken the United States as Africa's main trading partner. Soon after that, rationalizing and facilitating tighter continental economic relationships with BRICS countries became one of Pretoria's leading objectives, according to deputy foreign minister Marius Fransman (2012): "South Africa also presents a gateway for investment on the continent, and over the next 10 years the African continent will need $480 billion for infrastructure development."

Not just a gateway but a vanguard, for as Nkoana-Mashabane correctly observed, "In 2012, South Africa invested in the rest of Africa more than any other country in the world" (Mataboge 2013). In 2010, seventeen out of Africa's top twenty companies were South African, even after the capital flight a decade earlier (Laverty 2011). As Ernst and Young's *Africa Attractiveness Survey* (2013) recorded, thanks to predictable mining houses and MTN cellphone service, Standard Bank, Shoprite retail, and Sanlam insurance, South Africa's foreign direct investment in the rest of Africa had risen 57 percent since 2007.

The results were mixed, however. Central African Republic (CAR) investments, for example, followed the forging of close ties between several individuals at the top level of the ANC and its Chancellor House investment arm, in search of a diamond monopoly facilitated by a well-known CAR fixer, Didier Pereira. In 2006 these deals were codified by presidential-level relations involving Mbeki. But contradictions emerged and intensified as France dropped its traditional support for the CAR's dictator Francois Bozizé. He then visited Pretoria to request urgent military support (Amabhungane 2013). In January 2013 Zuma sent hundreds more SANDF troops to Bangui for a five-year commitment whose cost was officially estimated at R1.28 billion. "We have assets there that need protection," according to deputy foreign minister Ebrahim Ebrahim (Patel 2013a).

Tragically, the day before BRICS dignitaries arrived for the Durban summit, on March 25, 2013, more than a dozen corpses of South African soldiers were recovered in Bangui after a two-day battle in which hundreds of local fighters and bystanders were killed. Two hundred SANDF troops were apparently trying to *guard the South African assets* against the Chad-backed Seleka rebel movement. Bozizé fled to safety and Seleka invaded his presidential compound, taking state power that day in spite of resistance from the SANDF men they labeled "mercenaries." Two *Sunday Times* reporters (Hosken and Mahlangu 2013) offer quotations from interviews with SANDF troops who made it back alive:

> Our men were deployed to various parts of the city, *protecting belongings of South Africans*. They were the first to be attacked. Everyone thought it was those who were ambushed, but it was the guys outside *the different buildings—the ones which belong to businesses in Jo'burg*.... We were lied to straight out.... We were not supposed to be here. We did not come here to do this. We were told we were here to serve and protect, to ensure peace. (emphasis added)[2]

This tragic episode cold potentially have led to the "Vietnam syndrome," in which after a humiliating military experience, popular support waned for other US government attempts to protect its corporate allies' assets. Zuma approached the quandary with fortitude, however, calling for "decisive intervention: an African Standby Force for rapid deployment in crisis areas" (Msimang 2013).

A few weeks later he sent another 1,350 SANDF troops to the resource-rich eastern Democratic Republic of the Congo, making up nearly one-half of a UN force, alongside Tanzanian and Malawian troops. It was the first known UN peace-keeping mission that was authorized to go on the offensive, and immediately after South Africa's formidable helicopter firepower (three Rooivalks and five Oryx) flew five sorties, the M23 rebel movement surrendered in October 2013. According to *Jane's Defence Weekly* (Heitman 2013b), "the Rooivalks were extremely effective, firing 70 mm rockets with great accuracy at M23 defensive positions." In observing that the helicopter was originally designed to fight Cuban troops defending Angola from apartheid, industry analyst Simon Shear (2013) ruefully remarked, "We should not forget that the Rooivalk, as with so many of the country's advanced weapons, was conceived and designed in the service of brutal wars fought by an illegitimate regime."

The DRC battlefield was, notably, not far from where Zuma's nephew Khulubuse had bought into a $9 billion oil-exploration project with the apparent assistance of Pretoria, as DRC president Joseph Kabila personally approved the concessions for the "Zuma family" (Pauw 2014). So with the hubris of renewed subimperial ambitions and capabilities, it was now time, said Nkoana-Mashabane, to do business:

> The new South Africa is 19 years old, but we're always confronted with this history of the 101-year-old political movement [ANC]. The 101-year-old grandfather wants to go around making peace everywhere. The 19-year-old has got to look at every aspect of a relationship, needs to be impatient, and say: *"Hey, we need to make our people get the peace dividends"* ... South African companies need *to be more aggressive, but we can do better if we are co-ordinated.* This 19-year-old who's beginning to discover that there's no place overseas where we can go and make money, but that *we can make money in our own neighborhood,* needs to move faster.
>
> We've moved beyond talking, we've established an economic diplomacy tool for our diplomats. Our White Paper on international relations says *our diplomats must play an important role in advancing the cause of South African businesses* beyond our borders and attracting investments in their respective countries of accreditation. (Mataboge 2013; emphasis added)

A few weeks before, Zuma himself had made a public appeal to South African corporations to become more active on the continent: "It is always good to get there first. And if we don't get there as African business then people from far away get there first, then we complain later to say they are interfering with us" (De Wet 2013). South African capital's drive to accumulate up-continent was already moving at a rapid rate, as Johannesburg business sought out new opportunities, especially in mining, retail, banking, breweries, construction, services, and tourism. The largest South African corporations benefited from the African financial liberalization that Pretoria strongly promoted (Mminele 2012), so they could repatriate profits with increasing ease. However, most of the money did not stop in Johannesburg, as was the case prior to 2000. The financial flight went mainly to London, where Anglo American Corporation, DeBeers, Old Mutual insurance, South African Breweries, Liberty Life insurance, and other huge South African firms had relisted at the turn of the millennium, thanks to permission from Mbeki and Manuel (Bond 2003).

How would BRICS affect these relations? On one hand there would be even more intense competitive pressures transmitted through trade, finance, and investment. These became so severe in mid-2013 in relation to import of chickens from Brazil, as one example, that South African trade minister Rob Davies imposed an 82 percent import tariff, throwing into question whether in reality BRICS was a genuine bloc of like-minded allies. More generally, however, to enhance the extraction process for South Africa's benefit, the National Planning Commission (2012) argued,

> The country's diplomats should work *closely with business and industry leaders*, with research and academic institutions and with epistemic communities, to facilitate relationships with counterparts in BRICS.... The Department of International Relations and Cooperation, in collaboration with South Africa's research institutions and professional bodies, should lead a strategic drive to *engage China on minerals, mining, research and development and infrastructure expansion on the continent....*
>
> Strengthen economic diplomacy and build *effective partnerships with the private sector and state-owned enterprises*. In areas such as science, culture, higher education, sport and environmental protection, there is a need to showcase South Africa and promote its presence and leadership on strategic issues as part of its "soft power" in international relations, without losing sight of the increased value of mental power—the ability of countries to *show restraint on emotional impulses and maintain a relatively stable mind-set in getting along with each other* during international negotiations, and in general.
>
> Involve the business community in foreign relations. South Africa's sophisticated business community needs to be intimately involved in foreign relations. Diplomats may strike foreign cooperation deals, but it is private companies that actually trade across borders. They are, therefore, central to wealth creation. *The local business community is willing and able to provide managerial, administrative and general capacity-building services to South Africa's regional institutions.* It is a resource that needs to be fully explored. (emphasis added)

The difference from a decade earlier was palpable. In mid-2002, in spite of a high-profile endorsement of the New Partnership for Africa's Development

(NEPAD) by 187 business leaders and firms led by Anglo American, BHP Billiton, and the Absa banking group, Johannesburg business was skeptical about the continental market. In 2004 there were still no investments made in twenty key infrastructure projects, only vocal corporate complaints that the APRM had insufficient teeth to discipline errant politicians. According to the chief reporter of (pro-NEPAD) *Business Day*, "The private sector's reluctance to get involved threatens to derail NEPAD's ambitions" (Rose 2004).

On the other hand, the prospect that Johannesburg-based corporations would be "new imperialists" was of "great concern," according to Pretoria's then–public enterprises minister, Jeff Radebe, in early 2004: "There are strong perceptions that many South African companies working elsewhere in Africa come across as arrogant, disrespectful, aloof and careless in their attitude towards local business communities, work-seekers and even governments" (SAPA 2004). The same sentiment was expressed by veteran Namibian political economist Henning Melber (2013) because Pretoria "also always protected its own industry and destroyed infant industries in other countries. At the same time SA [South African] companies ruthlessly destroyed local enterprises to create monopolies in the Southern African Customs Union states. I never had any illusions that SA economic interests were only pursuing exactly these. Yes, from a Namibian perspective SA is subimperialist and a junior partner to imperialism."

To illustrate drawing upon a telling incident in 2012, the Johannesburg parastatal firm Rand Water was forced to leave Ghana after failing—with a Dutch for-profit partner (Aqua Vitens)—to improve Accra's water supply. This followed similar expulsions in Maputo (Saur sent back to Paris) and Dar es Salaam (Biwater to London). Rand Water had long claimed its role in Ghana was part of both the NEPAD and Millennium Development Goals mandate to increase public-private partnerships in water delivery (Amanthis 2012). But this disdain was also true of Pretoria bureaucrats, according to the National Planning Commission (2012): "In six months of consultations, the NPC encountered, alongside the *perception of the country as a regional bully*, and that South African policy-makers tend to have a *weak grasp of African geopolitics*" (emphasis added). The regional-bully image was amplified in October 2013 when, during a discussion at the University of the Witwatersrand about a controversial new tolling system for Johannesburg-Pretoria highways, Zuma defended his semiprivatization strategy with an unfortunate choice of words: "We can't think like Africans in Africa. It's not some national road in Malawi."

## Subimperial Promotion of Hinterland Neoliberalism

Under Mbeki, official South Africa–Africa relations were similarly harsh, and also in the service of neoliberalism. The Johannesburg *Sunday Times* reported from the July 2003 African Union meeting in Maputo that Mbeki was viewed by other African leaders as "too powerful, and they privately accuse him of wanting to impose his will on others. In the corridors they call him the George Bush of Africa, leading the most powerful nation in the neighborhood and using his financial and military muscle to further his own agenda" (Munusamy 2003). These critics of Mbeki were joined by African intellectuals who demanded better from their leaders as well, including those who understand Pretoria's continental ambitions. To illustrate, at a joint conference in April 2002 in Accra, Ghana, the Council for the Development of Social Science Research in Africa and Third World Network-Africa (2002) identified the "most fundamental flaws of NEPAD" as follows:

(a) the neoliberal economic policy framework at the heart of the plan ... which repeats the structural adjustment policy packages of the preceding two decades and overlooks the disastrous effects of those policies;

(b) the fact that in spite of its proclaimed recognition of the central role of the African people to the plan, the African people have not played any part in the conception, design and formulation of NEPAD;

(c) notwithstanding its stated concerns for social and gender equity, it adopts the social and economic measures that have contributed to the marginalization of women;

(d) in spite of claims of African origins, its main targets are foreign donors, particularly in the G8;

(e) its vision of democracy is defined by the needs of creating a functional market....

Mbeki's APRM was conceived so that African regimes—including South Africa's, to great internal consternation—would essentially review themselves with kid gloves. When civil-society critique emerged, this was repressed (Bond 2009). According to Bronwen Manby (2008) from AfriMAP (a pro-APRM NGO),

> Although each country that has undergone the APRM process is supposed to report back to the APR Forum on its progress, there is no serious monitoring exercise of how effectively this is done. Nor any sanctions for failure to act. Nor, apparently, is there any real system to ensure that the commitments the government makes address the most important problems highlighted in the APRM review....
>
> With no formalized role for parliamentarians or civil society to hold the government's feet to the fire should it fail to perform ... the APRM process seems doomed to become little more than a cosmetic exercise without effect in the real world of policy and decision making.

NEPAD also endorsed liberalized trade, though this was an increasingly exploitative process because of the "Singapore issues" advanced by the G8 countries: investment, competition, trade facilitation, and government procurement. The new conditionalities amplified grievances of poor countries regarding the G8's vast agricultural subsidies, unfair industrial tariffs, incessant services privatization, and intellectual-property monopolies. Together, they prompted African-Caribbean-Pacific withdrawal from the ministerial summit of the WTO in Cancun in September 2003, leading to its collapse, with no subsequent improvements in the following years.

Although more recently there was loose talk of "Africa Rising" thanks to high GDP growth in several countries—mainly those that benefited from the commodity boom or civil wars ending—the actual wealth of Sub-Saharan Africa shrunk dramatically during the 2000s once we factor in nonrenewable-resource depletion. Thanks mainly to trade in commodities, at the height of the boom Africa recorded a 6 percent annual decline in "adjusted net savings," in which GDP is corrected for ecological and social factors, by even the World Bank (2011). In other words, by following NEPAD's orthodoxy and being drawn deeper into the world-economy, Africans suffered worsening resource curse in a variety of ways, including malgovernance, ecological damage, displacement, repression of protest, physical asset stripping, and capital flight (Bond 2012a). As we consider later in this chapter, this was also a major feature of South African financial relations in the region. But one issue stands above all others in threatening the continent's and indeed the planet's future.

## Climate Policy Fuses Imperialism and Subimperialism

The most extreme way that Pretoria has lubricated global-scale neoliberalism with adverse implications for Africa as a whole is in climate policy. Here, South African elite interests conflicted most with those of the broader hinterland (as well as of most South Africans). Pretoria's predominant desire was, first, to maintain extremely high emissions levels on behalf of the country's "minerals-energy complex" and, second, to sabotage global climate talks by wrecking the Kyoto Protocol at summits in Copenhagen in 2009 and again in Durban in 2011.

Indeed, an important pre-BRICS example of Zuma's personal role in adjusting rather than transforming global governance was the December 2009 lineup of the BASIC (Brazil, South Africa, India, China) countries' leadership with Washington to ensure climate catastrophe. At the COP 15 summit in Denmark, Zuma joined Barack Obama, Lula da Silva, Wen Jiabao and Manmohan Singh to foil the Kyoto Protocol's mandatory emissions cuts, thus confirming that at least 4 degrees of global warming will occur by 2100, translating to 9 degrees in the African heartland. This Naomi Klein (2009) called "nothing more than a grubby pact between the world's biggest emitters: I'll pretend that you are doing something about climate change if you pretend that I am too. Deal? Deal."[3]

A secondary objective of the Copenhagen Accord and Durban COP 17—aside from avoiding binding emissions cuts—was to raise investor confidence in the crashing carbon markets. This was especially vital for elites after the 2008 financial meltdown, when over the subsequent five years the price of carbon fell by 90 percent in the main EU market. The strategy, initially, was to continue the fiction of Northern corporate carbon offsetting via "Clean Development Mechanism" (CDM) carbon trading by the BASIC countries until they were discontinued at the end of 2012. After that, not only could BASIC's polluting industries intensify their own CDM project development in hinterland markets, but they also would establish new internal carbon markets, initially in Brazil and China. (Unlike the other BRICS nations, South Africa faced such adverse conditions for establishing a carbon market because of the $CO_2$ emissions dominance by two firms, Eskom and Sasol, that the 2013 Carbon Tax Policy downplayed prospects for this strategy.)

As Steffen Böhm, Maria Ceci Misoczky, and Sandra Moog (2012) argue,

> the subimperialist drive has remained the same: while domestic capital continues to invest heavily in extractive and monocultural industries at home, it is increasingly searching for investment opportunities in other peripheral markets as well, precipitating processes of accumulation by dispossession within their broader spheres of influence. This mode of development can be observed in many semi-peripheral nations, particularly in the BRICS countries. China's extensive investment in African arable land and extractive industries in recent years has been well documented. What is perhaps less well recognized in the development literature, however, is the extent to which financing from carbon markets like the CDM is now being leveraged by elites from these BRICS countries, to help underwrite these forms of subimperialist expansion.

In terms of global-scale climate negotiations, the Washington and BASIC negotiators explicitly act on behalf of their fossil-fuel and other extractive industries to slow emission-reduction obligations. But as witnessed again at the Warsaw COP 19, they all supported a financial-sector backup in the event a global climate regime did appear in 2020, as agreed at the Durban COP 17. Similar cozy ties between Pretoria politicians, London-based mining houses, Johannesburg "Black Economic Empowerment" tycoons, and sweetheart trade unions were subsequently exposed at the massacre of thirty-four workers on strike at the Lonmin Marikana platinum mine on August 16, 2012. Other BRICS countries have similar power configurations, and in Russia's case it led to a formal withdrawal from the Kyoto Protocol's second commitment period (2012–2020) in spite of huge "hot air" benefits the country would have earned in carbon markets as a result of the industrial economy's disastrous exposure to the world-economy during the 1990s. That economic crash cut Russian emissions far below 1990 Soviet Union levels during the first (2005–2012) commitment period. But given the 2008–2013 crash of carbon markets—where the hot-air benefits would have earlier been realized as €33/ton benefits but by early 2013 fell to below €3/ton—Moscow's calculation was to promote its own oil and gas industries helter-skelter, and hence binding emissions cuts were not in Russia's interests, no matter that 2010–2011 climate-related droughts and wildfires raised the price of wheat to extreme levels and did tens of billions of dollars of damage.

The same pro-corporate calculations are being made in the four other BRICS nations, although their leaders did sometimes posture about the need for larger northern-industrial-country emissions cuts. However, the crucial processes in which UN climate regulatory language was hammered out climaxed in Durban in December 2011 in a revealing manner: "The Durban Platform was promising because of what it did not say," bragged US State Department advisor Trevor Houser to the *New York Times*. "There is no mention of historic responsibility or per capita emissions. There is no mention of economic development as the priority for developing countries. There is no mention of a difference between developed and developing country action" (Broder 2012). COP 17 was also celebrated by financiers because of its commitment to "new market mechanisms" which at COP 19 led to a renewed fetish for a "global carbon market." The warnings from South Africa should have kicked in because the "Durban Platform" should have, according to a front-page *Financial Times* article (Clark 2011), provided

> a fresh stimulus to the world's floundering carbon markets, according to bankers and analysts. "The deal provides a significant boost for investors in low-carbon technology," said Abyd Karmali, global head of carbon markets at Bank of America Merrill Lynch, adding this was an achievement amid the woes of the eurozone crisis . . . he said the deal was "like a Viagra shot for the flailing carbon markets."[4]

In these and other ways, the Durban COP 17 deal squashed poor countries' ability to defend against climate disaster. With South African foreign minister Nkoana-Mashabane chairing, the climate summit confirmed this century's climate-related deaths of what will be more than 180 million Africans, according to Christian Aid. Already 400,000 people across the world die each year from climate-related chaos due to catastrophes in agriculture, public health, and "frankenstorms."

And as a final confirmation of the role of Pretoria as a reliable subimperial ally of Washington on climate, the critical question of climate finance repeatedly emerged, with Manuel playing an especially important role. He served on the UN's High-Level Advisory Group on Climate Change Finance in 2010, and there he joined former World Bank chief economist Nick Stern in suggesting that up to half the $100 billion Hillary Clinton promised for the Green Climate Fund be sourced from the private sector (Manuel and Stern 2010). In the same spirit South African Reserve Bank deputy governor Daniel Mminele (2012) acknowledged, "South Africa is aligned with advanced economies on the issue of climate finance"—i.e., not paying the "climate debt" the rich countries owe the main victims of climate change, and relying on global carbon markets to solve the worst crisis humankind has ever faced, notwithstanding the markets, crashes, corruption, and chaos (Bond 2012a).

## Subimperial Development Finance for the Hinterland

Finance ultimately rules, given the stage of the accumulation cycle the world-economy entered during the 1980s. Written in 1916, Vladimir Lenin's ([1917] 1986) booklet on imperialism considers the implications of a delinking (or "separation") between the crisis-ridden productive sector and the financial assets that are meant to represent underlying real values:

> Imperialism, or the domination of finance capital, is that highest stage of capitalism at which this separation reaches vast proportions. The supremacy of finance capital over all other forms of capital means the predominance of the rentier and of the financial oligarchy; it means the singling out of a small number of financially "powerful" states from among all the rest.

The same could be said today, and is one reason why the BRICS New Development Bank and Contingent Reserve Arrangement are the two most portentous aspects of the recent BRICS summits. With Gordhan's regular critiques of the World Bank and the IMF, there was certainly potential for BRICS to "talk left" about the global-governance democracy deficit. Yet in the vote for bank president in April 2012, for example, Gordhan's choice was Washington Consensus ideologue Ngozi Okonjo-Iweala, the Nigerian finance minister who, with IMF managing director Christine Lagarde, catalyzed the Occupy movement's near revolution in January 2012 as a result of the removal of oil subsidies. Brazil chose the moderate Keynesian economist Jose Antonio Ocampo and Moscow backed Washington's choice: Jim Yong Kim.

This was a repeat of the prior year's fiasco over the race for IMF managing director, won by Lagarde—in spite of ongoing corruption investigations against her by French courts in the wake of criminal charges against her predecessor (in both the IMF and French finance ministry jobs) Dominique Strauss-Kahn—because BRICS was divided and conquered. The "emerging" bloc appeared in both cases as incompetent, unable to even agree on a sole candidate, much less win their case in Washington. In July 2012 the BRICS treasuries had sent $75 billion in new capital to the IMF, which was seeking new systems of bailout for banks exposed in Europe. South Africa's contribution of $2 billion was a huge sum for Gordhan to muster against local trade union opposition. Explaining the South African contribution—initially he said it would be only one-tenth as large—Gordhan told *Moneyweb* (2011) that it was on condition that the IMF became more "nasty" to desperate European borrowers, as if the Greek, Spanish, Portuguese, and Irish poor and working people were not suffering enough. The result of this BRICS intervention was that China gained dramatically more IMF voting power while Africa lost a substantial fraction of its share. Gordhan (2012) then admitted at the September 2012 Tokyo meeting of the IMF and the World Bank that it was likely "the vast majority of emerging and developing countries [would] lose quota shares—an outcome that will perpetuate the democratic deficit." And given "the crisis of legitimacy, credibility, and effectiveness of the IMF," it "is simply untenable" that Africa only has two seats for its forty-five member countries (Gordhan 2012). Yet Gordhan's role in promoting the BRICS members' expanded capital commitment to the IMF was the proximate cause of perpetuating the crisis of legitimacy.

The G20 was a much more substantive site for the debates about world finance, having been resurrected in November 2008 to deal with the global meltdown. A few months later, in April 2009, the G20 was central to the push for re-empowering the IMF, first through increased Special Drawing Rights allocations to stimulate the world-economy, and later, in a full recapitalization in 2012, to generate more bailout financing options for European bankers at the expense of structural adjustment for poor and working people (Donnely 2012). Gordhan was implicated in the latter, while in the former Manuel (2009) had authored the main document proposing the IMF's $750 billion recapitalization. Although Dominique Strauss-Kahn postured about a Keynesian fiscal-expansionary policy during the 2008–2009 crisis, the IMF maintained neoliberal, contractionary measures in most of Africa. Likewise, Manuel had consistently promoted the kind of debt relief that resulted in low-income African countries paying a much *higher* percentage of export income on debt relief in the 2005–2008 period, because while the unrepayable capital was written off, the terms of the deal meant that ongoing repayment obligations increased substantially, from 5 to 7 percent of export earnings (Bond 2012a).

In some respects, South Africa was out of step with the other BRICS countries when it came to global finance. Mminele (2012) acknowledged in November 2012 that Pretoria stood alongside Washington in *opposing global regulation* such as the "Robin Hood tax" on financial transactions that was supported by more-enlightened countries, including those from Europe being roiled by global financiers.

The squeeze of poorer countries through South Africa's financing power has been a long-standing problem, as Johannesburg became the continent's premier hot-money center. In mid-2002, Manuel (2002) promised the Commonwealth Business Council he would "fast-track financial market integration through the establishment of an internationally competitive legislative and regulatory framework" for the continent. But without any Africa-wide progress to report two years later, Manuel's director-general Lesetja Kganyago (2004) announced a new "Financial Centre for Africa" project to amplify the financialization tendencies already evident in Johannesburg's exclusive new Sandton central business district: "Over the five years to 2002, the financial sector grew at a real rate of 7.7 percent per year, more than twice as fast as the economy as a whole." Such financial bubbling would ordinarily be understood as a sign of a parasitic and dangerous economy, but not by Pretoria financial officials. Responsible for a full quarter of post-apartheid South African GDP growth, the sector now required further room to expand, according to Kganyago (2004):

> What is needed is a financial hub especially focused on the needs and circumstances of the region, much in the same way that Singapore and Hong Kong cater for the capital needs of the Asian continent.... International financial centers tend to have a foundation in common. Elements include political stability, free markets, and what is best described as the rule of commercial law.

Pretoria's specific aims included "opening South Africa's markets to African and global issuers; global lowest trading costs and trading risk; global leadership in investor protection; and a global hub for financial business process outsourcing." Concluded Kganyago, "Africa's economies cannot wait for the slow maturing of national financial markets to provide the necessary channel for large-scale foreign capital flows for development. Only a regional financial center will be in a position to provide these services in the foreseeable future." Ironically, by 2012 Mbeki (2012) was reinventing himself as a leading critic of illicit capital flight from Africa.

A telling incident in mid-2002 illustrated the responsibility that the South African government had taken on to police such world financial mechanisms. A cabinet meeting in Pretoria concluded with this statement: "The meeting noted the provision by South Africa of a bridge loan to the Democratic Republic of the Congo of Special Drawing Rights (SDR) 75 million. This will help clear the DRC's overdue obligations with the IMF and allow that country to draw resources under the IMF Poverty Reduction and Growth Facility" (Republic of South Africa, Government Communications and Information Service 2002). In ensuring the rollover of the debt, Pretoria thus sanitized the earlier generation of IMF loans made to Mobuto Sese Seko, riven with corruption and capital flight to European banks. In fact, continuities with an earlier subimperial project were obvious, for the people of the DRC were previously victims of South Africa's apartheid-era allegiance with Mobuto, an arrangement that especially suited the ecology-destroying mineral-extraction corporations headquartered in Johannesburg.

The people's struggle against oppression had initially spawned another ruler in 1996, Laurent Kabila, who unfortunately refused democracy and later fell to an assassin's bullet. Thanks to Kabila's son Joseph's connections in Pretoria's union buildings and the finance ministry, the old "odious" Mobutu loans were honored and serviced with Pretoria's new credits. They should have been repudiated. In addition, IMF staff would be allowed back into Kinshasa with their own new loans, and with neoliberal conditionalities again applied to the old victims of Mobutu's fierce rule. A similar process began with lending to regimes such as Mugabe's Zimbabwe and King Mswati's Swaziland, for the purpose of repaying the IMF first and foremost, without a care for human rights and other noneconomic values.

Indeed, had the subimperialist boost to global neoliberal financing not been so central to the BRICS countries' positioning, it would have been logical for them to instead have supported the Bank of the South. That project—with $12 billion in capital by 2013—was dreamt of by the late Hugo Chavez, although repeatedly sabotaged by more conservative Brazilian bureaucrats and likewise opposed by Pretoria, which refused to join it during the Mbeki era. Even if the Bank of the South continues to be ignored, another option is to finance development in a completely different way, as economists Nick Stern and Joe Stiglitz (2011)—both former World Bank senior vice presidents—told the BRICS:

> A new institution is required to ensure a better allocation of hard-earned savings of developing and emerging economies away from risky portfolios, much of which is in rich countries, and onto sound investments in the developing and emerging world. Low-carbon infrastructure and technologies, in particular, are crucial to lay different and more resilient foundations for growth in the next decades. Investments are urgently required to both mitigate the risks and adapt to climate change, generate economic growth, reduce poverty and promote stability and security. These are the great challenges of the 21st century. Failure on one is likely to imply failure on the others. Developing and emerging countries are in the position to both lead on the efforts to rebalance savings and investments and to make significant progress in creating the infrastructure for a different type of economic growth.

Although these are extremely noble sentiments, they have little hope of ever being realized given the broader BRICS project. Ironically, Stern (2013) bragged to a conference that he was the co-instigator of the very idea of a BRICS bank, but in telling the story to his peers in a jovial way, he neglected the rationale for a "different type of economic growth" and instead purely emphasised the merits of a bank in facilitating a deal between states and multinational corporations:

> If you have a development bank that is part of a [major business] deal then it makes it more difficult for governments to be unreliable.... What you had was the presence of the European Bank for Reconstruction and Development (EBRD) reducing the potential for government-induced policy risk, and the presence of the EBRD in the deal making the government of the host country more confident about accepting that investment. *And that is why Meles Zenawi, Joe Stiglitz and myself, nearly three years ago now, started the idea—and are there any press here, by the way? OK, so this bit's off the record. We started to move the idea of a BRICS-led development bank* for those two reasons.
>
> Coupled with the idea that the rich countries would not let the balance sheets of the World Bank and some of the regional development banks expand

very much, and they would not allow their share in those banks to be diluted. So essentially by refusing to come up with more money and by refusing to let other people come up with more money by not allowing those shares to be diluted, you're essentially limiting what the existing World Bank and existing regional development banks can do. (emphasis added)

## South Africa's Development Bank Disaster

One such institution, the Development Bank of Southern Africa (DBSA), is especially ill-equipped to serve as a model for a decent BRICS bank. One reason is the distinct gap between the DBSA and the Southern African Development Community (SADC), as acknowledged in the National Development Plan: "South Africa is critically under-represented in organizations like the African Development Bank and SADC. The latter is critical as South Africa is a major funder of the group.... To fulfill South Africa's obligations in the BRICS and in the region, the DBSA should be strengthened institutionally...." (Republic of South Africa, National Planning Commission 2012). The strengthening took the form of a $820 million recapitalization by Gordhan in early 2013.

But did the DBSA deserve the funding? Here is a well-grounded complaint by SADC deputy executive secretary João Samuel Caholo from less than a year before:

> There is resentment towards the DBSA in certain quarters because it is in South Africa, and South Africa is the only shareholder. SADC has no say in what the DBSA does and although the bank does work on a bilateral level with SADC countries, we need our own bank.... The name of the DBSA is misleading, as it was established by the apartheid government that saw Southern Africa as consisting of apartheid South Africa and the former homelands. (*City Press* 2012)

After leaving his job, Caholo renewed his criticism in October 2013, arguing that the DBSA "only exists in name," while in contrast "a regional bank is supposed to have regional representation of all SADC member states, or at least the participating members in the governance structure. This is still not the case for DBSA" (cited in Van Hove 2013). Just as it was deployed to become Pretoria's core representative as the BRICS bank was being conceptualized, the DBSA fell into disrepute within South Africa for recording R430 million in net losses in 2011–2012, based on (unspecified) investments. Around 14 percent of its assets were in the region outside South Africa, with future SADC lending anticipated at $2.3 billion, of which $400 million would be in semiprivatized infrastructure. In late 2012, the new DBSA CEO, Patrick Dlamini, announced a "new restructuring process, staff would be retrenched [from 750 to 300] and corruption would not be tolerated. We can no longer allow the DBSA to be associated with shoddy work" (Mungadze 2012).

Dlamini's prior job was as an executive with the Air Traffic and Navigation Services company, and he had no prior development-finance experience (Barron 2013).

In late 2013 the complaints and confessions were the same. In a *Sunday Times*, interview (Barron 2013) Dlamini stated, "We have huge room for improvement. Our job is to fund infrastructure development at municipal level, but if you look at this space you see a serious collapse of infrastructure." His own infrastructure had also collapsed, for Barron's sources noted "the departure of staff members with valuable information technology, project management and other skills ... [who] have been snapped up by the big commercial banks, which will be competing with the DBSA to provide infrastructure funding." As Barron pointed out, "Hard-earned taxpayers' money was invested in Sol Kerzner's One&Only hotel.... It lost a fortune on five-star luxury hotels, platinum jewelry and other such projects instead of investing it in boring things like water-treatment plants, roads, schools and hospitals." The loan and investment amounted to nearly $320 million, or 7 percent of the portfolio.

Yet in addition to managers of inappropriate investments, the entire social and environmental division was dismissed, including leadership of an important fund to promote employment. Moreover, as Carol Paton (2013) of *Business Day* remarked,

> When it comes to project work, the bank will be in the same position as most state departments: it will need to put out to tender. There is also another problem. The business model of the bank remains tenuous ... it does not take deposits and so does not have a source of cheap money, the capital injection provided for in this year's budget being a rare event.

The man tasked with ensuring the revitalization of the DBSA in the region was Mo Shaik, who trained as an optometrist but became the leading spy in the Zuma government prior to numerous internal crises in the National Intelligence Agency. One problem was his revelation of important and highly embarrassing political secrets to US embassy officials, which in turn were published by WikiLeaks (Rademeyer 2011). Shaik's forced resignation from the security services in 2012 was followed by studies in a brief Harvard executive course, after which he was controversially appointed the DBSA's main liaison to the region (Molatlhwa 2012).

A final case of a leading Pretoria official who apparently fused personal priorities with what should have been development finance is International Relations director general Jerry Matjila, South Africa's "sherpa" to BRICS. In September 2013 he was subject to an investigation regarding corruption in a state fund worth R530 billion, as well as the irregular funding of dictatorships, including Zimbabwe's:

> Matjila allegedly ignored instructions from the Treasury to channel R250 million from the UN World Food Program to African states. Instead, without

the consent of the finance and international relations ministers, he allegedly selected two companies personally, gave them contracts to do work on behalf of the African Renaissance Fund (ARF) in Africa and paid them millions before any work had been done.

Information presented to Parliament's international relations portfolio committee in 2010 showed that South Africa had provided millions to "rogue" African states. The international relations and co-operation department director of NEPAD, Harvey Short, provided the information showing that more than R770 million of South African state funds had been used to prop up rogue states and countries that had a history of human rights abuses or non-democratically elected governments, over the past three years and under the auspices of the ARF. (SAPA 2013)

## Conclusion

In sum, we need to now return to theoretical questions of defining and refining subimperialism. The preceding pages have illustrated various ways in which South Africa can be considered a subimperialist ally of global finance with, first, support for neoliberal global governance no matter its failure to deliver; second, growing regional clout on behalf of Johannesburg-based corporate plunder of the subcontinent, no matter that much of the capital then flowed out to the world financial headquarters of what were formerly South African firms; and third, a neoliberal orientation to development banking. The BRICS alliance is revealing and may, in the future, be vital if the BRICS New Development Bank gets off the ground and further financing is required to expand the extractive systems. This is no surprise, for harking back a century to South Africa's chilling past of subimperial regional conquest in the interests of global-imperial domination, it could easily have been said, and indeed was by Nelson Mandela (SAPA 2003d), "that Cecil John Rhodes [Britain's most avaricious imperial settler] would have given his approval to this effort to make the South African economy of the early 21st century appropriate and fit for its time."

What would "fit for its time" mean in an era of Africa's worsening resource curse? For one, like Rhodes's own British South Africa Company, which took advantage of the Berlin 1884–1885 Scramble for Africa to gain concessions as far north as Malawi, extraction is the central objective. In post-apartheid South Africa, a variety of cross-fertilizing intracorporate and state-corporate relationships emerged, symbolized in mid-2012 by the way the Lonmin company (formerly Lonrho, named by British prime minister Edward Heath as the "unacceptable face of capitalism" in 1973) benefited from leading ANC politician Cyril Ramaphosa's substantial shareholding and connections to Pretoria's security apparatus. Breaking a strike was deemed necessary at Lonmin's Marikana platinum mine, and Ramaphosa used his influence with the mining and police minister to ensure sufficient troops came out. They carried live ammunition and the result was a premeditated massacre of thirty-four miners, with seventy-eight wounded.

In carrying out these and other less violent forms of accumulation by dispossession, the traditional South African, US, European, Australian, and Canadian mining houses that operated in the region for decades were more recently joined by major firms from China, India, and Brazil. Their work relied upon and rebuilt the colonial infrastructural foundations—road, rail, pipeline, and port expansion—for the sake of mineral, petroleum, and gas extraction. The Chinese are especially capable of decisive project implementation and have also provided no-strings-attached credits, including a $5 billion loan in March 2013 to Transnet for its coal transport and port expansion.

According to Sam Moyo and Paris Yeros (2011, 19) imperialism's relations with subimperialism entail "the *super-exploitation* of domestic labor. It was natural, therefore, that, as it grew, it would require external markets for the resolution of its profit realization crisis." This notion, derived from Rosa Luxemburg's ([1913] 1968, 396) thinking a century ago when she wrote *The Accumulation of Capital*, focuses on how capitalism's extraeconomic coercive capacities loot mutual aid systems and commons facilities, families (women especially), the land, all forms of nature, and the shrinking state:

> The relations between capitalism and the non-capitalist modes of production start making their appearance on the international stage. Its predominant methods are colonial policy, an international loan system—a policy of spheres of interest—and war. Force, fraud, oppression, looting are openly displayed without any attempt at concealment, and it requires an effort to discover within this tangle of political violence and contests of power the stern laws of the economic process.

According to J&J Group executive director Michael Solomon, "The current Chinese investment in Africa is not that different from the European push of 100 years ago, except that today's world demanded far greater transparency" (Creamer 2013). An even more important voice of the African economic establishment, Nigerian central bank governor Lamido Sanusi (2013), was yet more explicit:

> China takes our primary goods and sells us manufactured ones. This was also the essence of colonialism. The British went to Africa and India to secure raw materials and markets. Africa is now willingly opening itself up to a new form of imperialism.... Africa must recognize that China—like the US, Russia, Britain, Brazil and the rest—is in Africa not for African interests but its own.

*Super*-exploitation is intensifying in all of this. Along with renewed looting, various symptoms of internal crisis and socioeconomic oppressions are common within the BRICS bloc, including severe inequality, poverty, unemployment, disease, violence (again, especially against women, as India unveiled in early 2013), inadequate education, and prohibitions on labor organizing. Rising BRICS inequality—except in Brazil, whose minimum-wage increase lowered the extreme Gini coefficient to a bit below South Africa's—is accompanied by worsening social tensions. As Brazilians showed in 2013, these in turn are met with worsening political and civil-rights violations, increased securitization of societies, militarization and arms trading, prohibitions on protest, rising media repression and official secrecy, debilitating patriarchy and homophobia, activist jailings, torture, and even massacres. In Durban, a notorious police hit squad killed more than fifty people in recent years, and this assassination of activists continued into 2013. In all these respects, South Africa is lubricating world neoliberalism, hastening world eco-destruction, serving as coordinator of hinterland looting, and generating unbearable internal pressures. This is logical, for the "new imperialism" entails—as Harvey (2003) suggests—much greater recourse to "accumulation by dispossession": the appropriation of "noncapitalist" aspects of life and environment by an increasingly super-exploitative capitalism.

A century ago, Luxemburg ([1913] 1968) considered how capitalist crisis "spurs capital on to a continual extension of the market," today called "globalization." Her core insight—as distinct from those of Lenin, Bukharin, Hilferding, Hobson, and others of her era—was to show, especially using southern African examples, that "capital cannot accumulate without the aid of non-capitalist" relations and "only the continuous and progressive disintegration of non-capitalist organization makes accumulation of capital possible" (see Bond, Chitonge, and Hopfmann 2007). With the current renewal of this process—crisis, extension of the market, and amplified capitalist-noncapitalist super-exploitative relations— serving as the basis for a "new imperialism," Harvey (2003) adds the layer we now know as the BRICS:

> The opening up of global markets in both commodities and capital created openings for other states to insert themselves into the global economy, first as absorbers but then as producers of surplus capitals. They then became competitors on the world stage. What might be called "subimperialisms" arose.... Each developing center of capital accumulation sought out systematic spatio-temporal fixes for its own surplus capital by defining territorial spheres of influence.

Overaccumulation of capital is a constant problem everywhere, often rising to crisis levels. As a result, in several BRICS countries (including South Africa) there are powerful impulses for local capital to both externalize and financialize. Judging by Harvey's criteria of seeking "spatio-temporal fixes," South Africa and the other BRICS members offer some of the most extreme sites of new subimperialism in the world today.

If the subimperial impulse remains and becomes collaborative instead of competitive, the territorial alliance represented by BRICS could be innovative.

As former Brazilian president Lula put it as early as 2005, the goal is "to create a new economic geography" (Gindin 2005). In theory, that process will work most decisively through development financing, in which the circulation of overaccumulated financial capital will occur fastest through mega-infrastructure projects (constructed by BRICS-based corporations) in the BRICS New Development Bank. To a great extent, these would in turn open up further routes for capital accumulation in sites like Africa's mines, oil patches, and gas fields. This territorial strategy is envisaged within BRICS as a coherent approach, but in reality there are no substantive indications that the accumulation process counteracts the broader processes of imperial economic and ecological practices, even if geopolitical tensions continue to emerge, and even if at some point China and Russia graduate from sub-imperial to inter-imperial positioning.

Internally, too, the older generation of arguments about South Africa's apparently unique historical mode of apartheid super-exploitation—which Wolpe (1980) called "articulations of modes of production"—recognized the internal dimension of subimperial accumulation. Migrant male workers from Bantustans long provided "cheap labor," thanks to black rural women's unpaid reproduction of children, sick workers, and retirees generally without state support. This stance seems to apply even more so within the BRICS these days. Consider the notorious Chinese pass-laws so spatially similar to apartheid's (though not racially determinant), or the expansion of the South African migrancy model much deeper into the region in the wake of apartheid, notwithstanding tragic xenophobic reactions from the local working class.

Moreover, like the political carving of Africa in Berlin in 1884–1885, the BRICS 2013 Durban summit had as its aim the continent's *economic* carve-up, unburdened—now as then—by what would be derided as "Western" concerns about democracy and human rights, with twenty-five African heads of state present as collaborators. Reading between the lines, its resolutions would do the following:

- support favored corporations' extraction and land-grab strategies, including through provision of army troops;
- worsen Africa's retail-driven deindustrialization (South Africa's Shoprite and Makro—soon to be run by Walmart—were already notorious in many capital cities for importing even simple products that could be supplied locally);
- revive failed projects such as NEPAD; and
- confirm the financing of both African land-grabbing and the extension of neo-colonial infrastructure through a new BRICS New Development Bank.

Lubricated by finance, with a South African gateway, are the BRICS doing deputy-sheriff duty for global corporations while controlling their own angry populaces as well as their hinterlands? The eco-destructive, consumerist-centric, overfinancialized, climate-frying maldevelopment model throughout the BRICS grouping works very well for corporate profits, but is generating crises for the majority of its people and for the planet. Hence the label "subimperialist" is tempting.

Marini (1974) argued that 1970s-era Brazil was "the best current manifestation of subimperialism" because of regional economic extraction, "export of capital" (always associated with subsequent imperialist politics), and internal corporate monopolization and financialization. But as we have seen, there are two additional roles for BRICS regimes if they are genuinely subimperialist. The first is ensuring regional geopolitical "stability"; for example, Brasilia's hated army in Haiti and Pretoria's deal making in African hotspots like South Sudan, the Great Lakes, and the Central African Republic.

The second is advancing the broader agenda of neoliberalism so as to legitimate deepened market access. Evidence includes the BRICS nations' role in IMF recapitalization; South Africa's NEPAD; the attempt by China, Brazil and India to revive the WTO; and Brazil's sabotage of the left project within Venezuela's "Bank of the South" initiative. As Nkoana-Mashabane puts it, "BRICS' focus is on a new approach to win-win economic development. It's pro-South, but not anti-North" (Mataboge 2013). At the best of times, that attitude translates into entering—and legitimating—the fora of the world-economy like the WTO, in search of minor concessions. To take the WTO as an example, the South African role was mainly destructive, especially under Alec Erwin's international leadership. With the 2013 Bali ministerial round negotiations potentially reviving the WTO, some of the BRICS members showed a degree of opposition to the Northern agenda. That agenda combined free-trade corporate expansion and ongoing self-interested protectionism, but BRICS opposition was well within the broader agenda of neoliberalism.

According to one of the coordinators of the Our World Is Not for Sale civil society network (James 2013), the mid-2013 move of the Brazilian ambassador—Roberto Azevêdo—to the WTO to become the body's director general was debilitating for resistance by the South's "G-110" bloc. Brazil, however, continues to oppose US/EU agribusiness subsidies. While the Indian WTO ambassador has been a strong opponent of the North, at higher levels the state is more prone to neoliberal concessions. With China and Russia relatively quiet, the importance of South Africa's relatively stronger recent critique of global trade should be more important. The cancellation of bilateral investment treaties by South African trade minister Rob Davies was seen as inspiring (James 2013).

Indeed, the forms of BRICS subimperialism are diverse, for as Moyo and Yeros (2011, 19) remark,

> Some are driven by private blocs of capital with strong state support (Brazil, India); others, like China, include the direct participation of state-owned enterprises; while in the case of South Africa, it is increasingly difficult to speak of an autonomous domestic bourgeoisie, given the extreme degree of de-nationalization of its economy in the post-apartheid period. The degree of participation in the Western

military project is also different from one case to the next although, one might say, there is a "schizophrenia" to all this, typical of "subimperialism."

As a result, all these tendencies warrant opposition from everyone concerned. One recent voice—that of Zambian vice president Guy Scott—was surprising for its frankness: "I dislike South Africa for the same reason that Latin Americans dislike the United States" (Smith 2013). More appropriate, however, would be "BRICS-from-below" projects to link up the dissidents. Earlier inklings were the solidaristic projects that linked antiapartheid activists from not only the West but also the other BRIC to South Africa prior to 1994. In more recent times, perhaps the best example of this solidarity was the protest around the region when a Chinese ship, the *An Ye Jiang*, docked in Durban's harbor to offload a major ammunition and weapons delivery for the then illegitimate Zimbabwe regime in 2008, after Robert Mugabe lost the presidential election (Biti 2013). Dockworkers, religious leaders, and social movements—acting in solidarity with Zimbabweans—prevented the ship from unloading.

The opportunities for more such activity will increase in the coming months and years:

- the more that BRICS leaders prop up the IMF's pro-austerity financing and catalyze a renewed round of World Trade Organization attacks;
- the more Africa becomes a battleground for internecine conflicts between subimperialists intent on rapid mineral and oil extraction (as is common in central Africa);
- the more the hypocrisy associated with BRICS/US sabotage of climate negotiations continues or offsetting carbon markets is embraced;
- the more that specific companies targeted by victims require unified campaigning and boycotts to generate solidaristic counterpressure, whether Brazil's Vale and Petrobras, South Africa's Anglo or BHP Billiton (albeit with London and Melbourne headquarters), India's Tata or ArcelorMittal, or Chinese state-owned firms and Russian energy corporations; and
- the more a new BRICS bank exacerbates World Bank human, ecological, and economic messes.

## References

Africom Public Affairs. 2012. "Ham Discusses AFRICOM Mission with African Journalists, PAOs at Symposium." Garmisch, Germany, August 29. www.africom.mil/getArticle.asp?art=8266&lang=0 (accessed June 10, 2014).

Amabhungane. 2013. "Is This What Our Soldiers Died For?" *Mail & Guardian*, March 28. http://mg.co.za/article/2013-03-28-00-central-african-republic-is-this-what-our-soldiers-died-for.

Amanthis, Judith. 2012. "How the Private Sector Didn't Solve Ghana's Water Crisis." *Pambazuka*, July 27.

Andes. 2013. "The Banco del Sur Initiates Operations in Caracas." *Andes*, June 12. www .andes.info.ec/en/economia/banco-sur-initiates-operations-caracas.html (accessed June 10, 2014).

Aslund, Anders. 2013. "Now the BRICS Party Is Over, They Must Wind Down the State's Role." *Financial Times*, August 22. www.ft.com/intl/cms/s/0/0147b43c-040b-11e3 -8aab-00144feab7de.html#axzz2keJpWM2W (accessed June 10, 2014).

Associated Press. 2004. "Mandela Extends Conciliatory Hand to the US." *Washington Post*, May 25.

Barron, Chris 2013. "Development Bank of Southern Africa: New CEO, Same Promises." *Sunday Times*, October 6.

Bello, Walden. 2009. "U-20: Will the Global Economy Resurface?" *Foreign Policy in Focus*, March 31.

Biti, Tendai. 2013. "Mbeki Privatized Zimbabwean Crisis." *Nehanda Radio*, September 17. http://nehandaradio.com/2013/09/17/mbeki-privatized-zimbabwean-crisis-biti (accessed June 10, 2014).

Böhm, Steffen, Mari Ceci Misoczky, and Sandra Moog. 2012. "Greening Capitalism? A Marxist Critique of Carbon Markets." Organization Studies 33, no. 11 (November): 1629.

Bond, Patrick. 2003. *Against Global Apartheid*. London: Zed Books.

———. 2005. *Elite Transition*. London: Pluto Press.

———. 2006a. *Talk Left Walk Right*. Pietermaritzburg: University of KwaZulu-Natal Press.

———. 2006b. *Looting Africa*. London: Zed Books.

———. 2009. "Removing Neocolonialism's APRM Mask: A Critique of the African Peer Review Mechanism." *Review of African Political Economy* 36, no. 122: 595–603.

———. 2012a. "South Africa's Dangerously Unsafe Financial Intercourse." *Counterpunch*, April 24. www.counterpunch.org/2012/04/24/south-africas-dangerously-unsafe -financial-intercourse (accessed June 10, 2014).

———. 2012b. "Who Will Get 'Whacked' Next in Africa?" *Black Agenda Report*, October 16. http://blackagendareport.com/content/who-will-get-%E2%80%9Cwhacked %E2%80%9D-next-africa (accessed June 10, 2014).

Bond, Patrick, Horman Chitonge, and Arndt Hopfmann, eds. 2007. *The Accumulation of Capital in Southern Africa: Rosa Luxemburg's Contemporary Relevance*. Berlin: Rosa Luxemburg Foundation and Durban: Centre for Civil Society

Broder, John. 2012. "Signs of New Life as UN Searches for a Climate Accord." *New York Times*, January 24.

Bruce, Peter. 2003. "SA Needs a Market Economy That Works for All People." *Business Day*, June 4.

Business Day. 2003. "Mbeki's Gift." *Business Day*, July 11.

City Press. 2012. "SADC Banks on Own Development Bank." June 23. www.citypress.co .za/business/sadc-banks-on-own-development-bank-20120623 (accessed June 10, 2014).

Clark, Pilita. 2011. "'Viagra Shot' for Carbon Markets." *Financial Times*, December 12.

Cochran, Shawn. 2010. "Security Assistance, Surrogate Armies, and the Pursuit of US Interests in Sub-Saharan Africa." Strategic *Studies Quarterly* 4, no. 1. www.au.af.mil /au/ssq/2010/spring/cochran.pdf (accessed June 10, 2014).

Columbia University and Yale University. 2012. *Environmental Performance Index 2012.* New York: Columbia University.

Council for the Development of Social Science Research in Africa, Dakar and Third World Network-Africa. 2002. "Declaration on Africa's Development Challenges." Resolution adopted at the Joint Conference on Africa's Development Challenges in the Millennium, Accra, Ghana, April 23–26.

Creamer, Martin. 2013. "Looming China/Africa Head-On Collision—Solomon." *Mining Weekly*, April 17. www.miningweekly.com/article/looming-chinaafrica-head-on -collision-solomon-2013-04-17 (accessed June 10, 2014).

De Wet, Phillip. 2013. "Zuma to Business: Seize Africa, Settle with Labour." *Mail & Guardian*, October 10.

Desai, Radhika. 2013. "The BRICS Are Building a Challenge to Western Economic Supremacy." *Guardian*, April 2.

Donnely, Lynn. 2012. "Throwing Good Money at EU Troubles." *Mail & Guardian*, June 22.

*Economist.* 2009. "Economics Focus: Domino Theory." *Economist,* February 26. www .economist.com/research/articlesBySubject/displayStory.cfm?story_id=13184631 &subjectID=348918&fsrc=nwl (accessed June 10, 2014).

———. 2013. "The Great Deceleration." *Economist*, July 27. www.economist.com/news /leaders/21582256-emerging-market-slowdown-not-beginning-bust-it-turning-point (accessed June 10, 2014).

England, Andrew, and Harding, Robin. 2013. "Call for Aggressive Action over Emerging Markets Crisis." *Financial Times*, August 25. www.ft.com/intl/cms/s/0/91c89454- 0d89-11e3-9fbb-00144feabdc0.html#axzz2keJpWM2W (accessed June 10, 2014).

Ernst and Young. 2013. *Africa Attractiveness Survey.* Ernst and Young. www.ey.com/ZA /en/Issues/Business-environment/Africa-Attractiveness-Survey (accessed June 10, 2014).

Escobar, Pepe. 2013. "Brazil, Russia, India, China and South Africa: BRICS Go over the Wall." *Asia Times*, March 27.

Ford, Glen. 2013. "Throwing BRICS at the U.S. Empire." *Black Agenda Report*, March 28.

Fransman, Marius. 2012. "South Africa: A Strong African Brick in BRICS." South African Foreign Policy Initiative, November 21. www.safpi.org/speeches/south-africa-strong -african-brick-brics-21-november-2012 (accessed June 10, 2014).

Fry, Tom. 2012. "Kim Crowned World Bank President." *World Bank President*, April 16. www.worldbankpresident.org/tom-fry/uncategorized/kim-crowned-world-bank -president (accessed June 10, 2014).

Gindin, Jonah. 2005. "Venezuela and Other South American Countries Meet with Arab League." *Voltairenet,* May 12. www.voltairenet.org/article125183.html (accessed June 10, 2014).

Gordhan, Pravin. 2012. Statement by Pravin J. Gordhan, Minister of Finance, South Africa. International Monetary Fund International Monetary and Financial Committee, Tokyo, October 13. www.imf.org/External/AM/2012/imfc/statement/eng/zaf.pdf (accessed June 10, 2014).

*Guardian.* 2013. "Dilma Rousseff, the Brazilian President, Isn't Happy with Barack Obama." *Guardian Passnotes*, September 18. www.theguardian.com/world/shortcuts/2013 /sep/18/dilma-rousseff-barack-obama-isnt-happy (accessed June 10, 2014).

Harvey, David. 2003. *The New Imperialism.* Oxford: Oxford University Press.

———. 2007. *The New Imperialism.* Toronto: Knopf Canada.

Heitman, Helmoed. 2013a. "How Deadly CAR Battle Unfolded." *Star*, March 31. www.iol
.co.za/sundayindependent/how-deadly-car-battle-unfolded-1.1493841#.U5figSjQ50c
(accessed June 10, 2014).

———. 2013b. "Rooivalk Attack Helo Makes Combat Debut in DRC." *Jane's Defence
Weekly*, November 13, www.janes.com/article/30155/update-rooivalk-attack-helo
-makes-combat-debut-in-drc (accessed June 10, 2014).

Hosken, Graham, and Isaac Mahlangu. 2013. "We Were Killing Kids." *Sunday Times*,
March 31.

James, Deborah. 2013. Personal correspondence. November 19, Washington, DC.

Jobson, Elissa. 2013. "Outgoing US Envoy Warns African Union about South Africa."
*Business Day*, September 6.

Keet, Dot. 2013. "Perspectives and Proposals on the BRICS for and from Popular Civil
Society Organisations." Economic Justice Network, November.

Kganyago, Lesetja. 2004. "South Africa as a Financial Centre for Africa." Speech delivered
at the Reuters Economist of the Year Award Ceremony, Johannesburg, August 11.

Klein, Naomi. 2007. *Shock Doctrine*. Toronto: Knopf Canada.

———. 2009. "For Obama, No Opportunity Too Big to Blow." *Nation*, December 21.

Laverty, Alex. 2011. "Globalization in Emerging Markets: How South Africa's Relationship to Africa Serves the BRICS." *African File*, May 2. http://theafricanfile.com
/public-diplomacy/international-relations/globalization-in-emerging-markets-unit
ed-how-south-africa%E2%80%99s-relationship-to-africa-serves-the-brics (accessed
June 10, 2014).

Lenin, Vladimir. [1917] 1986. Imperialism. Moscow: Progress Publishers.

Leon, Tony. 2013. "BRICS Caught with Pants Down as Tide Changes." *Business Day*,
August 27. www.bdlive.co.za/opinion/columnists/2013/08/27/brics-caught-with
-pants-down-as-tide-changes (accessed June 10, 2014).

Luxemburg, Rosa. [1913] 1968. *The Accumulation of Capital*. New York: Monthly Review
Press.

Magalhaes, Luciana. 2013. "China Only BRIC Country Currently Worthy of the
Title—O'Neill." *Wall Street Journal*, August 23. http://stream.wsj.com/story/latest
-headlines/SS-2-63399/SS-2-308220 (accessed June 10, 2014).

Manby, Bronwen. 2008. "African Peer Review Mechanism: Lessons from Kenya." *Pambazuka News* 362 (April 15).

Mangcu, Xolela. 2013. "Obama No Enemy of Ours." *City Press*, June 30.

Manuel, Trevor. 2002. *Mobilizing International Investment Flows: The New Global Outlook*.
Speech delivered to the Commonwealth Business Council, Johannesburg, September
24.

———. 2009. Letter to Dominique Strauss-Kahn. Pretoria, March 31.

Manuel, Trevor, and Nicolas Stern. 2010. "Funding the Low-Carbon Revolution." *Financial
Times*, November 6.

Marini, Ruy Mauro. 1965. "Brazilian Interdependence and Imperialist Integration."
*Monthly Review* 17, no. 7: 22.

———. 1974. Subdesarrollo y revolución. Mexico City: Siglo XXI Editores. Translated
at http://mrzine.monthlyreview.org/2010/bt280210p.html#_edn13 (accessed June
10, 2014).

Martin, William. 2013. "South Africa and the 'New Scramble for Africa': Imperialist,
Sub-imperialist, or Victim?" *Agrarian South: Journal of Political Economy* 2, no. 2:
161–188.

Mataboge, Mmanaledi. 2013. "Nkoana-Mashabane: SA's Not Looting the Continent, We're Cultivating Peace and Trade." *Mail & Guardian*, November 15, http://mg.co .za/article/2013-11-15-00-sas-not-looting-the-continent-were-cultivating-peace-and -trade (accessed June 26, 2014).

Mbeki, Thabo 2012. "Tackling Illicit Capital Flows for Economic Transformation." Thabo Mbeki Foundation, Johannesburg. www.thabombekifoundation.org.za/Pages /Tackling-Illicit-Capital-Flows-for-Economic-Transformation.aspx (accessed June 10, 2014).

McKibben, Bill. 2009. "With Climate Agreement, Obama Guts Progressive Values." *Grist*, December 18, www.grist.org/article/2009-12-18-with-climate-agreement-obama-guts -progressive-values/#comments (accessed June 10, 2014).

Melber, Hennig. 2013. "SA Subimpi Choice within EU v. Southern Africa Trade War." *debate-list*, August 16.

Mminele, Daniel. 2012. "South Africa and the G20." Keynote address to the South African Institute of International Affairs G20 Study Group, October 12, www.bis.org/review /r121105e.pdf (accessed June 10, 2014).

Mohammed, Seeraj. 2010. "The State of the South African Economy." In John Daniel, Prishani Naidoo Devan Pillay, and Roger Southall, eds., *New South African Review*. Johannesburg: Wits University Press.

Molatlhwa, Olebogeng. 2012. "DBSA Not Backing Down on Mo." *Sunday World*, August 13. www.sundayworld.co.za/news/2012/08/13/dbsa-not-backing-down-on-mo (accessed June 10, 2014).

*Moneyweb*. 2011. "Special Report Podcast: Pravin Gordhan, Minister of Finance." *Moneyweb*, September 29. www.moneyweb.co.za/moneyweb-boardroom-talk/special -report-podcast-pravin-gordhan—minister-of?sn=2009+Detail (accessed June 10, 2014).

Morrison, Stephen, and Walter Kansteiner III. 2004. *Rising U.S. Stakes in Africa*. Washington: Center for Strategic and International Studies, http://csis.org/publication /rising-us-stakes-africa (accessed June 10, 2014).

Moyo, Sam, and Paris Yeros. 2011. "Rethinking the Theory of Primitive Accumulation." Paper presented to the Second International Initiative for Promoting Political Economy Conference, May 20–22, Istanbul.

Msimang, Sisonke. 2013. "Will the Real Superpower Please Stand Up?" *Daily Maverick*, May 8. www.dailymaverick.co.za/opinionista/2013-05-08-will-the-real-superpower -please-stand-up/#.UYti34IwNDp (accessed June 10, 2014).

Mungadze, Samuel. 2012. "DBSA to Cut Equity Investments." *Business Day*, December 12.

Munusamy, Ranjeni. 2003. "The George Dubya of Africa." *Sunday Times*, July 13.

Murphy, Jarrett. 2003. "Mandela Slams Bush on Iraq." CBS News, February 3. www .cbsnews.com/2100-500257_162-538607.html (accessed June 10, 2014).

National Union of Metalworkers of South Africa (NUMSA). 2013. "Ideological Reflections and Responses to Some of the Recent Attacks." NUMSA, September 20.

Nkoana-Mashabana, Maiti. 2013. "Speech by the Minister of International Relations and Cooperation at the BRICS Academic Forum Welcome Dinner." Durban, March 10, www.dirco.gov.za/docs/speeches/2013/mash0313.html (accessed June 10, 2014).

Onyango-Obbo, Charles. 2013. "Return to Crisis in the Great Lakes." *Naked Chiefs*, September 19. http://nakedchiefs.com/2013/09/19/return-to-crisis-in-the-great-lakes -star-of-the-zuma-clan-hits-a-jackpot-in-dr-congo (accessed June 10, 2014).

Palast, Greg. 2013. "Larry Summers and the Secret 'End Game' Memo." *Vice Magazine*, August 22. www.gregpalast.com/larry-summers-and-the-secret-end-game-memo (accessed June 10, 2014).

Patel, Khadija. 2013a. "Analysis: The World According to Dirco." *Daily Maverick*, January 25.

———. 2013b. "Francois Hollande Visit: Mopping Up Sarkozy's Mess." *Daily Maverick*, October 15.

Paton, Carol 2013. "Are the Right People Leaving DBSA?" *Business Day*, April 10, www.bdlive.co.za/business/financial/2013/04/10/are-the-right-people-leaving-dbsa (accessed June 10, 2014).

Pauw, Jacques. 2014. "Khulubuse Zuma's R100 Billion Oil Deal." *City Press*, May 18, www .citypress.co.za/news/khulubuse-zumas-r100bn-oil-deal/ (accessed June 10, 2014).

Pesek, William. 2013. "The BRICS Expose the West's Hypocrisy." *Bloomberg*, March 28. www.bloomberg.com/news/2013-03-28/the-brics-expose-the-west-s-hypocrisy.html (accessed June 10, 2014).

Pew Research Global Attitudes Project. 2013. *Climate Change and Financial Instability Seen as Top Global Threats.* Pew Research Global Attitudes Project. www.pewglobal .org/2013/06/24/climate-change-and-financial-instability-seen-as-top-global-threats (accessed June 10, 2014).

Prashad, Vijay. 2013. "China Finds Its Place." *CounterPunch*, March 27. www .counterpunch.org/2013/03/27/china-finds-its-place (accessed June 10, 2014).

Radebe, Kentse. 2012. "SA's Business Leaders Open Letter Courageous—DBSA CEO." *Moneyweb*, December 11. www.moneyweb.co.za/moneyweb-south-africa/sas-busi-ness-leaders-open-letter-courageous—dbsa- (accessed June 10, 2014).

Rademeyer, Julian. 2011. "WikiLeaks Exposes SA Spy Boss." *Beeld*, January 23. www .news24.com/SouthAfrica/News/Wikileaks-exposes-SA-spy-boss-20110123 (accessed June 10, 2014).

Republic of South Africa Department of National Treasury. 2012. "Contingent Reserve Arrangement." National Treasury. www.treasury.gov.za/brics/crp.aspx (accessed June 10, 2014).

Republic of South Africa, Government Communications and Information Service. 2002. "Statement on Cabinet Meeting." Government Communications and Information Ser-vice, June 26. www.gcis.gov.za/content/newsroom/media-releases/cabinet-statements /statement-cabinet-meeting-26-june-2002 (accessed June 10, 2014).

Republic of South Africa, National Planning Commission. 2012. "Positioning South Africa in the World." In *National Development Plan 2030: Our Future—Make It Work*, 235–257. National Planning Commission, August. www.npconline.co.za/MediaLib /Downloads/Downloads/NDP%202030%20-%20Our%20future%20-%20make %20it%20work.pdf (accessed June 10, 2014).

Republic of South Africa, the Presidency. 2013. "President Zuma Returns from the G20 Leaders' Summit." Presidency, September 7. www.thepresidency.gov.za/pebble .asp?relid=16066&t=79 (accessed June 10, 2014).

Reuters. 2013. "Gordhan: Floating Rand Helps Absorb Shocks." IOL, August 22. www .iol.co.za/business/markets/currencies/gordhan-floating-rand-helps-absorb-shocks-1 .1566777#.UoUbPfkwqch (accessed June 10, 2014).

Rose, Rob. 2004. "Companies 'Shirking' Their Nepad Obligations." *Business Day*, May 24.

Ross, Sherwin. 2010. "Rendition and the Global War on Terrorism: 28 Nations Have Supported the US in the Detention and Torture of 'Suspects.'" Global Research,

April 1. www.globalresearch.ca/index.php?context=va&aid=18419 (accessed June 10, 2014).

Sanusi, Lamido. 2013. "Africa Must Get Real about Chinese Ties." *Financial Times*, March 11. www.ft.com/intl/cms/s/0/562692b0-898c-11e2-ad3f-00144feabdc0.html #axzz2PKy79X3R (accessed June 10, 2014).

SAPA (South African Press Association). 2003a. "G8 Vows to 'Fully Commit' to Developing African Nations." *Financial Times*, June 2.

———. 2003b. "Texas Is Missing an Idiot." *Star*, July 9.

———. 2003c. "Anti-Bush Crowd Braves Cold." *Star*, July 9.

———. 2003d. "Mandela Criticises Apartheid Lawsuits." *Financial Times*, August 25.

———. 2004. "SA's 'Imperialist' Image in Africa." *Star*, March 30.

———. 2013. "Matjila on Special Leave after Half a Billion Rand Corruption Charge." *Mail & Guardian*, September 19. http://mg.co.za/article/2013-09-19-matjila-on -special-leave-after-half-a-billion-rand-corruption-charge (accessed June 10, 2014).

Schmitt, Eric. 2013. U.S. Army Hones Antiterror Strategy for Africa, in Kansas. *New York Times*, October 18.

Shear, Simon. 2013. "A Brief (Brutal), History of the Rooivalk." eNCA, September 1. www.enca.com/technology/brief-brutal-history-rooivalk (accessed June 10, 2014).

Shubin, Vladimir. 2013. "BRICS Viewed from Russia." *Pambazuka News*, March 20. www .pambazuka.org/en/category/features/86658/print (accessed June 10, 2014).

Smith, David. 2013. "Zambian Vice-President: 'South Africans Are Backward.'" *Guardian*, May 1.

South African International Marketing Council. 2013. "SA to Validate BRICS Member-ship." Brand South Africa, April 10. www.imc.org.za/news/853-sa-to-validate-brics -membership (accessed June 10, 2014).

Stern, Nicolas. 2013. "Emerging Powers as Emerging Economies." Statement at the Brit-ish Academy's Emerging Powers Going Global Conference, London, October 8–9. YouTube. www.youtube.com/watch?v=4ZKQ6wQ-29w (accessed June 10, 2014).

Stern, Nicolas, and Joseph Stiglitz. 2011. "An International Development Bank for Foster-ing South-South Investment: Promoting the New Industrial Revolution, Managing Risk and Rebalancing Global Savings." Unpublished paper, London and New York, September.

Stratfor. 2009. "Monography for Comment: South Africa." WikiLeaks, May 5. http:// search.wikileaks.org/gifiles/?viewemailid=951571 (accessed June 10, 2014).

Tatlow, Kirsten. 2012. "BRICS Agitate for a Seat at the Table." *New York Times*, April 19. www.nytimes.com/2012/04/20/business/global/brics-agitate-for-a-seat-at-the-table .html?pagewanted=all&_r=0 (accessed June 10, 2014).

Third World Network. 2013. "Whither the BRICS?" *Third World Resurgence* 274 (June). www.twnside.org.sg/title2/resurgence/2013/twr274.htm (accessed June 10, 2014).

Tian, Wei. 2013. "End to QE to 'Split' Emerging Markets." *China Daily*, September 14. www.chinadaily.com.cn/business/2013-09/14/content_16969677.htm (accessed June 10, 2014).

Van Hove, Kathleen. 2013. "Interview with João Samuel Caholo, former SADC Deputy Executive Secretary." *GREAT Insights* 2, no. 7 (October).

White House Press Office. 2006. "Press Release: Remarks by President Bush and President Mbeki of South Africa in Photo Opportunity." White House, December 8. http:// georgewbush-whitehouse.archives.gov/news/releases/2001/06/20010626.html (accessed June 10, 2014).

Wolpe, Harold, ed. 1980. *The Articulation of Modes of Production*. London: Routledge
    and Kegan Paul.
World Bank. 2011. *The Changing Wealth of Nations*. Washington, DC: World Bank Group.

## Notes

1.  Pretoria pays the salaries of several Dlamini-Zuma advisors, which according to Institute for
Security Studies analyst Paul-Simon Handy has become a major problem: "Politically it's dangerous
because it suggests that the only suitable talent is in Southern Africa" (Handy, quoted in Jobson 2013).

2.  The survivors had more to say about the SANDF modus operandi:

> We were told these rebels were amateurs. We were told there was nothing to worry about—
> that the thousands of Central African regional troops along with CAR government soldiers
> would help us.... But they were the first to run.... When those first shots were fired they
> disappeared.... When the sh*t really hit the fan the very okes [men] we trained started killing
> us.... They [the Seleka rebels] were not stupid.... They knew we had no support ... they had
> intelligence on us ... they knew our movements, our numbers, our capabilities ... everything
> about us.... It was only after the firing stopped that we saw we had killed kids.... We did
> not come here for this ... to kill kids. It makes you sick. They were crying, calling for help ...
> calling for [their] moms.

However, according to Helmoed-Römer Heitman (2013a) of *Jane's Defence Weekly*, "This
was one of the hardest-fought actions that the South African military have ever experienced, and the
soldiers fought well, even outstandingly. Their valour was underlined by the French force at Bangui
airport when it held a formal parade to bid farewell to those who had fallen." As Heitman explains,

> In the process the soldiers fired off more than 12,000 rounds of 12.7 mm machinegun
> ammunition, more than 60 rockets from 107 mm rocket launchers and 200 bombs from 81
> mm mortars, and thousands of rounds from 7.62 mm machineguns and 5.56 mm rifles. In
> all, they would appear to have used some ten tons of assorted munitions. In all, the fight cost
> 13 killed and 27 wounded. But the force retained its cohesion throughout and was able to
> fall back from two separate engagement areas to its base and to hold it until their attackers
> gave up trying to overrun them, offering, instead, a ceasefire and disengagement. By then they
> had suffered as many as 800 killed, according to the estimates of officers with considerable
> operational experience and by some NGOs in the country. Later reports say several hundred
> more may have died of wounds due to a lack of medical support.

One of the most effective weapons was the 19 kg rocket that fires up to 8 km, described
by Heitman as "Chinese weapons originally captured in Angola and kept in service, mainly with the
Special Forces," an unintended consequence of pre-BRICS, apartheid-era technology transfer from
China.

3.  Climate was not exceptional when it came to the BRICS countries' approach to environmental
preservation. As revealed in the Columbia University and Yale University (2012) Environmental Performance Index, four BRICS states (not Brazil) have been decimating their—and the earth's—ecology
at the most rapid rate of any group of countries, with Russia and South Africa near the bottom of
world stewardship rankings.

4.  It could have been pointed out how quickly Viagra fades (and South African cartoonist
Andy Mason did so). Indeed after a brief spike, the market resumed its free fall.

# 7

# ONE LOGIC, MANY WARS

## THE VARIETY AND GEOGRAPHY OF WARS IN THE CAPITALIST WORLD-ECONOMY, 1816–2007

**Raymond J. Dezzani and Colin Flint**

## Abstract

In this chapter we suggest a new approach to world-systems studies of hegemony that links a number of different literatures and concepts. Current analytical approaches do not consider the complexities of global political-economic structures or spatial variations in processes that give rise to hierarchy in the world-economy. As a result, conflict, contradiction, and war across scales have, under certain circumstances, been misrepresented. We argue that the interests of global and core elites as well as the spatial organization of urban networks culminating in hegemonic territorial integration give rise to specific types of conflict at specific times over the course of the cyclical development of global hegemony. We propose an analytical approach that is both spatial and temporal and permits the evaluation and assessment of the timing of conflicts of similar types across at least two hegemonic cycles (in Britain and USA). The goal of this work is to explain conflict as a consequence of structured economic activity in the arena of the world-economy and the timing and type of war as a consequence of hegemonic processes.

## Introduction

The basis of the world-systems approach is a conceptualization of the capitalist world-economy as a historical social system with structure, institutions, and dynamics driven by a single logic of capital accumulation that entwines political and economic processes (Chase-Dunn 1989, 154; Flint 2010). Using this approach, war is seen as a feature of capital accumulation stemming from three imperatives. Wars may represent struggles for control over the entire interstate system to fundamentally change the world-economy and create a world-empire (Chase-Dunn 1989, 159). Alternatively, wars may be the violent component of interstate competition reflecting the upward or downward mobility of individual states within the core-periphery hierarchy of the capitalist world-economy (Chase-Dunn 1989, 160). Finally, we consider that "wars may be used to restructure relations between core states and the periphery in keeping with relative changes in power among actors" (Chase-Dunn 1989, 160).

Our purpose in this study is to connect a number of literatures and concepts. We begin with the fundamental premises that current analytical approaches to conflict do not adequately consider the global political-economic structure, which we define as the core-periphery structure of the capitalist world-economy. Second, we raise the intriguing prospect that the causal processes of war have been fundamentally misconceptualized because the wrong actors have been identified. To address this concern, we focus on the actions of elites within the capitalist world-economy and their settings of cities, the loci of capital accumulation. Third, war is in danger of being an analytical chaotic conception (Sayer 1984) unless the variety of types of conflicts is taken into consideration. Finally, relationships across the core-periphery structure and the roles of city-based elites are not static but display a dynamism that is best represented through the paired-Kondratieff model of hegemony.

## Conceptualizing War

We start with a deceptively simple statement:

**Conflict = F(economics)**

We expand the left side of the equation to consider a variety of types of conflicts that reflect the processes of capital accumulation and the way they are expressed in competition for control over territory. Using the backdrop of the world-systems approach, O'Loughlin and van der Wusten (1993, 96–97; see also Johnston, O'Loughlin, and Taylor 1987) adopted an eightfold classification of war, which we will use in this analysis:

- *Frontier* wars—involving the geographic expansion of the world-economy and the incorporation of other social systems.
- *Imperialist* wars—the establishment of core control over the periphery and related intracore competition, most notably the two world wars.
- *Colonial* wars—peoples of the periphery attempting liberation from imperialist control.
- *Neocolonial* wars—core states and technically independent regimes that depend on core allies for survival working together to suppress challengers to the regime.
- *Collaborationist* wars—this type of violence is similar to neocolonial wars but is expressed as state repression, usually by a conservative pro-capitalist regime against internal opposition.
- *Resistance* wars—civil wars involving majority-minority conflicts and often mobilizing collective identities of ethnicity and religion and, to a lesser extent, ideology and class.
- *State resistance* wars—peripheral countries attacking core interests, perhaps best reflected in state-sponsored terrorism.
- *Territorial* wars—border disputes over the course of an international boundary.

The major difference in our interpretation of war in the capitalist world-economy is our emphasis upon restructuring as a means of gaining access to new pools of cheap labor, rather than the common resort to the explanation of seeking new markets. We believe that markets are about creating new pools of consumers and will largely involve intrastate competition within core and semiperiphery states, though some of the related social change may be reflected in border disputes as nationalist agendas are adopted as a political outlet.

An initial step is to focus on the purely economic driving forces that are likely to provoke particular types of wars. Frontier wars are processes of the expansion of the capitalist world-economy as a reflection of the imperative to increase the pool of cheap labor. Hence, these types of war are expected to occur in periods of economic restructuring. Imperialist wars are also a reflection of core states seeking access to labor in the periphery but also involve calculations of core competitors. The timing is likely to be complicated and manifold, as the positioning for imperial control may occur as signs of economic growth waning become evident (the peak of an A-phase) but war is delayed until the pressures of stagnation spike.

Inflation is the key, perhaps. Previous studies correlating price rises with outbreaks of war have suggested that expansion phases and the associated high prices reflect an ability for states to afford to conduct war (Boswell, Sweat, and Brueggemann 1989). However, if price rises are interpreted as the manifestation of inflation as a result of emerging shortages and wage demands, A-phases can be times when alternative sources of labor are being identified, foreshadowing military adventures into the periphery.

Colonial wars are expected to be a feature of B-phase restructuring as colonies seek to improve their position in the capitalist world-economy by seeking independence to enable them to develop their own strategies of economic development. Neocolonial and collaborationist wars, on the other hand, are likely to be features of A-phases as states colonized in previous A-phases (or colonies that were not successful in seeking liberation in a previous colonial war) resist colonial control. Resistance wars are expected to be most prevalent in B-phases as the expressions of economic restructuring within states. State resistance is likely to be a feature of the capitalist world-economy when a hegemonic power is at its peak, and in decline as states try to challenge the authority of the hegemon but realize it is too powerful to engage directly. Territorial wars are hard to conceptualize within the world-systems framework. Our tendency is to see them as a "chaotic conception" (Sayer 1984), a category that is unclear as it contains events occurring for different underlying reasons (Chi and Flint 2013). Hence, in this analysis we do not hypothesize any dominant temporal-spatial pattern for territorial wars.

At this stage of the project no definitive conclusions can be drawn from this conceptualization of conflict and our tentative attempts to connect them to particular manifestations of the process of capital accumulation. In other words, we are not able to make hypothetical statements and carry out a deductive analysis at this moment. In moving toward such an analysis our next conceptual step is to identify moments in the cycles of the capitalist world-economy when these different types of conflicts are most likely to occur.

## The Paired-Kondratieff Model

To interpret the rhythms of the capitalist world-economy we will utilize the paired-Kondratieff model of hegemony. Rather than focusing on the rise and fall in prices that define the fifty-year Kondratieff cycles and how they relate to the timing of war (Goldstein 1988; Boswell, Sweat, and Brueggemann 1989), the timing of war through the nineteenth and twentieth centuries can be related to the dynamic of the consecutive sequence of the rise and fall of British and then US hegemony. The paired-Kondratieff model explains the politics of intracore competition for hegemony through consideration of trade policies reflecting the economic rhythms of Kondratieff waves (Flint and Taylor 2011, 54–56). However, it would be a mistake to view the politics as simply intracore. The movement to and from free-trade policies over the course of the paired-Kondratieff has implications for economic relations connecting the core and periphery of the world-economy.

A hegemonic power rises to prominence on an economic foundation that is, in fact, a process. The emerging hegemonic power first achieves prominence in production, allowing it to become dominant in global trade, that in turn allows for dominance in global finance. The hegemonic process results in a country's wane as it loses prominence in the same sequence: first production, then trade, and finally finance (Wallerstein 1979). In this analysis, we assume that different sections of the capitalist elites of the hegemonic countries are prominent as their respective sectors emerge as being prominent: first production elites, etc.

The paired-Kondratieff model posits a period of ascending hegemony in the first of the two consecutive Kondratieff waves spanning the hegemonic process (Table 7.1). This is a period of rivalry followed by commercial victory as the emerging hegemonic power established a presence in a significant part of the periphery. Commercial victory is a period of restructuring that sees the emergence of the hegemon's role in the periphery. However, the important point to note for our analysis is that the hegemonic victory phases for Britain and the United States are expected to display different patterns of conflict. Though systemic processes will drive similar behavior for the United States as what was observed for Britain about 100 years earlier, the difference for the pattern in the B-phase of the third Kondratieff wave (IIIB) is that there are also dynamics of declining British hegemony and emerging US hegemony. The period of hegemonic maturity in the A-phase of the second Kondratieff wave is when the hegemon is expected to use its productive efficiency and commercial dominance to establish a global system of free trade. However, hegemonic dominance is soon challenged in two ways. Emulation of the hegemon's productive efficiency by other core states leads to a decline in the ability to dominate global trade, and challenges to the structure of dominance needed to establish global economic relations emerge as forms of resistance in the periphery.

Also, there is a linear trajectory to hegemony in the world-economy by which the transformations made by previous hegemonic powers have a legacy and will alter the landscape of subsequent political actions (Agnew 2005). Most notably, the period of US hegemony used a different framing of core-periphery relations than the previous period of British hegemony (Smith 2003). Formal colonialism was challenged. Hence, the manifestation of colonial and neocolonial wars is likely to be different between the British and US cycles of hegemony, though the general phenomenon of colonial violence is expected to be persistent.

The economic processes driving hegemonic rise and fall, and the related trade policies of hegemonic powers and challengers, are related to geopolitical strategies that, in aggregation, produce geopolitical world orders at the global scale (Table 7.2). The most important feature to highlight is a relatively limited period of stability (during hegemonic maturity) and the more pervasive condition of uncertainty and competition. The $A_1$ phase is one of competition and emerging

**Table 7.1 A Dynamic Model of Hegemony and Rivalry**

| | Britain | | United States | |
|---|---|---|---|---|
| A₁ Ascending hegemony | 1790/98 | Rivalry with France (Napoleonic Wars) Productive efficiency: Industrial Revolution | 1890/96 | Rivalry with Germany Productive efficiency: mass-production techniques |
| B₁ Hegemonic victory | 1815/25 | Commercial victory in Latin America and control of India: workshop of the world | 1913/20 | Commercial victory in the final collapse of the British free-trade system and the decisive military defeat of Germany |
| A₂ Hegemonic maturity | 1844/51 | Era of free trade: London becomes the financial center of the world-economy | 1940/45 | Liberal-economic system of Bretton Woods based on the US dollar: New York is the new financial center of the world |
| B₂ Declining hegemony | 1870/85 | Classical age of imperialism as European powers and United States rival Britain; "new" industrial revolution emerging outside Britain | 1967/73 | Reversal to protectionist practices to counteract Japan and European rivals |

*Source:* Flint and Taylor 2011, 55.

alliances that become central to the process of restructuring in $B_1$, which becomes finalized in what is posited to be the most stable period of the cycle of hegemony ($A_2$). Finally, a return to competition and challenge occurs in the $B_2$ phase.

### Table 7.2 Long Cycles and Geopolitical World Orders

| Kondratieff Cycles | Hegemonic Cycles | Geopolitical World Orders |
|---|---|---|
| 1790/98 A-phase | BRITISH HEGEMONIC CYCLE Ascending hegemony (grand alliance) | (Napoleonic Wars as French resistance to Britain's ascending hegemony) |
| 1815/25 B-phase | Hegemonic victory (balance of power through Concert of Europe) | Disintegration WORLD ORDER OF HEGEMONY AND CONCERT Transition (1813–1815) |
| 1844/51 A-phase | Hegemonic maturity ("high" hegemony: free-trade era) | (Balance of power in Europe leaves Britain with a free hand to dominate the rest of the world) |
| 1870/75 B-phase | Declining hegemony (age of imperialism, new mercantilism) | Disintegration WORLD ORDER OF RIVALRY AND CONCERT Transition (1866–1871) (Germany dominates Europe; Britain still the greatest world power) |
| 1890/96 A-phase | AMERICAN HEGEMONIC CYCLE Ascending hegemony (a world power beyond the Americas) | Disintegration WORLD ORDER OF THE BRITISH SUCCESSION Transition (1904–1907) |
| 1913/20 B-phase | Hegemonic victory (not taken up: global power vacuum) | (Germany and the United States overtake Britain as world powers; two world wars settle the succession) |
| 1940/45 A-phase | Hegemonic maturity (undisputed leader of the "free world") | Disintegration COLD WAR WORLD ORDER Transition (1944–1946) |
| 1967/73 B-phase | Declining hegemony (Japanese and European rivalry) | (US hegemony challenged by the ideological alternative offered by the Soviet Union) |
| 19?? | NEW HEGEMONIC CYCLE? | Disintegration "NEW WORLD ORDER" Transition (1989–?) |

*Source:* Flint and Taylor 2011, 56.

Two conclusions may be drawn from the paired-Kondratieff-model approach. First, similar patterns of war should not be expected when comparing the British and US cycles of hegemony. As Chase-Dunn (1989, 159) notes, war is transformative; it makes lasting changes to the system. One obvious case is the role of frontier wars in expanding the geographical extent of the world-economy. If frontier wars are successful then the possibility of the same type of war in that region at a future date is precluded. Also, the period of British hegemony was not immediately preceded by the hegemonic cycle of another power, but the cycle of US hegemony was. Hence, wars in the cycle of US hegemony will be a function of the aftermath of British hegemony as well as the establishment of, and challenges to, US hegemony. The difference in the form of colonial violence between the two cycles of hegemony has already been noted. Second, a multiscalar approach suggests that the domestic tensions that intensify during B-phases will be overlaid by, or integrated with, the interstate processes of hegemony and the construction and disintegration of geopolitical world orders. Hence, the rhythms of economic restructuring and geopolitical competition must be integrated and, as the one-logic approach would suggest, be seen as mutual components of the economic innovation, restructuring, and geopolitical competition.

## The Space-Time Complexity of Conflict in the Capitalist World-Economy

The integration of economic and geopolitical processes with a multiscalar approach leads to a more complex set of expectations of when (and where) conflict will occur within the capitalist world-economy (Table 7.3). A key driving impetus is the need to balance innovation within the core with the needs to expand the periphery and maintain colonial control. Imperial wars are a combination of intracore competition and control over the economy; their political ambition and geographic scope suggest that they will be evident across a broad time span, the two phases of each hegemonic cycle. Such a process of expansion into the periphery is expected to produce immediate resistance ($B_1$ phases) that is also a function of a period of global economic restructuring. In the $A_2$ phases, with the hegemon at the peak of its power, intracore competition will be limited and resistance in the periphery limited to neocolonial and collaborationist conflict rather than outright war. In the $B_2$ phases many processes come together to produce an expectation of heightened conflict in its many forms, the precursor to a new round of imperial conflict. Though resistance conflicts are identified in a separate column for heuristic purposes, it is understood that such tensions will be linked into global tensions, especially in the more competitive context of the $B_2$ phases. Finally, the successful prosecution of frontier wars by core powers in the British cycle of hegemony resulted in the world-economy becoming global in scope and, therefore, precluding the possibility of such wars in the US cycle.

Table 7.3 One Logic, Many Wars

| | Geopolitical Context | Type of War | Domestic Restructuring | Geographic Pattern |
|---|---|---|---|---|
| A$_1$ Britain | Rivalry | Imperial | | Global |
| B$_1$ Britain | Victory | (Imperial)/frontier Colonial | Resistance | Regional |
| A$_2$ Britain | Maturity | Neocolonial Collaborationist | | Regional |
| B$_2$ Britain | Decline | Colonial/neocolonial/collaborationist State resistance/frontier | Resistance | Global |
| A$_1$ United States | Rivalry | Imperial | | Global |
| B$_1$ United States | Victory | (Imperial) Colonial | Resistance | Regional |
| A$_2$ United States | Maturity | Neocolonial Collaborationist | | Regional |
| B$_2$ United States | Decline | Colonial/neocolonial/collaborationist State resistance/frontier | Resistance | Global |

## Identifying Geopolitical Actors

Returning to the equation at the beginning of this chapter, if economics is the driver of territorial conflict then serious consideration needs to be given to geopolitical actors. War is, and has been, primarily conducted by states. However, capital accumulation is led by business elites (Braudel 1984). A geography of capital accumulation that focuses on cities as the loci of wealth generation has contrasted cities as arenas of accumulation with states and their role as "guardians" (Taylor 2005; 2007). Taylor's work rests on the political economy of Tilly (1990) as well as Jacobs's (1992) discussion of the function of cities. Moreover, Taylor's world cities project has identified intercity relationships as the means by which the core-periphery structure of the world-economy is created and maintained. The important conclusion for our analysis is that if conflict is a function of economics, then somehow cities must be placed on the right-hand side of the equation rather than following the usual recourse to state aggregations of economic measures (usually GDP based).

To avoid the danger of reifying cities as economic actors, they are better seen as being the locations of capitalist elites (Dezzani and Chase-Dunn 2010). We identify five types of elites:

- Extractive (agriculture, mining, forestry, etc.)
- Manufacturing
- Trade (retail, commerce)
- Financial (banking and investment)
- Military/territorial (government and military)

Furthermore, we attempt to locate each of these different types of elites within particular geographical settings:

- Rural/hinterland (for extractive elites)
- Provincial (for manufacturing elites)
- Urban/entrepôt/depot (for trade elites)
- Financial urban centers (for financial elites)
- Capital cities and garrison towns (for military/territorial elites)

## Situating Geopolitical Actors

The final piece in the conceptual puzzle is to locate elites, and the cities within which they are based, within the structure of the capitalist world-economy using the standard three-tier hierarchy of core, semiperiphery, and periphery. Each state involved in a conflict will be classified as being a core, peripheral, or semiperipheral state.[1] Each city in the analysis will be identified as being located within a core, peripheral, or semiperipheral state. Though some justification could be made for defining core, periphery, and semiperiphery at a regional intrastate scale, data restrictions make a state scale definition most practical. Furthermore, the state scale of analysis reflects the role of the state as the monopolizer of the means of violence and coercion, and the institution that creates policy and has territorial legitimacy (Thomson 1994). Hence, the relationships we discover will be modeled in terms of the position of the actors (cities and states) and the type of connection or relationships across the tiers of the capitalist world-economy: core-core, core-periphery, core-semiperiphery, periphery-periphery, periphery-semiperiphery, and semiperiphery-semiperiphery. Furthermore, these relationships should be directional to show their purpose and potential impact (Dezzani 2002).

## Rational Conflict Decisions and Methodologies

To evaluate the conflict-in-world-systems framework described, a database consisting of both conflict variables and socioeconomic variables at the national and subnational scales must be constructed. No complete, single database of this type is currently extant. If the Kondratieff framework is to be effectively incorporated into the analysis, the period of study must cross at least two cycles. Thus, the spatial-temporal database should extend from roughly 1816 to 2005. In addition, a rational framework incorporating primary causes of conflict must be considered to render hypotheses for analysis. Fragmented or partially constructed data covering the time period for particular countries already exist. Hence, the first task in the validation of the proposed framework is to construct a single coherent database satisfying the basic requirements of the study parameters.

The primary issue with which we are concerned is the timing of a particular rationale to engage in conflict and how the economic situation may impact this decision. This rationale will be a function of the systemic Parsonian learning, potential contenders for hegemonic position, relative strength posture of the hegemon, and potential economic gains (e.g., new investment or resource/market growth opportunities [see Arrighi (1994) 2010; Mansfield 1994]). The decision to engage in war behavior will be based on the position of the hegemon in its own hegemonic cycle. The tradeoff in the decision will be between war and other system-maintenance and capital-expansion possibilities—so there is a computable utilities-possibilities frontier and this locus will change at different times in the hegemonic cycle (Powell 1999). The hypothesis is that early in the hegemonic cycle different types of war are more likely to occur than later in the cycle. This hypothesis is suggested by the war type patterns observed in Tables 7.2 and 7.3. Early-phase wars may be more likely to be regional conflicts while late-phase conflicts that challenge hegemony may be more likely to be global conflicts of long duration. During the phase of geopolitical world order, a variety of maintenance conflicts will ensue to stabilize and maintain the power base (e.g., the Cold War or the British colonial conflicts of the late nineteenth and very early twentieth centuries). If this is the case, then the geopolitical and economic conditions as well as the deterrence posture of the hegemon will have an impact on the rational decision to go to war. It is hypothesized that this rationality changes with position in the long cycle.

To provide a mechanism for classifying wars and linking these to processes operating in the world-system we need to address space and process functions of conflict. This will also serve to validate the hypotheses concerning types of wars occurring in certain phases of the Kondratieff cycle. The framework we propose is twofold: (1) for process-based classification of conflict, use discriminant analysis or some form of adaptive discrimination (Dillon and Goldstein 1984; James 1985); (2) for the temporal component, use transfer function methods to relate the conflict scope and intensity to position in the Kondratieff cycle or to expected temporal processes associated with cyclical behavior—particularly capitalization cycles and the role of finance in the economic development of the hegemonic state.

## Discriminant Analysis-Based Process Classification of Conflict

The conflict classification to be functionally estimated is described in Table 7.3. Then structural correlates of conflict will be used to construct a functional explanatory framework for each war class, as follows:

$$\text{WAR}_i = (\text{Conflict Class})_i = k_i + \sum \beta_{ik} Z_{ijk} + \varepsilon_i$$

The classification of the multinomial variable WAR with i classes is expressed as a linear or quadratic function of a series of functional explanatory independent variables determined by theoretical expectation. Then, in the linear expansion, k is a proportionality constant, $Z_{ijk}$ are the k unique explanatory variables for each country case j and class i; $\beta_{ik}$ are the coefficients or classification weights for the variable and conflict type, and $\varepsilon_i$ are the errors of a Gaussian white-noise process with mean 0 and constant variance $\sigma^2 I$. The contribution of explanatory variable to conflict type will be measured as the relative variance contribution of the $\beta$ values. These can be evaluated for significant contribution and thus test the corresponding hypothesis. The model parameters will use maximum likelihood estimation. Quadratic functional form and logistic (i.e., paired/binary dependent classification) approaches may also be used (Dillon and Goldstein 1984; McLachlan 1992; Ripley 1996). These models can be examined for their sensitivity using bootstrapping approaches and they can be calibrated using partial sample distributions (Efron and Tibshirani 1993; McLachlan 1992). Error rates can be estimated and the functional forms can then be used to classify new cases provided the models are statistically feasible.

Mansfield (1994) provides a series of models used to explain conflict behavior using several different theoretical foundations, including world-systems. The variables Mansfield (1994) uses include trade and power concentration, as well as the proportion of aggregate capabilities possessed by the core states that each major power state controls in a year. Such a variable implies a gradient of power-projection potential, which must also be assessed. Mansfield (1994) also uses a hegemonic indicator variable, which we will redefine as a country-specific characteristic for any given time. Other independent variables used for classification tied to a particular country j may be country j global trade contribution, country j relative position in global economic hierarchy (Dezzani 2001; 2002), country j finance capital expansion rate at time of consideration, country j average income level, trade diversity, trade concentration (Dezzani 2001), net trade flows, gross fixed domestic capital formation as a proportion of total capital formation, unemployment and inequality, growth of the financial sector ($\Delta t$—over time periods), rate of finance capital expansion ($\Delta t$—over time periods), country gross growth rate, GDP/GNP proportionate differential, percent GDP spent on defense, country defense concentration, country defense orientation (orthogonal contrast variable: defensive [−1], neutral [0], offensive

[+1]), trade and/or defense/policy bloc membership (multinomial or binary), internal economic integration, basic commodity gross domestic output (measure of autarky), government revenue growth rate, rate of domestic consumption, and measures of wealth concentration (e.g., Gini as well as changes in wealth concentration of the top 5 percent and top 1 percent). The role and importance of finance capital accumulation and the dominance of "mercantile" finance capital are described by Arrighi as a characteristic of late-hegemonic rent-seeking behavior by capital-controlling elites (Arrighi [1994] 2010, 163–246). We will use finance capital behavior as a predictor of conflict type and activity in the paired-Kondratieff cycle following Arrighi ([1994] 2010). In this way, we will differ slightly from Goldstein (1988), who used the time-lagged structure of commodity price changes. In sum, the discriminant analysis allows us to test hypotheses regarding how the timing of different types of wars are a function of the different phases of the hegemonic cycle.

## Integration of Processes across Space, Time, and Scale

As with most analyses of cyclical time series, we will employ linear and nonlinear models of cross-correlation among series (Goldstein 1988; Berry 1991). However, we will extend the analysis beyond war and price-fluctuation description through intervention and examine stochastic processes of conditional dependence. The transfer function provides a ready instrument for such analysis among time series (Enders 1995, 277–290). The transfer function permits the estimation of lagged relationships among time series through a relation such as the following:

$$Z_t = \alpha_0 + \Gamma(L)\, Z_{t-1} + \Lambda(L)\, X_t + \Pi(L)\varepsilon_t$$

Here $\Gamma(L)$, $\Lambda(L)$, and $\Pi(L)$ are polynomials of the time-lag operator L. The lag operator is defined as $L^i Z_t = Z_{t-i}$, where distributivity and associativity across different lag orders hold. The endogenous variable is $Z_t$, the exogenous variable is $X_t$, and data are collected for both. The parameters of the model and the polynomials are then estimated such that a specific deterministic path is not assumed; the exogenous variable may reflect any stochastic process and the polynomial $\Lambda(L)$ is referred to as the transfer function because it is used to demonstrate how change in the exogenous variable influences/is transferred to the time path of the dependent/endogenous variable (Enders 1995, 277). As an example we could express the number of occurrences of the onset of war or the rate of war occurrence at time t and relate this to changes in the rate of mercantile capital/finance transfers of specific types or, alternatively, trade transactions may be used:

(Conflict rate)t $= \alpha_0 + \Gamma(L)$ (conflict rate)$_{t-1} + \Lambda(L)$ (mercantile capital investment rate)$_t + \Pi(L)\varepsilon_t$

The model consists of an autoregressive component and a transfer-function component. When expanded using the lag operator, the function might appear as follows:

$$Z_t = \alpha_0 + \alpha_1 Z_{t-1} + k_0 + \sum_j k_j X_{t-j} + \Pi(L)\varepsilon_t = (\alpha_0 + k_0) + \alpha_1 Z_{t-1} + \sum_j k_j X_{t-j} + \varepsilon_t$$

$$(1 - \alpha_1 L)Z_t = (\alpha_0 + k_0) + \sum_j k_j X_{t-j} + \varepsilon_t$$

$$Z_t = (\alpha_0 + k_0)/(1 - \alpha_1) + \sum_j k_j \sum \alpha_1^j X_{t-j} + \sum \alpha_1^j \varepsilon_t$$

Then $\partial Z_{t+1} / \partial X_t = k_0 + \sum_j k_j \alpha_1^j$ is the impact function of the effect of X on Z, where $k_0$ is the proportionality constant (direct effect/impact of $X_{t+1}$ on $Z_{t+1}$) for $X_t$ and if it is zero then $\{X_t\}$ may be a leading indicator of the observations $\{Z_t, Z_{t-1}, Z_{t-2}, \ldots\}$, and j is defined for 0 to maximum lag, where the sum is taken over all lags. Through the use of transfer functions, relationships between series and cycles may be explicated.

State-space Markov models and "change of regime" frameworks will also be employed in the analysis of classifiable behaviors. These state-space models of change (Bishop, Fienberg, and Holland 1975) can be used to capture models of hegemonic cycles and state "maneuver" behaviors similar to the regime-transition-rate models used in Dezzani (2002) and Fingleton (1999). We will employ this type of stochastic analysis to assess state-space position in a Kondratieff cycle or to assess position and change in a hegemonic cycle. The models employed in this approach are similar/analogous to stochastic social-mobility models (Boudon 1973).

Hierarchical modeling involves a complex interaction of processes across different levels. The levels may reflect spatial or geographical units such as cross-scale aggregations of process effects feeding into other processes at larger spatial aggregations or smaller scales. The process interaction can usually be described by a directed acyclical graph. For example, we might express resource-production processes occurring at a large regional scale or as a city hinterland. Processes at each scale would feed into and influence levels of production of goods/commodities at the urban and national scales. The trade and sale of these goods would produce a surplus that can be used as finance capital at a large transnational scale of aggregation that may influence the conflict behavior of a country. There may also exist systemic effects such as economic or power stratification that can influence the likelihood of a country starting a war, and these likelihoods may in turn be influenced by the general state space of the global political system (multipolarity, hegemony, hegemonic decline, etc.). To be able to capture these interactions across scales and among processes, a framework that accounts for data, processes, and parameter estimation must be specified and the Bayesian framework is then useful for specification, parameter estimation, and inference. Such a model might be delineated for the influence of war onset due to influences from finance capital and trade structure and may be initially specified as follows:

DATA MODEL: $[\{Z_{war,i}\}, \{Z_{capital,i}\}, \{Z_{trade,i}\}|$ WAR, CAPITAL, TRADE, $\theta_{war}, \theta_{capital}, \theta_{trade}]$

PROCESS MODEL: [WAR, CAPITAL, TRADE $| \eta_{war}, \eta_{war|capital}, \eta_{war|trade}, \eta_{capital|trade}]$

PARAMETER MODEL: $[\theta_{war}, \theta_{capital}, \theta_{trade}, \eta_{war|capital}, \eta_{war|trade}, \eta_{capital|trade}]$

The actual model specified will be based on the sampling distribution of the variables. In general, Gaussian models may be used as initial estimates where appropriate and conditional autoregressive models may be used as priors. Markov random fields may also be used as priors for Poisson and binary processes such as the number of wars per unit time or within an interval or the binary classification of wars. Spatial Markov random fields depend on the type of spatial structure or connection as intercommunicating units termed cliques. In spatial Markov random fields, the clique defines the structure of conditional dependence.

Finance capital usually follows log-normal distributions, as does trade behavior. Therefore, auto-Gaussian Markov random fields may also be specified as priors. In sum, the transfer analysis enables a multiprocess, multiactor, and multiscale analysis of the timing of different types of war that places cities as the key economic drivers on the right-hand side of the conflict equation and is a function of the economic relations that either directly or indirectly are the causes of war.

## Conclusion

Our initial goal for this project is to make an empirical linkage between different types of wars in different phases of the twin paired-Kondratieff model of hegemony (for the British and US periods of hegemony), with different processes of capital accumulation in different cities. We expect that different types of war will occur in different phases, as demonstrated in Table 7.3. Moreover, we expect to see these periods of war related to activity in, and flows between, the different types of cities. The goal is to identify an empirical connection between different types of elites in different cities, with different types of conflict in particular phases of the twin hegemonic cycles.

If we are successful in these empirical goals, a connection between the accumulation processes in cities and the violent behavior of states may be demonstrated. The implication will be that though states and cities may indeed have separate moral syndromes (Taylor 2007), the imperatives of accumulation and war are connected in the one logic of the capitalist world-economy (Chase-Dunn 1989).

# References

Agnew, John. 2005. *Hegemony: The New Shape of Global Power*. Philadelphia, PA: Temple University Press.

Arrighi, Giovanni. [1994] 2010. *The Long Twentieth Century: Money, Power and the Origin of Our Times*. London and New York: Verso.

Banerjee, Sudipto, Bradley P. Carlin, and Alan E. Gelfand. 2004. *Hierarchical Modeling and Analysis for Spatial Data*. Boca Raton, FL: Chapman and Hall/CRC.

Berry, Brian J. L. 1991. *Long-Wave Rhythms in Economic Development and Political Behavior*. Baltimore: Johns Hopkins University Press.

Bishop, Yvonne M. M., Stephen E. Fienberg, and Paul W. Holland. 1975. *Discrete Multivariate Analysis: Theory and Practice*. Boston: MIT Press.

Boswell, Terry, Mike Sweat, and John Brueggemann. 1989. "War in the Core of the World-System: Testing the Goldstein Hypothesis." In *War in the World-System*, edited by R. Schaeffer, 9–26. Westport, CT: Greenwood Press.

Boudon, Raymond. 1973. *Mathematical Structures of Social Mobility*. Amsterdam: Elsevier.

Braudel, Fernand. 1984. *The Perspective of the World: Civilization and Capitalism 15th–18th Century*. Vol. 3. New York: Harper and Row.

Carlson, Lisa J., and Raymond Dacey. 2006. "Sequential Analysis of Deterrence Games with a Declining Status Quo." *Conflict Management and Peace Science* 23: 181–198.

———. 2009. "A Note on Second Order Probabilities in the Traditional Deterrence Game." *Peace Economics, Peace Science and Public Policy* 15, no. 1.

———. 2013. "The Influence of Domestic Constraints on Crisis Initiation and Termination." Paper prepared for presentation in the Domestic Political Constraints and International Behavior panel at the 2013 ISA meeting, San Francisco, April 3–6.

Chase-Dunn, Christopher. 1989. *Global Formation: Structures of the World-Economy*. Cambridge, MA: Blackwell.

Chase-Dunn, Christopher, Alexis Alvarez, and Dan Pasciuti. 2005. "Size and Power: Urbanization and Empire Formation in World-Systems." In *The Historical Evolution of World-Systems*, edited by Charles Chase-Dunn and E. N. Anderson, 92–112. London: Palgrave.

Chi, Sang-Hyun, and Colin Flint. 2013. "Standing Different Grounds: The Spatial Heterogeneity of Territorial Disputes." *Geojournal* 78: 553–573.

Cressie, Noel, and Christopher K. Wikle. 2011. *Statistics for Spatio-Temporal Data*. Hoboken, NJ: John Wiley and Sons.

Dezzani, Raymond J. 2001. "Classification Analysis of World-Systems Regions." *Geographical Analysis* 33: 330–352.

———. 2002. "Measuring Transition and Mobility in the Hierarchical World-Economy." *Journal of Regional Science* 42: 595–625.

Dezzani, Raymond J., and Christopher Chase-Dunn. 2010. "The Geography of World Cities." In *The International Studies Encyclopedia*, edited by Robert A. Denemark, 2969–2986. Chichester, UK: Wiley-Blackwell Publishing.

Dillon, William R., and Matthew Goldstein. 1984. *Multivariate Analysis: Methods and Applications*. New York: John Wiley and Sons.

Efron, Bradley, and Robert J. Tibshirani. 1993. *An Introduction to the Bootstrap*. New York: Chapman and Hall.

Enders, Walter. 1995. *Applied Econometric Time Series*. New York: John Wiley and Sons.

Fingleton, Bernard. 1999. "Estimates of Time to Convergence: An Analysis of Regions of the European Union." *International Regional Science Review* 22, no. 1: 5–34.

Flint, Colin. 2010. "Geographic Perspectives on World-Systems Theory." In *The International Studies Encyclopedia*, edited by Robert A. Denemark, 2828–2844. Chichester, UK: Wiley-Blackwell Publishing.

Flint, Colin, Paul Diehl, Jürgen Scheffran, John Vasquez, and Sang-Hyun Chi. 2009. "Conceptualizing ConflictSpace: Towards a Geography of Relational Power and Embeddedness in the Analysis of Interstate Conflict." *Annals of the Association of American Geographers* 99, no. 5: 827–835.

Flint, Colin, and Peter J. Taylor. 2011. *Political Geography: World-Economy, Nation-State, and Locality*. 6th ed. Harlow, UK: Pearson.

Ghosn, Faten, Glenn Palmer, and Stuart Bremer. 2004. "The MID3 Data Set, 1993–2001: Procedures, Coding Rules, and Description." *Conflict Management and Peace Science* 21: 133–154.

Goldstein, Joshua S. 1988. *Long Cycles: Prosperity and War in the Modern Age*. New Haven, CT: Yale University Press.

Groningen Growth and Development Centre. 2010. Historical National Accounts Database, March. www.rug.nl/research/ggdc/data/historical-national-accounts (accessed May 16, 2014).

Jacks, David S., Christopher M. Meisser, and Dennis Novy. 2008. "Trade Costs, 1870–2000." *American Economic Review, Papers and Proceedings* 98, no. 2: 529–534.

———. 2011. "Trade Booms, Trade Busts, and Trade Costs." *Journal of International Economics* 83, no. 2: 185–201.

Jacks, David S., Kevin H. O'Rourke, and Jeffrey G. Williamson. 2011. "Commodity Price Volatility and World Market Integration since 1700." *Review of Economics and Statistics* 93, no. 3: 800–813.

Jacobs, Jane. 1992. *Systems of Survival*. New York: Random House.

James, Mike. 1985. *Classification Algorithms*. New York: John Wiley and Sons.

Johnston, R. J., J. O'Loughlin, and P. J. Taylor. 1987. "The Geography of Violence and Premature Death: A World-Systems Approach." In *The Quest for Peace*, edited by Raimo Vayrynen with Dieter Senghaas and Christian Schmidt, 241–259. Beverly Hills, CA: Sage.

Maddison, Angus. 1995. *Monitoring the World Economy, 1820–1992*. Paris: OECD.

Mansfield, Edward D. 1994. *Power, Trade and War*. Princeton, NJ: Princeton University Press.

McLachlan, Geoffrey J. 1992. *Discriminant Analysis and Statistical Pattern Recognition*. New York: John Wiley and Sons.

Meissner, Christopher M. 2005. "New World Order: Explaining the International Diffusion of the Gold Standard, 1870–1913." *Journal of International Economics* 66, no. 2: 385–406.

Mitchell, Brian R. 2003a. *International Historical Statistics: Africa, Asia and Oceania, 1750–1988*. New York: Stockton Press.

———. 2003b. *International Historical Statistics: Europe, 1750–1988*. New York: Stockton Press.

———. 2003c. *International Historical Statistics: The Americas, 1750–1988*. New York: Stockton Press.

O'Loughlin, J., and Herman van der Wusten. 1993. "Political Geography of War and Peace." In *Political Geography of the Twentieth Century*, edited by P. J. Taylor, 63–113. London: Belhaven Press.

Powell, Robert. 1999. *In the Shadow of Power*. Princeton, NJ: Princeton University Press.

Riley, S. 2007. "Large-Scale Spatial-Transmission Models of Infectious Disease." *Science* 316: 1298–1301.

Ripley, B. D. 1996. *Pattern Recognition and Neural Networks*. Cambridge: Cambridge University Press.

Sarkees, Meredith Reid, and Frank Wayman. 2010. *Resort to War: 1816–2007*. Thousand Oaks, CA: CQ Press.

Sayer, Andrew. 1984. *Method in Social Science: A Realist Approach*. London: Routledge.

Smith, Neil. 2003. *American Empire: Roosevelt's Geographer and the Prelude to Globalization*. Berkeley: University of California Press.

Taylor, P. J. 2005. "New Political Geographies: Global Civil Society and Global Governance through World City Networks." *Political Geography* 24: 703–730.

———. 2007. "Problematizing City/State Relations: Towards a Geohistorical Understanding of Contemporary Globalization." *Transactions of the Institute of British Geographers* 32: 133–150.

Thomson, Janice E. 1994. *Mercenaries, Pirates, and Sovereigns: State-Building and Extraterritorial Violence in Early Modern Europe*. Princeton, NJ: Princeton University Press.

Tilly, Charles. 1990. *Coercion, Capital, and European States, AD 990–1990*. Cambridge, MA: Blackwell.

Wallerstein, Immanuel. 1979. *The Capitalist World-Economy*. Cambridge: Cambridge University Press.

## Endnote

Peace scientists have done a tremendous job in collecting data pertaining to the manifestations and likely causes of war. The two important sets of data are the Correlates of War (COW) data (Sarkees and Wayman 2010) and the Militarized International Disputes (MIDs) data (Ghosn, Palmer, and Bremer 2004). Within each of these databanks smaller datasets have been housed focusing upon aspects of conflict and political economy. The COW and MIDs data are collected at the state scale, extend back to the early 1800s, and are coded at the dyad-year level of analysis. They are usually coded as a 0 or 1; i.e., France-Germany were not at war in 2012 and hence coded as a 0. From these data we can identify conflict and other forms of political economic relations between states formally recognized as members of the inter-state system. Furthermore, recently collected data have included certain relations between political entities other than states, such as protectorates and other colonial possessions (Sarkees and Wayman 2010). The collection of datasets within the suites of COW and MIDs data will be used extensively in our analysis.

However, the right-hand side of our equation also requires a large amount of data on economic linkages between geopolitical actors other than states. At this stage of the project we are still searching for relevant and useful databases: ones that provide consistent measures across most of the nineteenth and twentieth centuries. For example, Jacks has collected numerous data on trade, trade costs, and market integration (Jacks, Meisser, and Novy 2008, 2011; Jacks, O'Rourke, and Williamson 2011). Groningen Growth and Development Centre (2010) hosts data on agricultural production and trade, which complements the extensive collections of Maddison (e.g., 1995) and Meissner (2005). These specific datasets will be supplemented by relevant data in the numerous volumes of the International Historical Statistics (e.g., Mitchell 2003a, b, and c).

# Note

1. These terms are shorthand for the accurate but more complicated recognition that a core state is one within which core processes predominate, a peripheral state is one within which peripheral processes predominate, and a semiperipheral state is one with a relatively even balance of core and peripheral processes.

# PART III

Social Movements in Struggle

# 8

# INDIGENOUS ALTERNATIVES TO THE GLOBAL CRISES OF THE MODERN WORLD-SYSTEM

**James V. Fenelon**

## Abstract

The modern world-system "developed" global crises based on principles and practices that supported European expansion over the Americas and creation of industrial capitalism. These crises include devolution of the environment, competitive states during hegemonic decline, decreasing lands for resource extraction, increasing inequality locally and globally, and lessening involvement of community. The same crises are products of 500 years of concentrated destruction of existing indigenous societies with healthy social systems. I review historical processes, identify existing indigenous peoples' movements, and proffer alternative "developments" with indigenous social-systems models that do not threaten states but allow local, community-based, and sustainable societies to flourish within existing global orders. I analyze indigenous peoples' movements in Central and South America, South Asia, the Pacific region, North America, Africa, and Australia.

## Introduction

I start with a set of observations—indigenous peoples have certain social constructs useful in facing critical global issues that threaten to destabilize and possibly bring down contemporary capitalist-controlled market economies and countries. I identify indigenous social systems with respect to globalization (Hall and Fenelon 2008; 2009), using world-system analysis, with strong doses of resistance and revitalization discussions from earlier works, including the United States' intentional destruction of "culture" and collective organizing by Native Nations (Fenelon 1998). The modern world-system has "developed" into a set of global crises that put the entire world into conflict and increasing chaos. Premier among these crises are competitive strong states during the hegemonic decline of the United States, associated with global climate change—partly the result of centuries of unrestrained industrial development. I observe early development of the modern world as European expansion and colonization of the Western Hemisphere, fueled by wealth production and resource extraction from Native Nations. Ultimately this gave rise to state structures in North America that industrialized, building capitalism into powerful economies. Here we see crises of centralized systems and their militaries, operating globally in neoliberalism and based on systemic production of inequality.

The central construct of much analysis of considering "development" of the modern world-system along with notions of civilization are based quite simply on size—the larger and more globally dominant the "system" the greater importance it has in our understanding world-system analysis. This feeds into what Andre Gunder Frank termed "the development of under-development" in so-called Third World countries, which in ancient times had been First World in their regions (Wolf 1982). Many of these peoples and countries devolved under pressure into colonies and smaller nation-states, what social scientists call "tribes" even as other peoples, already smaller in scope, simply survived.

Essentially, newly created social groupings began to emerge as European nations took over the Americas; the indigenous peoples were later termed Indians, "tribes," and sometimes nations, and much later were called hunter-gatherers, terms that clearly put indigenous peoples surviving four centuries of the increasingly violent onslaught of European and then Euro-American societies into categories of the "underdeveloped." However, less studied is what was lost or submerged with development of the modern world-system over "less developed" regions (Bunker 1985: 100) and how that produced structured inequality.

Dominant Western-based societies have expanded over much of the globe under systems of colonization, neoimperialism of capitalist markets, and the twentieth-century systems called neoliberalism, with neverending extraction of natural resources, large-scale agricultural markets, and industrial growth—all without concern for land, the environment, or atmospheric changes that such systems have caused. Now the globe has come under threats to overall stability, in addition to what human societies have done directly in world wars, also conducted partly in competitive conflict over valued resources such as oil.

I place this discourse into adapted world-systems analysis by addressing the basic relationships of core-periphery power dynamics, precisely the product of inequality developing over centuries of Euro-American domination. For this I will use a presentation by one of the leading world-systems analysts, Christopher Chase-Dunn (2013):

> Another way to look at the core/periphery hierarchy is as a multidimensional set of power hierarchies, that includes economic, political and military power forming a continuous hierarchy that is a relatively stable stratification hierarchy.…
>
> The labels of core, periphery, and semiperiphery are just convenient signifiers of relative overall position in a continuous hierarchy rather than truly discrete categories.…

The semiperiphery, and to a large extent the periphery, is thereby understood in its totality in relation to the core economic-power hierarchies, a set of relationships built on the last couple hundred years of the increasing power of Euro-American core countries, which created peripheral dynamics for many of the peoples conquered and dominated in their conquest and "development" of the Americas. The Aztecs stand out in this regard, in that their regional hegemonic power had to be destroyed by the Spanish, with all "indigenous" social systems entirely wiped out to the extent of cultural genocide or "culturicide" (Fenelon 1998) that also destroyed legitimacy and historical hierarchies. Not only was Mexico City built upon the ruins of Tenochtitlán, but the racialized polity of the "mestizo" was created to further deny indigeneity and its historical situation. Thus the periphery and semiperiphery are created by the invasive colonizing-dominating powers that become hegemonic. Understanding this as the basis of inequality is central to analyzing contemporary global crises, especially those of "movements" emanating from these hierarchies of power. Chase-Dunn (2013) explains, "These differences may be related to how a national society, or the movements that are based in these national societies, behave in world politics."

However, indigenous societal analysis finds that many indigenous peoples, Native Nations or American Indians, are those that survived large processes of global power convergence in various forms and that retained sociocultural systems fundamentally different from modern nations and powers:

> I contend that the question of cutting points between allegedly discrete core, peripheral and semiperipheral zones is largely a matter of convenience in what is, in the long run, a continuous set of distributions of different kinds of power. (Chase-Dunn 2013)

In this analysis, size matters. Overreliance on existing systems of power overwhelms all other modes of understanding, especially smaller systems, existing in defiance of larger systems using capitalist modes. We have missed fundamental differences in social construction, existing irrespective of "incorporation" into larger systems, typified as "resistance" rather than alternative social patterns. Only when larger societies come to crisis, threatening the entire system, do indigenous societies come in focus.

## The Crises Facing the World

Ironically, these crises are based on the same set of principles and practices—taking of lands for large-scale agricultural development (*encomienda* under the Spanish, plantations under the English) and sublimating and destroying existing indigenous populations—that supported the European expansion over the Americas. Euro-American countries contributed to growing crises when creating capitalism and global industrial economies—with centralized political economies furthering growth of systems predatory in both system and size, forever altering the world by developing immense trading systems shipping products and people to different parts of the world. These very large systems subordinated smaller systems, maximizing displacement and creating a vortex of social problems that destroyed community cohesion, distributive economies, and land-tenure relations of indigenous societies practicing reciprocity and holistic interaction. Although the markets increased inequality and centralized power, effects on global climate change were proving to be greater problems:

> Environmental catastrophe is far more serious: The externality that is being ignored is the fate of the species.... For the first time in human history, humans are facing the significant prospect of severe calamity as a result of their actions—actions that are battering our prospects of decent survival. (Chomsky 2013)

Herein we see one of the crises that could endanger the entire world. Although we clearly have the ability to identify the problem and its consequences, there is apparently little we will do to limit or counteract it since any such action means curtailing the system itself in terms of capitalism's required growth and powerful corporation-states' continued predation.

> The scientific consensus on climate change is by now well established, and in dispute only in the United States, where powerful fossil fuel corporations spend millions ... to shape the political debate.... [If limits are exceeded] scientists predict a centuries-long epoch of extreme weather, sea level rise, extinction of species, and untold social unrest due to mass human migrations, famines, and wars. (Foran and Widick 2013)

Rich capitalist countries profiting from corporations support status quo operations, even as the only "effort to preserve conditions in which our immediate descendants might have a decent life are the so-called 'primitive' societies: First Nations, tribal, indigenous, aboriginal" (Chomsky 2013). Some analysts are seeing this as "tantamount to genocide" for certain regions of the world and the most marginalized, enacting "climate apartheid" to benefit the richest 1 percent while sacrificing the other 99 percent (Foran and Widick 2013). This great anomaly is ironic; those peoples thought left behind to be "underdeveloped" or those that are simply surviving centuries of predation, suppression, and destruction by the large-scale "civilized" societies may well hold the keys to future survival:

> The countries with large and influential indigenous populations are well in the lead in seeking to preserve the planet. The countries that have driven indigenous populations to extinction or extreme marginalization are racing toward destruction. (Chomsky 2013)

I deconstruct this simple observation, identifying an intentional process of destruction of indigenous populations thought necessary, or at least efficacious, in order for countries to become leaders of large capitalist systems, and identifying "hegemonic powers as the source of inequality and wealth" in the contemporary world, to the level of calling it "structural genocide" (Leech 2013).

"Grow or die" has been the mantra of capitalist "development" for the last two centuries, and since then has been based on industrialism, fueled by the power sources of oil and coal, while much larger effects, including whole-scale destruction of the environment upon which all countries depend, are ignored in the pursuit of growth and profits. However, Chomsky credits countries with large indigenous populations, such as Ecuador or Bolivia, rather than the indigenous societies themselves creating alternative social patterns. (Ecuador tried to auction Amazonian oil reserves to China, while Bolivia wants to build highways in "undeveloped" regions without consulting indigenous governance.)

> This observation generalizes: Throughout the world, indigenous societies are struggling to protect what they sometimes call "the rights of nature," while the civilized and sophisticated scoff at this.... (Chomsky 2013)

The global crises include devolution of the environment, probably to the point of chaos, or what some scientists are calling a global "tipping point" of no return in nature where we are "approaching a state shift in Earth's biosphere" (Barnosky et al. 2012), because of the burning of fossil fuels, greenhouse-gas emissions, rising sea levels, and altered climates causing perturbations in the agricultural and industrial sectors of all societies, notably negative and possibly irreparable. World-systems analysts are drawing attention to these models as potentially causing sociopolitical unrest and resource wars across regions, over water, food, and survival itself (Foster 2012; Ciplet and Roberts 2012).

> Localized ecological systems are known to shift abruptly and irreversibly from one state to another when they are forced across critical thresholds.... The global ecosystem as a whole can react in the same way and is approaching a planetary-scale critical transition as a result of human influence. The plausibility of a planetary-scale "tipping point".... It is also necessary to address root causes of how humans are forcing biological changes. (Barnosky et al. 2012)

The global ecological crisis alone threatens humanity and makes a strong foundation for this chapter. Even so, mankind's deviltry in exacerbating these issues is furthered by sociopolitical problems arising from conflicts over valuable limited resources. Survival itself may already be in play, such as rising sea levels forcing populations of Bangladesh inward toward India, which is already building massive walls to keep out the unwanted peoples. Related water shortages are likely to cause wars:

> Mr. Ehrlich [a national-security specialist] said he foresees a series of dire threats to humanity, many virtually untouched by political leaders, including climate change, water shortages, and widespread use of man-made toxins. Even a single repercussion of one of those, such as water scarcity leading to nuclear war between India and Pakistan, could devastate populations worldwide.... (Basken 2012)

This leads to another crisis, interactive with the global ecological crisis—competitive states coming into conflict during the decline of a hegemon (Wallerstein 2004). Of course, nuclear-war possibility, whether regional or global between competing world powers, increases during hegemonic decline. Yet what is more important is how that links with disastrous effects from the interactions between "environmental catastrophe and nuclear war" (Chomsky and Polk 2013).

> We are in the midst of a structural transition from a fading capitalist world-economy to a new kind of system. But that new kind of system could be better or worse. That is the real battle of the next 20–40 years. (Wallerstein 2013)

When the ensuing global climate-change crisis reaches its tipping point, this will preclude movement into the next structural transition. As the United States declines in its global hegemonic influence and powers like China attempt to move into competing spheres of increasing hegemony, lesser or smaller countries coming into conflict or war with each other and with declining and inclining hegemons increase the possibilities for regional and global warfare, with attendant effects stemming from nuclear war. This means interactive effects are on a global scale, suggesting proposed resolutions cannot further destabilize existing powers.

I observe decreasing new lands for resource extraction, connected to destruction of the remaining rainforests and extensive old-growth groundcover around large waterways that act as the lungs of the earth by taking in carbon dioxide and producing oxygen. Increasing uses for agricultural production (related to rising world population and to waste from global agribusiness—connected to increasing world inequality) decreases the ratio of food-producing lands to those occupied by humans, another set of interactive effects noted by scientists studying this globally (Barnosky et al. 2012). Alternatives to large agribusiness production are ignored and instead there is a focus on increasing yield, almost always on crops for markets.

In recounting traditional planting practices of the Ifugao in the Philippine Highlands, Peter and Jessica Jacques (2012) find that "green" technology "openly belittles traditional knowledge as useless folk-beliefs" while the major agricultural institutes advance high-yield varieties, industrial fertilizer, and chemical pesticide approaches that are all about maximizing yield with no concerns for their impact on local or regional environments or the destruction of rice-growing knowledge on an indigenous village level.

Jacques and Jacques find that core power nodes have exploited power relationships and "must then seek out new energy … in peripheral areas that have not reduced or over-simplified their ecology" and "thus the core eats the periphery literally and metaphorically," producing "unequal exchange" within the periphery, as well as between the state and indigenous peoples, as an outgrowth of colonizing processes (Bunker 1985). Overall, these world-systemic agricultural processes discourage and destroy local diversity, replacing a "globalization of culture, food-ways, languages, export crops, and exotic invasive species" with distributions so wide that some call this the "homogocene" era (Jacques and Jacques 2012).

Food production has moved into a larger world-system with transnational rules and patterns of trade, production, and consumption. In contrast are the "pockets of abandonment and autonomy that exist outside the global economy," where we find smallholder farmers who plant thousands of crop varieties (Jacques and Jacques 2012). Premier among such farmers are indigenous peoples who have maintained seed banks that are now used to diversify and even save genetically modified monocrops that are prey to pesticide-resistant insects and diseases, which were "developed" for transportation and distribution and standardized for ease and predictability of market profit and growth. Indigenous farming stands opposed to agribusiness, which is destructive to community or local production and consumption, and requires transportation, packaging, and marketing—deep-level processing that forces local growers into selling wage-labor, breaks up family and community, increases commodification in capitalist markets, and is connected to environmental decay on many levels. Indigenous systems are more productive locally, adapt to changing environmental conditions, and have nonmaterial (e.g., spiritual, ethical, or emotional) meaning alienated by consumer-based systems, and that contributes to sustainability and decreases biodiversity loss, homogenization of cultures, and systemic inequality.

Native Americans have adapted to live in a specific place, interdependent with nonhumans and ecological cycles that generate intense cultural meaning, identity, and traditional life-ways. More importantly, they hold alternative views on the human condition in society as well as in the world (Deloria 1979). These social systems are interactive with the natural world and are symbiotic with philosophical and spiritual understandings, including seeing land as sacred and holding steward responsibilities of "being a relative."

Frances Moore Lappé, as early as 1971, demonstrated that local, small-scale food production was actually more effective than agribusiness in terms of feeding people, and that when these differences in production were taken into account, food scarcity was a myth (Lappé and Collins 1977). Complexity exists on a small scale and agricultural use has a set of interactive effects that become compounded when producing diets primarily for rich elites and the middle classes, versus sustainable diets for the working class or peasants in poorer countries. These effects (interaction between types and diversity of crops, yields, harvest methods, and replanting) are further connected to biodiversity and local ecosystems (crop rotation, individual adaptive strategies, food use). It is important to distinguish between peasant groups and indigenous peoples, in that peasants (and their urban counterparts, the proletariat) are understood in relationship to other class structures in the same society, not as social systems or full societies in their own right. By including examples of the historical Mayan construction of maize with contemporary systems, corn production, and distribution, we see accomplishments in complex, local, indigenous societies.

The focus on economies of scale is also hardly new, as in "giantism," seeing all cost-benefit analysis in terms of markets and monetary or capital value and maintaining accumulation as the primary model—materialism measured by individual profits, accumulation, or ownership of the amount of consumption.

E. F. Schumacher ([1973] 1989) critiqued the capitalist world-system, including reliance on utilizing technology for profiteering and endless accumulation. He found that "small is beautiful" when viewing "economics as if people mattered." Size does matter, in that small systems, indigenous societies, cannot compete or thrive—can barely survive—in large world-systems and are given no credence.

Therefore, even agricultural sectors are contributing to an increasing inequality both locally and globally, and lessening involvement of community for sociopolitical representation. Edwin Wilson (2012) captures this discussion by questioning whether these developments are about a better or simply a larger earth system. Some indigenous scholars question all evolutionary progress, sociobiology, and group-behavior explanations, seeing most conflict around basic competition as compared to community interests (Deloria 1990).

Processes that maximize personal property and deemphasize community and collective goods create an individuation, or more broadly an industrialism and capitalism that erode community and families—leaving a sense of being fundamentally alienated from ecological cycles and systems and the web of life, as in what happened to the Guaraní after the destruction of rainforests and agricultural production in Paraguay "recoded" cultural groups that were fragmented and assimilated through alienation from traditional lands, use values, and means of life (Jacques and Jacques 2012). Indigenous peoples form or are linked to resistance groups that reclaim land bases, restore culture, and maintain traditional practices in new ways, such as by keeping seed banks. For instance, the Terena people in Mato Grosso do Sul, western Brazil, are in conflict with ranchers, farmers, and resource-extraction companies over the land, biodiversity, and subsistence, and are further linked to transnational peasant movements demanding self-determination.

Here we see the intersection of food production and culture as world-view and practice, all in resistance to and opposition over further penetration of indigenous lands and societies by global powers literally changing the ecological and sociopolitical relationships that have sustained them through the years. Religious leaders of Native Nations from North America produced a document reiterating these values. In the Statement of Vision Toward the Next 500 Years from the Gathering of United Indigenous People at the Parliament of World Religions, Chicago, 1993 (Fenelon 1998, 310), indigenous leaders declared their "honoring ... future generations ... continuing survival with our sacred homelands." They saw this as

> lived in a spiritual way in keeping with sacred laws, principles and values given to us by the Creator. That way of life is predicated on a sense of honor and respect for the Earth, a sacred regard for all our relations, and a continuation of our languages, cultures and traditions.... We call for recognition of the past, acknowledgement of the present, and a commitment to support our just demands for dignity, justice and human rights. These rights include: the right to practice our *spiritual traditions* without interference or restrictions, the right to raise our children in *our own cultures*, and the right to *sovereignty and self-determination*. (emphasis added)

These crises are partly the product of 500 years of concentrated destruction of existing indigenous societies with healthy social practices. Creation of the state has been especially powerful in determining the flow of capital and resources, cultural domination, and often exclusivity of citizenship based on race and ethnicity, which causes further destruction to indigenous local communities and cultures. Borders are created that overlay and erode national origin identities. Champagne (2005, 4) differentiates indigenous claims toward "government, land ownership ... resource management and community organization and identity," calling for "multinational" state structures that respect indigenous peoples' rights and societies.

International borders often run across and divide traditional lands of indigenous peoples, so that US "border crossings" with Mexico in the case of the Kumeyaay and Tohono O'odham and with Canada in the case of the Iroquois and Blackfoot Confederacy share policy shifts over two centuries that are still fracturing communities and tribal identities, which somehow manage to survive. Nearly all these peoples use symbolic language similar to *mitakuye oyasin* (we are all relatives) as sociophilosophic statements.

Mayan-descent peoples in Guatemala and in the states of Chiapas and Oaxaca, Mexico, are moving away from liberation theology to a new indigenous "liberation philosophy" partly based on traditional understandings of culture, the land, and community. These are epistemological movements that reject not only the hierarchy of European social orders, but the very nature of their social organization.

Some examples demonstrate how these indigenous communities come under pressure from many forces, including the Nicaragua Miskito communities when they attempted to realize their "autonomous" zones of Zelaya Norte, first in armed conflict with the Sandinistas, who were in low-intensity war with US-funded Contras, and later with coalition governments under the influence of neoliberal policies.

Mapuche peoples in Chile have organized resistance along cultural lines, relating struggle to community and land. While many of these interethnic conflicts find flash points around major economic activity, such as mining or land appropriation for large agricultural development, their underlying issues remain focused on maintaining traditional lifestyles in order to retain community cohesion (Fenelon and Hall 2005).

As indigenous leader Felipe Quispe Huanca describes in the quote below, as Evo Morales speaks to the elected head of Bolivia, and as traditionalists spoke throughout the historical reality of the North American indigenous struggles, the essence of community, economic cooperatives, traditional decision making, and land-tenure relations sometimes leads to violent uprising or a more localized economic reorganization. Yet indigenous peoples rely on these foundations to resist in their individual situations and within global networks (Ramirez 2003). These new movements have a collective orientation toward communities, are transparently antiglobalization, and specifically target neoliberalism as a modern evil for poor, indigenous, marginalized peasants making up their constituency. Examples such as coca-leaf growing in Bolivia, an indigenous horticultural practice disconnected from US cocaine markets, challenge regional dominance and hegemony operated by corporate economic practices. Indigenous identity revolves around relationships to relatives and those living close by, even if that "community" is fluid and transmorphic. For instance, consider the words of Felipe Quispe ("El Mallku" the Aymara, head of the Pachacuti movement):

> We believe in the reconstruction of the Kollasuyu, our own ancestral laws, our own philosophy.... We have ... our political heritage [that] can be successful.... It is community-based socialism.... That is what the brothers of our communities hold as a model.... In the Aymara and Quechua areas, primarily in La Paz, we have been working since 1984 on fostering awareness of community-based ideologies. (América Profunda 2003)

Indigenous peoples are involved in struggles over local autonomy, land tenure, community relations, and socioeconomic "development" that are often viewed as antiglobalization efforts when viewed through the lens of world-systems analysis. In many parts of the world, these struggles take on forms of decolonization strategies, none more poignantly than in Mexico and other Latin American countries.

## Conflicting World Paradigms—Global Crises and Indigenous Peoples

In reviewing the predictions of impending global crisis in relation to a declining hegemon and conflicts between states, I observe a connection and convergence with global climate change, economic and political crises and breakdown, along with control over land and national resources, all in conflict with modes of indigenous resistance and revitalization, outlined in the model in Figure 8.1 (Fenelon and Hall 2008).

This ideal type is not any romantic or pristine set of relations, but rather a redress of primitive accumulation as it is only in respect to more advanced, larger-scale, and capitalistic accumulation that these relations are stereotyped and denigrated. One critical point to note is that many of these peoples are not

**Figure 8.1 Four Modes of Indigenous Resistance and Revitalization**

attempting to move up into wealthier social groups, but instead are focusing on maintaining their traditional systems.

Bonfil Batalla (1996, 18) identified a targeted cultural destruction of individual "Indian" or indigenous communities, nations, cultures, and collectivities for the purposes of domination, and the subsequent building of racialized concepts of "the Indian" that no longer has these diverse relationships, but only represents the primitive and undeveloped. Stark contrasts on the nature of the land, autonomous sociopolitical relationships, and community as a collectivity emerge in relationship to "modernity" and capitalist expansion over increasingly large territories.

Activist scholars in Mexico call indigenous communities *pueblos indígenas* in order to identify important differences from other groups resisting potential erasure or assimilation. The following is the United Nations definition:

> Indigenous communities, peoples and nations are those who have a continuous historical connection with pre-colonial societies that preceded the invasion ... that have the determination to preserve, develop and transmit to future generations their ancestral lands and their ethnic identity. (Cobo 1987)

Basic relationships of indigenous peoples are to the land, often sacred, rarely of direct economic value, and usually held collectively rather than by individuals (Bonfil Batalla 1996, 88). This orientation to land is in direct opposition to modern capitalistic society, with direct economic values and individual title.

> The larger problem for the Indians was the struggle against breaking up the communal lands. The Liberals made *private property sacred* ... the *communal ownership* of land in Indian communities became an obstacle to be removed. (Bonfil Batalla 1996, 100; emphasis added)

Bonfil Batalla identifies areas of social organization that differ markedly from dominant mainstream modern society, including medicine, community service, and cargo systems in Mexico that are "simultaneously civil, religious, and moral." I observe that it is the collective nature of indigenous life that appears to be in conflict with modern social systems, invading and incorporating an indigenous collectivity that includes the land, distributive economics, shared decision making, and the community. Invasive systems want to privatize and take land, stratify the economy, and centralize political systems into controlled hierarchies. Since indigenous peoples utilize alternative social organization and do not dissolve relationships, they are seen as obstacles, and if they resist they are seen as enemies (Bonfil Batalla 1996, 103–104).

> The struggle over land involved one side, which wanted free trade and individual property, while the other side protested the land was communal and inalienable. (Bonfil Batalla 1996, 105)

"To civilize" is meant to pacify them, domesticate them, end their violence.

The key issues in the conflict of the identified global crises versus ideal types of the indigenous model can be found in four questions (Champagne 2005):

- Where does responsibility for the environment lie?
- Who really benefits or is hurt by decisions, especially in regard to natural-resource extraction and profiteering and resultant toxicity?
- What is the relationship to land in terms of privatization and suppression of collective voices (tribal or ethnonational relations, care for the sacred)?
- What is the nature of community?

I now consider examples of how these modalities come into conflict and what indigenous peoples do.

In India, the Adivasi (specifically, the Gond), after a thousand years of basic tributary dominance before undergoing colonial domination by the British and then independence, were subsumed as "tribals" near the bottom of the caste system, but now they are regrowing teak forests and maintaining armed guards to repel illegal timber companies and resist further devastation of lands (Bijoy 2008).

In South Africa, the Zulu (conglomerated peoples) who resisted *voortrekkers*, the Boers, were subsumed under colonialism by the English; put into a South African racial apartheid state that saw them as blacks, tribal minorities, or tribal nations (Lesotho, Swaziland); and dominated culturally by Afrikaans or English, even in post-apartheid South Africa. Within neoliberal economic systems, their uncertain future includes participation in corrupt political practices that accept capitalist market structures.

The Mapuche militarily resisted conquest, the colonial forces, and then independence for a Chilean state that did not recognize indigenous peoples. Later indigenous agreements made with the government during the Allende regime were overturned after the coup by Pinochet backed by neoliberal forces, with suppression and alienation of land still in conflict over privatization of land rights, timber resources, and mining. Sociopolitical conflict over Mapuche conservancy and collective land rights, replete with political prisoners and intermittent armed standoffs, still partially controls Mapuche resistance, now with efforts to set up schools and colleges with indigenous history and perspectives.

Finally, there are the Mohawk in North America, first colonized by the British with French involvement, then, after the American Revolutionary War, sharply divided between what ended up as the Canadian and US sides of the border. Differences between First Nations in Canada and the sovereignty struggles in the United States became clear when conflicts emerged in Mohawk communities such as the Oka, referred to as Kahnesatake on the Canadian side and Akwesasne St. Regis on the US side. This illustrates how states divide and subordinate indigenous nations.

In these examples I observe long-term processes of conquest, colonial and later cultural domination, and imposition of state structures of sovereignty that deny or distort indigenous autonomy (Fenelon and Hall 2008). Furthermore, I note how struggle becomes primarily internal to states, though connected through neoliberal capitalism to globalization processes that then contain and suppress authentic, autonomous representation and participation by most indigenous peoples in the state.

The problems with accepting interstate systems and transnational economic market structures are illustrated by the thirty-year struggle for recognition, addressed by the United Nations Declaration on the Rights of Indigenous Peoples of September 2007. The United States, with other core states such as Canada, New Zealand, and Australia, resisted the declaration, and the United States was the last holdout on its full recognition.

Other examples of transnational border issues for indigenous peoples include the Yaqui and Kumeyaay along the border with Mexico; Kurds in tripartite border issues with Iraq, Turkey, and Iran; Pashtun in Afghanistan and Pakistan; Aymara in Bolivia and Ecuador; Maasai in Kenya and Tanzania; Tibetan peoples in Chinese-held Tibet and Nepal; the Penan in Malaysia and Indonesian Kalimantan; the diverse Mayan-descent peoples straddling Mexico and Guatemala; and a host of other indigenous peoples with transborder issues, relocation issues, or both.

Essentially, then, states and hegemons control their internalized populations through continual denial of indigenous history, ethnonational presence, and claims to national autonomy and cultural sovereignty. I have reviewed historical processes, identified existing indigenous peoples' movements, and observed commonalities of indigenous struggles, whether that of the *Ina Maka* (Lakota for "Mother Earth") philosophy maintaining symbiotic sacred relationships with the environment; or Idle No More, started by Canadian indigenous grandmothers then spread over North America; or the Warli, with Mother Earth guiding philosophies; and Adivasi activism within India. Furthermore, we see ancient philosophies similar to these taking new political forms, such as *Pachamama* in Ecuador and throughout South America.

I identify four thematic issues among indigenous peoples that are construed by states as a challenge: first, economic relationships are redistributive; second, political relations of "cultural sovereignty" and "community autonomy" predominate; third, environmental relationships tend to be symbiotic, less destructive to life forms than capitalist societies; and fourth, indigenous communities value inclusive relationships that promote common goals.

While Western-based societies and now virtually the entire world accept some form of a central state system of government, most indigenous peoples identified an indigenous equivalent of *autoridad* (authority) with the "communal authority [of] the whole community in its assembly" including elders and others sharing in decision making. I found that "the central idea is to maintain harmony within the community," or what Felipe Quispe Huanca calls "fostering awareness of community-based ideologies" (Hall and Fenelon 2009, 26, 82–84).

Indigenous peoples have collective orientations toward land tenure, extending to environmental issues: "Land is given as a sacred gift and a sacred stewardship. People do not own land, but must care for the land as part of their sacred task within the purpose and direction of the cosmic order" (Champagne 2005, 7). This orientation to land is in direct opposition to how modern capitalist society approaches private property with economic value and private title. This created a conflict over the "breaking up the communal lands," and the "communal owner-ship of land in Indian communities became an obstacle to be removed" (Bonfil Batalla 1996, 100). Thus, communal land-tenure relationships, compounded by the less destructive and symbiotic interactions with the environment, became a central point of conflict with neoliberalism and globalization processes, even as alternatives are viewed as threats by modern states.

## Origins of Crises in the Modern World-System in the Americas

The basis of creating an exploitable, racialized labor force—an essential feature of the modern world-system in development—took different directions depending on the particular dynamics, spatial and temporal, in areas of initial conquest. In Hispaniola it was a fast-developing genocide of Taino-Arawak on the island's western half, morphing into replacement labor of peoples taken from African nations, called negroes or black. Attempts by the Spanish to introduce this race-based slavery into larger land bases were less effective, although the Portuguese in Brazil destroyed native peoples (enslaved first) and uprooted African "blacks" to be slaves on a massive scale, greater than that of any other Western state.

Not only have these systems overwhelmed and destroyed smaller systems in their way; they have also quite purposefully destroyed midsized societies and even very large systems in the conquest of the Americas, and later the world in patterns of colonization that became global. A perfect example is Tenochtitlán—Cortez's conquest of the Aztecs, disassembling of the regional empire, and building of the colonized and then contemporary "state" of Mexico, with stratified and racialized populations, in what is now Latin America: European peoples in the top echelons controlling most socioeconomic power, and creation of midlevel, racialized pop-ulations called mestizo or *mestizaje*. The Spanish, and to an extent the Portuguese in Brazil, created fluid constructs of racialized stratification along similar lines in the first "conquests" in Española. This system maximized ethnoracial inequality and destroyed indigenous social systems by land and labor exploitation, quite intentional in the Vallodolid debates controversy, and now seen as an emerging "coloniality of power" in the Caribbean.

Land was expropriated on the most massive scale in the world under the dual ideologies of "discovery" and "conquest" by European sovereigns, with the taking of vast resources. Entire forests were leveled to become timber for structures and ships to further form fleets expanding new markets from the Western Hemisphere back to European nations (a critical leg of the triangular trade, including the Middle Passage of slaves to the Americas). Vast mineral resources (Zacatecas silver, gold mining everywhere along the periphery, and other valuable ores) enriched the coastal European nations, with new foods as wealth for burgeoning empires—see tobacco, sugar, corn, and the potato as fodder for working populations tied to the land (Weatherford 1988)—and new areas for excess population growth as a basis for "settlers" or "settlement." (Note the ironic use of Eurocentric civilization as a basis for humanity, what Blumenbach did 200 years later, defining "Caucasians" as evolution and "development" as social Darwinism.)

As powerful and pervasive as these transoceanic processes would become—the setting of knowledge-based systems forming all perspectives of "civilization" that became the basis for the Western separation of the social sciences and humanities (Wallerstein 2004)—they introduced deep distortions that would affect under-standings of the modern world and global dominance to this day. Deloria (1979) called these the "Metaphysics of Modern Existence" for comparative analysis with indigenous peoples, describing how these separate scientific knowledge of the physical world from that of human societies and holistic spiritual philosophy.

What is critically important to understand—and little understood in the academy—are the massive and often complete suppression and destruction of communities and smaller social groups or societies with reflexive relationships to (local) environmental and socioeconomic concerns of people.

These effects would be magnified by the rise of industrialism as a key element of empire and power, further turning communities (ranging from construction of family households as a first basis of society to extensive migration across societies in the pursuit of employment) from cohesive social groups with the ability to adapt to local or regional circumstances, into sources of labor—increasingly based on the dynamics of wage labor. This forced permanent changes to the family-to-community-to-society-to-"state" dynamics of ordinary peoples' lives.

The other, and ultimately more powerful, social force of change, partly arising from conquest of the Americas and an enriching of Europe leading to colonization of much of the world, is capitalism. Banking as large-scale financing became ever more necessary to support global systems of conquest, colonization, taking of lands/exploiting of labor, and the rise of industrialism and capitalism itself.

Even initial "risk capital" of the Columbus voyages and development of shipping and market systems—Triangle Trade of the Atlantic building markets that required transportation of goods (raw, manufactured) and people—meant many expensive operations could not have single-source support, or be entirely reliant on single nation-state centralized operations. Markets and bank-based financing became more important than people or community (on any scale)—social con-structions already under corrosive effect if not actual assault by racialized systems growing in the Americas. Vast, diverse societies of peoples were categorized as "tribal" and "savage," and as inferior in their essence. Other peoples were given racial constructs to be enslaved not as individuals, or as a family or community members, but generationally passed down in what is called "social death"—without rights or any mobility.

These ideologies co-occur with development of wage labor as central class-based relations—transitions from large-scale agricultural, textile-based economies, (using slave labor) to industrial-based economies (using wage labor; the US Civil War is indicative of how powerful this change becomes). Later immigrating peoples sought work across border economies, as in the case of the Zapotecs from Oaxaca, Mexico, working in Los Angeles, both states denying them community.

## Crises in Conflict over the Twentieth-Century Paradigms of the "Modern World-System"

Another aspect of this devolution of societal responses to environmental disasters resulting from human-influenced climate change is the intensification of these effects, operating from capitalist models driven by profiteering and growth rather than problem analysis (carbon "caps" and greenhouse emissions). Here I note fossil-fuel extraction has increased with new technologies that add to environmental issues, such as destructive applications of "fracking" that pollute groundwater, or the tar sands in Canada and the United States. Related consumption and control areas include corporate market manipulation such as Monsanto's genetic modification of food crops for large-scale agribusiness (destructive to family and small-scale farming), which has generated political support to the point where it has sought and received protection from lawsuits, which no other industry enjoys.

The cases of genetically modified foods and of oil extraction are mired in the new forms of resistance, wherein indigenous peoples negatively affected by the industries bring lawsuits and international claims for reparations or to stop operations. These pursuits are pretty much to no avail in stopping the environmental effects and socioeconomic changes to their communities.

For instance, indigenous and family farmers in Oaxaca, Mexico, once self-sustaining even in bad times (people were able to feed their own families and generate barter-level crops when unable to sell to local markets), cannot stand up to legal staffs of genetically modified–corn producers sold to the supermarkets. Once-self-sufficient farmers are forced into seeking employment as wage laborers, usually outside of Oaxaca and Mexico, perpetuating immigrant labor forces crossing state borders and breaking up families. Ironically, this is done in Oaxaca and the central valley of Mexico, where indigenous peoples first domesticated corn for healthier crops thousands of years ago. Today, there are communities of Zapotec and Mixtec wage earners in Los Angeles with ties to their homes in Oaxaca. They send money back to their families to sustain traditional households. Zapotec communities have charged *cargo* system members (a civil-religious hierarchy, *fiesta* or *mayordomía* system) with returning to their home villages periodically, as revitalization in the face of expatriation.

Even as indigenous peoples in Ecuador and Peru fight to protect their lands from corporate predators, especially oil companies, and have famously won some international lawsuits over environmental losses, the state is coerced (and enticed) to sell or even auction oil rights in its most sensitive regions.

Fuller analysis of indigenous struggles demonstrates that the dominant society will only measure the negative effects on the local environment and communities, often if not always disregarding the claims of American Indians and indigenous peoples generally. Consider the fight over the Pick-Sloan Plan and the Missouri River "dammed Indians" in the Dakotas, and more recently the relocation and environmental effects of dams in southern Chile, affecting Pehuenche and Mapuche peoples, and the huge Belo Monte Dam under construction in Brazil— among the largest in the world, with strong negative effects of land takings and relocations for "tribes" living in this Amazon region. Whole communities protest projects in Brazil, seeing effects on their lives and biospheres. These construction projects are done under a guise of power production and profits without engendering local inputs. Indigenous peoples' lands, socioeconomic livelihoods, and communities are upended and destroyed, often while political decision makers repress the democratic participation of peoples over these life changes.

Examples are not limited to forest and riverine destruction; they include the dead zones in the oceans that are changing ocean currents and affecting atmospheric air currents, as noted by many seagoing indigenous peoples. Interactive effects include negative intensified greenhouse gases, or what I directly observed when visiting the Maori peoples in New Zealand, in radio announcements of current "burn times" when exposed to direct sunlight because of the ozone holes opening in the atmosphere. Indigenous-community leadership, more responsive to concerns because they are likely to answer to councils of elders or sometimes the community as a whole, addresses environmental destruction, labor exploitation, increased inequality, and relations to the land in terms of what is good for the people in general rather than what is good for some business, corporation, or larger governmental interest.

Navajo "peacemaker" courts are an example of modern organizing principles, even as Dakota councils were disbanded by the Bureau of Indian Affairs. I observed Warli Adivasi leadership, acting in council, moving to save and regenerate entire teak forests, similar to the Gond Adivasi community meetings allocating resources for guards against rogue timber operations in central India. The Zapatistas of Mexico are near-perfect examples of combined resistance-revitalization models, in that much of their revolutionary activity was/is in reaction to Plan Panama—"development" of the Chiapas region into dammed rivers, power-generating stations, roads, and extractive industries, with resulting community destruction, relocation, and pushing of Indian peoples into farm wage labor, all with central control by banking interests and strong-arm government. The Zapatistas established focus on *normas y costumbres* (community norms and customs), with *pueblos indígenas* changing to *comunidades indígenas* (indigenous communities) providing local leadership and decision making through *juntas de buen gobierno* (good-government committees) for each community to decide what is best for the people. Newer resistance deals with inculcated dysfunctionality of long-term conquest and internal colonialism.

The effects of coercive assimilation and culturicide systems are why Noam Chomsky wisely points us to places where significant numbers of indigenous peoples have survived and thrived, such as Ecuador or Bolivia. After more than a century of breaking up collective *tiyospaye* kinship-based land holdings among the Lakota in the Dakotas, and similar moves among the Hidatsa with the Three Affiliated Tribes of the Fort Berthold Reservation, with coerced corruption by fracturing traditional political societies (*ominiceye*) when oil or mining or grazing leases are negotiated, many "Indian" land owners do not act in collective or community interests in relation to land and local economy, but rather in self-interest. Fracking on the Fort Berthold Reservation is an example of this, as are leasing rights on the Standing Rock Reservation and coal on the Crow Reservation in Montana, to name a few. Those increasingly are seen as resources to be developed with "tribal status," which is how distributing is to be accomplished—better than dominant neoliberal practices, but based in capitalism nonetheless.

Large-scale system examples also abound, such as how the People's Republic of China uses capitalist or neoliberal principles in "developing" strong economic practices, all the while becoming the worst polluters, with horrific environmental issues. I saw this when working in Shanghai during the early 1980s, when China's notions of communism (versus communalism) or socialism connected conflict with capitalism (as economic "development" first in special economic zones) becoming sociopolitical rather than socioeconomic organizing principles. This is where "movement" starts to matter.

As stronger indigenous people collectively coordinate or share resistance modalities and revitalization strategies, they become more resilient and more likely to be targeted by even stronger states driven by neoliberal capitalist expansion. The deeper consciousness initiated by the Zapatistas (typically found among indigenous peoples' movements) within their international *encuentros* (invited encounters with other indigenous peoples) is now reflected in similar groups in Ecuador, sponsored by indigenous leadership in Bolivia, and increasingly found in other Amazonian regions in South America, such as with the Guaraní.

Individual resistance is easily circumvented or minimized, as seen at Standing Rock and Fort Berthold. However, as indigenous groups share experiences and are further influenced by continental and global group consciousness (with a focus on decolonization) they become more adept at countering neoliberal forces of corporate mining and oil-extraction industries and sponsor states. The long-term struggle of the Adivasi indigenous peoples taking over an entire state in India is an example.

## Indigenous Alternatives

Arguably the most basic societal difference between indigenous peoples and the dominant societies of the modern world-system are "Mother Earth" philosophies of relationships to the earth, environmental consciousness, and humans as an interconnected whole with a strong basis in community. I use societal ("tribal") connections of the Lakota, linked to similar constructs of the Warli, Maori, Tzotzil, and Mapuche, among other indigenous peoples, to illustrate this universality as a social construct.

The basis of Lakota relationships between people and the environment uses *Ina Maka* (Mother Earth) as key. For instance, the Lakota greet relatives with *Hau Mitakuyepi* (for everything that is related): the *tiwaye* (family), *tiyospaye* (extended relatives—community), *Unci Maka* (Grandmother Earth), *Tunkashila* (grandfather or ancestors), *Oyate* (nation or those belonging together—*wanbli* for eagle, *pte* for buffalo nations), *unma oyate* (people outside the group, or others). *Ikce Wicasa* means just a common human and *Omidakuye oyasin* means we are all related, including animals and other living things in the environment. The Lakota have kinship relationships, encompassing an environment of all life.

The Dakota in Minnesota and North Dakota have similar relationships. The Warli in northwestern Maharashtra, India, use the term "the earth is our mother" with four cardinal directions, also found in symbology of the earth with the Tzotzil in southern Chiapas, Mexico, and in patterns with the sea of the Maori in Aotearoa, New Zealand. The Mapuche in southern Chile pray to four directions, within patterns shared by the Maasai in Kenya, the Sami in Scandinavia, and indigenous Filipinos.

Four interactive components of indigenous peoples are found in each of the cases, including a focus on community providing group/local coherence; an economy with redistribution to community members; land (tenure) relationships with the local environment; and a decision-making orientation with sociopolitical leadership responsive to all of those elements. I observe interactive societal practices in these ideal types, depending on local/traditional ways of "the people," so "leaders" must come from and answer to communities themselves, and elders' councils become steering and selection bodies rather than central powers. Economic interests often resist agribusiness and are related to community and land (environment) so that use of genetically modified products and pesticides, as well as supermarkets and shelved products, is less preferable than local fixes to problems. Interestingly, these four modes are the same divisions that Wallerstein (2004) observes as distortions to knowledge and the academy of (social) sciences.

These modes have become operative with the Zapatistas in their *junta del buen gobierno*, governance that is responsive to the community *normas y costumbres*; with Adivasis (Warli and Gond) resistance, food production, forest regeneration, and community laws as in *ghotul* (youth enclosures); with Maori rebuilding of *marae* (communal) community structures and the *wananga* ("tribal") colleges; with Mapuche political resistance and with reforesting practices; and with the Zapotecs in Oaxaca community building and restoration of *maize* values versus Monsanto. Many other indigenous peoples in resistance and revitalization modes do not threaten states (or the neoliberalism that emerged last century) but do allow local, community-based, and sustainable societies to flourish within the existing global orders.

Finally, we must observe the strength of these indigenous efforts, each based on community values, relative to movement and organizational efforts on regional, national, and international levels. When discussing a Kichwa woman's frustration about the Confederation of Indigenous Nationalities of Ecuador (CONAIE) activity pushing for "constitutional recognition of indigenous collective rights, plurinationality" of the Ecuadorian state, Casas (2014) reports the woman "explained that the CONAIE was only as powerful as its base organizations and communities." In other words, indigenous communities drove the movement, not organizational interests, and indigenous "people living in Intag [Ecuador] were fighting to protect the valley . . . yet they were not the ones benefitting from leadership conferences, scholarships, or from international summits."

Indigenous peoples in Central and South America, and their movements, are necessary to understand, such as how Casas (2014) captured these dynamics in her work on the September 2008 Ecuador constitution "that granted rights to living things and their environment." The Ecuadorian Constituent Assembly said, "nature has the right to exist, persist, maintain and regenerate its vital cycles, structure, functions and its processes in evolution" (Article 71). Importantly, the assembly acknowledges a "Kichwa indigenous concept and project of *sumak kawsay*, or 'living well' for all natural systems." *Sumak kawsay* has a "critique of traditional development strategies focused on growth and exploitation of resources rather than seeking to live and coexist within dynamic systems of interdependence and relations. This practice and concept integrates (and unites) peoples and communities with *Pachamama* (Mother Earth)" (Casas 2014).

Clearly, then, concepts of a living relationship with the earth and community as collective responsibility are operative among indigenous peoples in Latin America, and indeed around the world. This is clear in Bolivia, which passed *Ley de Derechos de la Madre Tierra* (Law of the Rights of Mother Earth) in 2011, defined as "the living dynamic system comprised of the indivisible community of all living systems and all living beings that are interrelated, interdependent, and complementary, and that share a common destiny. . . . Mother Earth is considered sacred" (Article 3) (Casas 2014).

The very real challenge from community interests—such as oil in the Amazon, dams in the Americas, and forests in Asia—results in clashes of paradigms of development, progress, and what is valued. Global interests pit economic calculus against ecological calculus and dismiss most indigenous claims as primitive or less progressive rather than viewing these as different paradigms of social life on Earth. We need to affirm and support communities (indigenous peoples) to determine their own futures—over use of nonrenewable and unsustainable resources and redistribution of money from "developing" resources, infrastructures, and societies. Chilean indigenous struggles of the Mapuche and Pehuenche are classic examples of neoliberal corporate interests toppling democracies while native communities take control over "development" by what they value, with profits in redistribution to the people.

## Conclusion

While common "defense" such as use of militaries and so on is a firm reality, these forces should not be used internally, externally, or internationally to enforce neoliberal market structures and mechanisms. In order to reduce the possibility of using these forces, no major disruptive challenges to current states or their structures should be made. Even so, I must reiterate that states and governments that contain, dominate, and control Native Nations and indigenous peoples do not confer these sociopolitical rights "of Nature" upon the indigenous, so they have no real representation. Overarching principles of human organization and global society have to be our common destiny: what some indigenous peoples call "Mother Earth" (environment and climate), not an economy maximizing profits or centralizing power in large states.

From this analysis we can make four observations.

Major environmental accords are unlikely to produce results, especially as they all answer to capitalist, industrialist (including large agribusiness) states and economic forces such as corporations. Significant change must acknowledge the indigenous peoples in their region and find ways not to disrupt their lives, especially when producing neoliberal policies of "development."

States must not be disrupted, especially with a declining hegemon, as potential for war is increased and interactive effects of all the other components thus become stronger. In that way, places where levels of sovereignty are already recognized (the United States and Canada, New Zealand, etc.) can continue to gain ground over these matters while those without recognition focus more on cultural sovereignty.

Communities must decide on their own food, resource, and environmental policies, along with distribution strategies. What some analysts are calling "food sovereignty" is really an interactive, holistic set of relationships between food, land, and more, not fully understood. This is a base of production, consumption, and of life itself.

Leadership with decision making needs to be responsive to communities, and not centralized power sources and political parties with corrupt representatives no longer directly linked to home groups. Rights of collective human groups, whether community, village, or tribe, need to be understood in the context of the United Nations Declaration on the Rights of Indigenous Peoples, similar to the Mother Earth platforms in Ecuador's and Bolivia's constitutional improvements.

However, perhaps the most difficult challenge is for more of the world to embrace and understand concepts like "Mother Earth" and spiritual-social-biological relationships with land, air, sea, and all life that walks, flies, swims, or crawls upon it. Rather than view these alternative philosophies as primitive, we need to see they are holistic approaches better suited to the powerful and potentially lethal changes we will see as a result of global climate change.

## References

América Profunda. 2003. América Profunda colloquium, December, Mexico City, Mexico.

Barnosky, Anthony, Elizabeth A. Hadly, Jordi Bascompte, Eric L. Berlow, James H. Brown, Mikael Fortelius, Wayne M. Getz, John Harte, Alan Hastings, Pablo A. Marquet, Neo D. Martinez, Arne Mooers, Peter Roopnarine, Geerat Vermeij, John W. Williams, Rosemary Gillespie, Justin Kitzes, Charles Marshall, Nicholas Matzke, David P. Mindell, Eloy Revilla, and Adam B. Smith. 2012. "Approaching a State Shift in Earth's Biosphere." *Nature* 486, no. 7401 (June 7): 52–58.

Basken, Paul. 2012. "U.S. Is Urged to Step Up Research Linking Climate Change to National Security." *Chronicle of Higher Education*, November 9. https://chronicle.com /article/US-Is-Urged-to-Step-Up/135724 (accessed June 24, 2013).

Bijoy, C. R. 2008. "Forest Rights Struggle: The Adivasis Now Await a Settlement." *American Behavioral Scientist* 51, no. 12: 1755–1773.

Bonfil Batalla, Guillermo. 1996. *Mexico Profundo—Reclaiming a Civilization*. Translated by Phillip A. Dennis. Austin: University of Texas Press.

Bunker, Stephen. 1985. *Underdeveloping the Amazon: Extraction, Unequal Exchange, and the Failure of the Modern State*. Chicago: University of Chicago Press.

Casas, Tanya. 2014. "Transcending the Coloniality of Development: Moving beyond Human/Nature Hierarchies." *American Behavioral Scientist* 58, no. 1: 30–52.

Champagne, Duane. 2005. "Rethinking Native Relations with Contemporary Nation-States." In *Indigenous Peoples and the Modern State*, edited by Duane Champagne, Karen Jo Torjesen, and Susan Steiner, 3–23. Walnut Creek, CA: AltaMira Press.

Chase-Dunn, Christopher. 2013. "Crisis of What: The End of Capitalism or Another Systemic Cycle of Capitalist Accumulation?" Paper presented at the Global Studies Association conference, Marymount College, Los Angeles, California, June 7–9.

Chomsky, Noam. 2013. "Will Capitalism Destroy Civilization?" *Truthout*, March 7. http://truth-out.org/opinion/item/14980-noam-chomsky-will-capitalism-destroy -civilization/ (accessed June 1, 2014).

Chomsky, Noam, and Laray Polk. 2013. *Nuclear War and Environmental Catastrophe*. New York: Seven Stories Press.

Ciplet, David M., and J. Timmons Roberts. 2012. "Power in a Warming World: Consent and Inequality in Global Climate Change Politics." Paper prepared for the Political Economy of Global Climate Change and Other Environmental

Disruptions panel at the American Sociological Association meetings in Denver, Colorado, August 20.

Cobo, Jose R. Martinez. 1987. *Estudio del problema de la discriminación contra las poblaciones indígenas*. Vol. 5: *Conclusiones, propuestas y recomendaciones*. New York: United Nations.

Deloria, Vine. 1979. *The Metaphysics of Modern Existence*. San Francisco: Harper and Row.

———. 1990. "Knowing and Understanding." *Winds of Change* 5, no. 4: 26–31.

Fenelon, James V. 1998. *Culturicide, Resistance and Survival of the Lakota ("Sioux Nation")*. New York: Garland (Routledge).

———. 2002. "Dual Sovereignty of Native Nations, the United States, and Traditionalists." *Humboldt Journal of Social Relations* 27, no. 1: 106–145.

———. 2012. "Indigenous Peoples, Globalization, and Autonomy in World-Systems Analysis." In *Routledge Handbook of World-Systems Analysis*, edited by Salvatore J. Babones and Christopher Chase-Dunn, 304–312. New York: Routledge.

Fenelon, James V., and Thomas D. Hall. 2005. "Indigenous Struggles over Autonomy, Land and Community: Anti-Globalization and Resistance in World-Systems Analysis." In *Latin@s in the World-System: Towards the Decolonization of the US Empire in the 21st Century*, edited by Ramón Grosfoguel, Nelson Maldonado-Torres, and Jose David Saldivar, 107–122. Boulder, CO: Paradigm Publishers.

———. 2008. "Revitalization and Indigenous Resistance to Globalization and Neoliberalism." *American Behavioral Scientist* 51, no. 12: 1867–1901.

Foran, John, and Richard Widick. 2013. "Breaking Barriers to Climate Justice." *Contexts* 12, no. 2: 34–39.

Foster, John Bellamy. 2012. "The Planetary Rift and the New Exemptionalism: A Political-Economic Critique of Ecological Modernization Theory." Paper prepared for the Political Economy of Global Climate Change and Other Environmental Disruptions panel at the American Sociological Association meetings in Denver, Colorado, August 20.

Hall, Thomas D., and James V. Fenelon. 2008. "Indigenous Movements and Globalization: What Is Different? What Is the Same?" *Globalizations* 5, no. 1: 1–11.

———. 2009. *Indigenous Peoples and Globalization: Resistance and Revitalization*. Boulder, CO: Paradigm Publishers.

Jacques, Peter J., and Jessica R. Jacques. 2012. "Monocropping Cultures into Ruin: The Loss of Food Varieties and Cultural Diversity." *Sustainability* 4, no. 11: 2970–2997.

Lappé, Frances Moore. 1971. *Diet for a Small Planet*. New York: Ballantine Books, 1991.

Lappé, Frances Moore, and Joseph Collins. 1977. *Food First: Beyond the Myth of Scarcity*. New York: Ballantine Books, 1979.

Leech, Garry. 2013. *Capitalism: A Structural Genocide*. New York: Zed Books.

*Narco News*. 2002. "El Mallku Speaks: Indigenous Autonomy and Coca." January 15. www.narconews.com/felipe1eng.html (accessed June 1, 2014).

Ramirez, Gloria Munoz. 2003. *EZLN: 20 y 10, el fuego y la palabra*. Mexico City: Revista Rebeldía.

Schumacher, E. F. [1973] 1989. *Small Is Beautiful: Economics as if People Mattered*. London: Blond and Briggs (Harper Perennial).

Wallerstein, Immanuel. 2004. *World-Systems Analysis: An Introduction*. Durham, NC: Duke University Press.

———. 2013. "Uprisings Here, There, and Everywhere." Commentary No. 356. Immanuel Wallerstein, July 1. www.iwallerstein.com/uprisings (accessed July 6, 2013).

Weatherford, Jack. 1988. *Indian Givers: How the Indians of the Americas Transformed the World.* New York: Fawcett Columbine.

Wilson, Edwin O. 2012. *The Social Conquest of Earth.* New York: Liveright Publishing Corporation.

Wolf, Eric R. 1982. *Europe and the People without History.* Berkeley: University of California Press.

# 9

# GLOBAL INTEGRATION AND CARBON EMISSIONS, 1965–2005

Jennifer E. Givens and Andrew K. Jorgenson

## Abstract

We take a theoretically integrative approach and analyze the effects of two types of global integration on per capita carbon dioxide ($CO_2$) emissions of nations. The political economic theory of ecologically unequal exchange suggests that the global economy is characterized by an unequal flow of value to higher-income nations and the externalization of environmental degradation to lower-income nations. Neoinstitutional world polity theory suggests that connection to the global environmental regime may be associated with decreased levels of production of environmental harms and may mitigate negative environmental effects of integration in the global economic system. Results of panel analyses for a large sample of nations from 1965 to 2005 provide support for both theoretical orientations and suggest that the relations of ecologically unequal exchange may have an even greater effect on $CO_2$ emissions in less developed countries than in others. Our results suggest the need for further research on how different types of global integration interact and may drive or reduce the production of anthropogenic $CO_2$ emissions and other forms of environmental degradation.

## Introduction

It is well established that carbon dioxide ($CO_2$) emissions contribute to modern climate change (Solomon et al. 2009), and human activities driving $CO_2$ emissions include fossil-fuel combustion for energy and transportation, industrial processes, and land-use changes. Recently, according to data from the Mauna Loa Observatory in Hawaii, for the first time in recorded history the global concentration of $CO_2$ in the atmosphere passed 400 parts per million, leading climate scientists at NASA to use the words "alarming" and "scary" in response and to comment that we are not yet on a sufficient track toward limiting emissions (NASA n.d.). The design and implementation of effective strategies for curbing anthropogenic carbon emissions require an adequate understanding of their causes, which emanate from coupled human and natural systems (Liu et al. 2007). Responding to the pressing need for a better understanding of the drivers of climate change, sociological research on carbon emissions has flourished in recent years and represents an area of rich theoretical inquiry (see Jorgenson 2012; Jorgenson and Clark 2012; Jorgenson, Dick, and Shandra 2011; Rosa and Dietz 2012). Research in this area has indicated the importance of considering how forms of global integration impact the production of environmental harms such as $CO_2$ emissions. Furthermore, researchers have demonstrated that global environmental change requires analysis at the global level (Roberts and Grimes 2002). Finally, there is also a need for more theoretically integrative approaches that look simultaneously at different types of global integration and how these interact to influence both the production of environmental harms and possibilities for reduction or mitigation (Jorgenson, Dick, and Shandra 2011; Shorette 2012).

In this study of carbon emissions we analyze two types of global integration—world-economy integration and world society integration—utilizing political economy and world polity perspectives. Research utilizing the political-economic theory of ecologically unequal exchange has found a detrimental environmental effect of such integration, especially in less developed countries (Jorgenson 2012). Research in the world-society tradition points to the growth of a global environmental regime (Frank, Hironaka, and Schofer 2000a; Meyer, Frank, et al. 1997) and the increasing diffusion of global environmental concern (Givens and Jorgenson 2013). While there is some evidence that this environmental regime and civil society action may have some ability to mitigate the detrimental effects of economic integration into the highly unequal global capitalist system (Jorgenson, Dick, and Shandra 2011; Shorette 2012), the power of this political/social/cultural integration and its interaction with economic integration demands further empirical analysis.

## Ecologically Unequal Exchange

In analyzing economic integration into the world-system, the political-economic theory of ecologically unequal exchange focuses on how particular types of world-economic integration contribute to uneven environmental outcomes. This perspective builds on Emmanuel's (1972) concept of unequal exchange and Bunker's (1984; see also Bunker and Ciccantell 2005) attention to the unequal relationships involved in resource extraction, global trade, and development within nation-states (Jorgenson 2012). Via this theory, the global distribution of environmental harms can be seen as structurally determined, dependent on the relations of trade and materials traded, and based on historical relationships. This perspective, emphasizing both the historical and the material, helps to explain globally unequal levels of economic and social development and consumption, power, and environmental degradation.

In the world-system, the pattern of trade relationships is asymmetrical; more developed countries are advantaged at the expense of less developed countries. The theory of ecologically unequal exchange posits that the vertical flow of exports from lower-income, less developed countries to more developed countries is a structural mechanism that in part creates and maintains inequality in the global system. Value, in the form of energy and matter, flows vertically from low-income countries to high-income countries; through this unequal relationship more developed nations gain disproportionate access to resources and are able to externalize the environmental harms associated with high levels of consumption to less developed nations, a situation known as environmental load displacement (Hornborg 2009). Conversely, less developed nations exchange environmental resources for environmental harms and are treated as both a tap for raw materials and a sink for wastes, including air and water pollution. This leads to a situation termed the consumption/degradation paradox, where the degradation associated with high levels of consumption is spatially displaced to less developed areas (Jorgenson 2003) and is related to the concept of the Netherlands Fallacy, which points out the error in thinking that environmental harms of rich nations are contained within their borders. This unequal ecological relationship, to which all of these concepts refer, combines with parallel relations of labor exploitation to produce uneven levels of capital accumulation between nations and consequent high levels of global inequality (Jorgenson and Rice 2012).

In addition to increasing resource consumption in high-income countries above globally sustainable levels, this structural relationship also results in the suppression of consumption below sustainable levels in low-income nations, leading to some devastating effects for human well-being (Jorgenson and Rice 2005; Rice 2007a). Ecologically unequal exchange theory illustrates that these unequal global economic relationships create and perpetuate a lack of development in some nation-states despite the neoliberal market-based recommendations for development of attracting foreign direct investment and export-oriented production as a path to development for low-income countries via the concept of comparative advantage and other neoliberal propositions (Jorgenson 2012; McMichael 2008).

Another consequence of this historic trajectory of uneven ecological exploitation is that it brings us globally ever closer to ecological limits (Rockström et al.

2009). Research from this orientation has analyzed the impact of global economic integration on various environmental harms, including carbon emissions of nations (Jorgenson 2012; Jorgenson, Dick, and Shandra 2011; Jorgenson and Clark 2009; Roberts and Parks 2009), biodiversity loss (Shandra, Leckband, McKinney, and London 2009), deforestation (Jorgenson 2006; Jorgenson, Dick, and Shandra 2011; Shandra, Leckband, and London 2009), and water pollution (Jorgenson, Dick, and Shandra 2011; Shandra, Shor, and London 2009). Adequate challenges to the status quo may be limited by the circumstances that those whose consumption levels are contributing the most to global degradation are also the most insulated from its effects, as illustrated by the consumption-degradation paradox—and in the short term, at least, they also benefit from the uneven rewards that the unequal system confers. This does not bode well for challenges to this structurally unequal relationship, changes to this ecologically unsustainable system, or the future development prospects for currently disadvantaged populations.

Based on the premises of ecologically unequal exchange theory, we hypothesize that a higher percentage of exports sent to high-income countries will be associated with higher levels of per capita $CO_2$ emissions.

## Institutional Theory and World Society

Research from the neoinstitutional world polity perspective (also referred to as world society theory) developed in response to the perception that other macro-level sociological theories were unable to adequately identify and make available for analysis the existence of a global society consisting of more than purely economic relations (Boli and Thomas 1997; Meyer 2009). World society theory calls attention to the phenomenon of globally shared understandings of reality, including concepts of a collectivity and the diffusion of institutional structures. World society theory, however, is not necessarily contradictory to political-economic approaches (Jorgenson, Dick, and Shandra 2011; Meyer 2009; Shorette 2012) since both emphasize different but related global structures and relationships.

World society theory draws on Durkheimian notions of social cohesion and Weberian concepts of legitimate authority and societal institutions. This neoinstitutional analysis sees modern society as based on faith in rationalization and the conceptual creation of the individual as an actor with agency (Meyer 2007; 2010). World polity theory claims, however, that rather than individuals and institutions such as nation-states having rational choice–type agency, those institutions are better seen as exogenously socially constructed entities enacting scripts of the world society (Meyer, Boli, et al. 1997). These scripts are created by a complex of occidental individuals and groups at the top of the global stratification system consisting of university-educated experts, professionals, and consultants who construct models of accepted thinking and action based on rational logic for the agentic actor in the world polity (Meyer 2009). Thus individuals and institutions, rather than responding to local conditions, are socially constructed via a top-down process of global cultural diffusion. International nongovernmental organizations (INGOs) are key entities in terms of both the creation and spread of these norms (Boli and Thomas 1997).

Among other institutions, world polity theorists identify the creation of a world environmental regime in the world polity (Frank, Hironaka, and Schofer 2000a; Meyer, Frank, et al. 1997). Environmental international nongovernmental organizations (EINGOs) are actors that construct and spread the concepts of the global environmental regime, and connection to the global environmental regime can be measured by the presence of such organizations. Concern for the environment is increasing globally (Givens and Jorgenson 2011), as are the number of EINGOs (Jorgenson, Dick, and Shandra 2011; Smith and Wiest 2005) and overall levels of many environmental harms, such as $CO_2$ emissions (Jorgenson and Clark 2010; 2012).

A question for research is, Does connection to the world polity, specifically the world environmental regime, make a difference to real environmental outcomes? Buttel (2000) questions the ability of global civil society actions to counteract global structural inequalities (see also Frank, Hironaka, and Schofer 2000a; 2000b). Meyer also notes that the concept of actorhood that is spread in world society may "vastly transcend the realistic capabilities of the participating actors" (Meyer 2009, 59). Meyer, Frank, et al. (1997, 647) write, "it is plausible to expect continuing rapid creation and discovery of environmental issues, continuing conceptions of failure to deal with them effectively, and continuing world-level social mobilization around them."

There is growing empirical support for the beneficial effect of connection to the world polity. In terms of real environmental outcomes, Jorgenson, Dick, and Shandra (2011) find that in less developed countries world polity connection has a direct effect on reducing deforestation and mitigates the effects of foreign direct investment on $CO_2$ emissions and industrial organic water pollution (see also Jorgenson 2009). Other research finds that world polity connection, measured by EINGO presence, slows deforestation (Shandra 2007a; 2007b; Shandra, Shircliff, and London 2010) and biodiversity loss (Shandra et al. 2009; 2010). World polity connection has also been found to reduce organic water pollution in developing nations (Shandra, Shor, and London 2009) and reduce the carbon emissions of nations (Roberts and Parks 2007).

Mechanisms through which such connections could lead to real outcomes include increased awareness, collective action, and institutional change. Previous research finds that world polity connection is associated with increased individual environmental concern (Givens and Jorgenson 2013) and world polity influences of the global environmental regime affect individual behavior such as personal recycling practices and environmental-social-movement participation (Hadler and Haller 2011). With EINGO encouragement and support individuals and groups become involved in political processes such as treaty creation, support for international treaty participation, and treaty-compliance monitoring (Shandra, Shor, and London 2009). Individuals and groups may also help construct rules and monitor compliance with a host of environmental policies from the local to the national level (Frank, Longhofer, and Schofer 2007). Schofer and Hironaka (2005) find support for the idea that agentic actors both act locally and make global linkages through involvement with and participation in EINGOs, thus connecting with the global environmental regime to foster and sustain effective action at a variety of levels. Keck and Sikkink (1998) find INGOs support social-movement activities; Frank, Hironaka, and Schofer (2000a; b) find world polity links are associated with increases in domestic environmental movements (see also Long-hofer and Schofer 2010); and Smith and Wiest (2005) find world polity links encourage transnational activism in less developed countries. Furthermore, Frank, Robinson, and Olesen (2011) find world polity top-down diffusion is a better predictor of the spread of environmental education in universities around the world than local needs and interests. Thus world polity theory sheds important light on macro-to-micro-and-back-to-macro connections within society; the world polity constructs the scripts that individuals act upon, and in such acting and EINGO involvement individuals are able to influence the norms of global institutions and have potentially real effects on environmental outcomes.

Based on this theorization and previous research, we hypothesize that world polity connection and the individual and institutional action it fosters do matter, and thus EINGO presence is associated with decreased national-level per capita $CO_2$ emissions.

## Methods and Data

We use Prais-Winsten regression two-way fixed effects panel model estimates (with unit-specific and period-specific intercepts) with panel-corrected standard errors and an AR(1) correction. The general two-way fixed effects model is $y_{it} = \beta x_{it} + u_i + w_t + e_{it}$, where subscript i represents each unit of analysis (i.e., country), subscript t represents the time period (i.e., year of observation), and $y_{it}$ is the dependent variable for each country at each year of observation. $\beta x_{it}$ represents the vector of coefficients for predictor variables that vary over time, $u_i$ is the country-specific disturbance term, $w_t$ is the period-specific disturbance term that is constant across all countries, and $e_{it}$ is the disturbance term unique to each country at each point in time. We calculate and employ dummy variables to control for the country-specific and period-specific disturbance terms. Country-specific dummy variables control for unobserved heterogeneity that is temporally invariant within countries (unit-specific intercepts). Period-specific dummy variables control for potential unobserved heterogeneity that is cross-sectionally invariant within periods (period-specific intercepts). Including both is comparable to estimating a two-way fixed-effects model; this lessens the likelihood of biased model estimates that result from outcomes and predictors that follow similar time trends (Wooldridge 2005).

We have a balanced panel dataset with nine observations per country every five years during 1965–2005 for sixty-four developed and less developed countries, all with populations of at least one million. Of the countries included in the analyses, forty-three are designated as less developed countries, meaning they fall below the World Bank's upper quartile of country income-classification rankings (World Bank), so technically this category includes both low- and middle-income countries. Box 9.1 lists the countries included in the analyses and indicates which are designated as less developed.

The dependent variable is per capita $CO_2$ emissions in metric tons per person, logged to correct for its positively skewed distribution. This is obtained from the World Resources Institute's Climate Analysis Indicators Tool (CAIT) and represents the mass of $CO_2$ produced during the combustion of solid, liquid, and gaseous fuels, as well as from the manufacture of cement and gas flaring. CAIT compiles data from three sources, the Carbon Dioxide Information Analysis Center, the International Energy Agency, and the Energy Information Administration, to provide a comprehensive and comparable database of greenhouse-gas-emissions data including all major sources and sinks.

We have three independent variables of interest. First, trade as a percent of GDP measures the extent to which a country is integrated in the world-economy. This variable is obtained from the World Bank's World Development Indicators.

---

**Box 9.1  Countries Included in the Analyses**

| | | | |
|---|---|---|---|
| Algeria* | South Africa* | Mexico* | United States |
| Haiti* | Cameroon* | Syria* | Finland |
| Paraguay* | Italy | Denmark | Nigeria* |
| Argentina* | Spain | Morocco* | Uruguay* |
| Honduras* | Canada | Thailand* | France |
| Peru* | Japan | Dominican | Norway |
| Australia | Sri Lanka* | Republic* | Venezuela* |
| India* | Chile* | Netherlands | Ghana* |
| Philippines* | Kenya* | Togo* | Pakistan* |
| Austria | Sudan* | Ecuador* | Zambia* |
| Indonesia* | Colombia* | New Zealand | Greece |
| Portugal | Korea, Rep. | Tunisia* | Panama* |
| Bolivia* | Sweden | Egypt, Arab Rep.* | Guatemala* |
| Ireland | Costa Rica* | Nicaragua* | Papua New |
| Senegal* | Madagascar* | United Kingdom | Guinea* |
| Brazil* | Switzerland | El Salvador* | |
| Israel | Cote d'Ivoire* | Niger* | |

\* Denotes countries coded as a less developed country (LDC)

Prior analyses show a positive correlation between relative level of trade and $CO_2$ emissions (Jorgenson 2012; Roberts and Parks 2007).

Second, proportion of exports to high-income countries is obtained from the online version of the World Bank's World Development Indicators. These data refer to the sum of merchandise exports from the reporting country to high-income countries according to the World Bank classification of country incomes. The measure is expressed as a proportion of total merchandise exports and computed only if at least half of the recipients in the partner country group had nonmissing data. Prior cross-national tests of ecologically unequal exchange theory use this as a measure of the vertical flow of exports for hypothesis testing (e.g., Jorgenson 2012; Rice 2007b; Shandra, Leckband, and London 2009; Shandra et al. 2009).

Our third independent variable of interest is the presence of EINGOs. This variable consists of a nation-state's number of ties to or chapters of twenty-five such organizations, randomly sampled from the population of all EINGOs. These data come from the Union of International Associations' (UIA) 2007 Yearbook of International Organizations. INGOs are treated here as environmental (i.e., EINGOs) if their main goal is environmental protection (based on "environment" entries in subject indices in the UIA yearbook), and not mainly agriculture, animal welfare, or natural science. These data were compiled and used by other researchers in this field (e.g., Frank, Robinson, and Olesen 2011) and the authors of this study thank David John Frank for these data. We divide the EINGO counts by the total population of nations (measured in millions), the latter of which we obtained from the World Bank. Then the ratio is logged to normalize the distribution. As a sensitivity analysis we include the EINGO variable not weighted by population in additional model estimations.

To compare the effects of the three key independent variables for developed countries and less developed countries, we calculate and employ an interaction between each of them and a dummy variable for the less developed countries included in the dataset. As a time-invariant measure, the dummy variable for the less developed countries is excluded from the estimated models since it is perfectly correlated with and thus accounted for by the unit-specific intercepts that operate as fixed effects. If the interaction term is statistically significant it indicates that the effect of the variable of interest differs for more developed and less developed countries; summing the coefficients for the significant interaction and the reference group provides the actual effect of the predictor on the outcome for the less developed countries.

All control variables in the reported models are obtained from the World Bank. We control for GDP per capita logged to minimize skewness, measured in 2000 constant US dollars, as a measure of a nation's level of economic development, in line with a majority of prior cross-national research. Prior research suggests GDP per capita and $CO_2$ emissions are positively correlated (Jorgenson and Clark 2012; Rosa and Dietz 2012). We also include the squared version of

GDP per capita to account for a potential Kuznets distribution, which resembles an inverted *U* shape.

We control for urban population as percent of total population. Prior research from urban political economy perspectives has shown emissions levels and levels of urbanization to be associated (Jorgenson and Clark 2010; Rosa and Dietz 2012; York 2008).

Finally, we control for manufacturing as percent of GDP. This indicates the domestic focus on secondary-sector activities, and conventional wisdom suggests that manufacturing activities tend to be relatively carbon intensive and thus associated with higher levels of carbon emissions. There are missing data on this variable, and therefore the models that include manufacturing as a percent of GDP involve an unbalanced dataset that is smaller than the balanced datasets; models including this variable include fifty-eight countries rather than the full dataset of sixty-four countries for the other models. The countries that are excluded in these two models are Greece, Haiti, Guatemala, Israel, Nigeria, and Switzerland. Several other control variables were employed in unreported sensitivity analyses available upon request.

## Results

Findings for the analyses are reported in Table 9.1. Unstandardized coefficients (flagged for statistical significance) are provided for the predictors, as well as

**Table 9.1  Unstandardized Coefficients for the Regression of per Capita Carbon Dioxide Emissions, 1965–2005**

|  | Model 1 | Model 2 | Model 3 | Model 4 |
|---|---|---|---|---|
| GDP per Capita (ln) | .394*** | .452*** | .431*** | .433*** |
| Urban Population as Percent of Total Population | .012*** | .010*** | .011*** | .011*** |
| Trade as Percent of Total GDP | .001* |  | .001* | 0.001 |
| Proportion of Exports to High-Income Countries | .064 |  | .096* | .095* |
| EINGOs / Population (ln) |  | −.224*** | −.233*** | −.222*** |
| Trade as Percent of Total GDP × LDC |  |  |  | .001 |
| Proportion of Exports to High-Income Countries × LDC |  |  |  |  |
| EINGOs / Population × LDC |  |  |  |  |
| GDP per Capita (ln) Squared |  |  |  |  |
| Manufacturing as Percent of Total GDP |  |  |  |  |
| EINGOs (raw count, ln) |  |  |  |  |
| R-squared | 0.963 | 0.967 | 0.968 | 0.968 |
| N | 576 | 574 | 574 | 574 |
| Number of Countries | 64 | 64 | 64 | 64 |
| rho | 0.507 | 0.453 | 0.449 | 0.449 |

*** p < .001 (one-tailed tests); ** p < .01 (one-tailed tests); * p < .05 (one-tailed tests); # p < .10 (one-tailed tests)

R-square values, sample size characteristics, and rho for each estimated model. Eleven models are reported, and all models include unreported unit-specific and period-specific intercepts, which commonly lead to relatively high R-square values. Model 1 consists of GDP per capita (ln), urban population as a percent of total population, trade as a percent of total GDP, and proportion of exports to high-income countries. Model 2 includes GDP per capita (ln), urban population as a percent of total population, and EINGOs divided by population then logged. Model 3 includes all predictors in Model 1 as well as EINGOs divided by population and then logged. Models 4 through 6 build on Model 3, including separately the interaction of the three key independent variables of interest with the dummy variable for less developed countries (LDCs). Model 4 includes the interaction of trade as a percent of total GDP with the LDC dummy, Model 5 includes the interaction of proportion of exports to high-income countries with the LDC dummy, and Model 6 includes the interaction of EINGOs divided by population then logged with the LDC dummy. Model 7 includes the variables in Model 3 plus the GDP per capita logged then squared to look for evidence of a Kuznets-type distribution. Model 8 adds manufacturing as a percent of total GDP to Model 7. Model 9 includes this without the GDP per capita squared term. Models 10 and 11 are Models 2 and 3 but with the EINGO raw count included instead of the EINGOs standardized by population.

As expected, GDP per capita and urban population as a percent of total population have a positive and significant effect on $CO_2$ emissions across all the models. Our first independent variable of interest, world-economic integration,

**Table 9.1 continued**

| Model 5 | Model 6 | Model 7 | Model 8 | Model 9 | Model 10 | Model 11 |
|---|---|---|---|---|---|---|
| .429*** | .434*** | .065* | .059* | .423*** | .453*** | .433*** |
| .011*** | .011*** | .011*** | .011*** | .011*** | .010*** | .011*** |
| .001* | .001* | .001* | .001* | .001* | | .001* |
| −.176 | .096* | .096* | .099* | .096* | | .097* |
| −.224*** | −.235*** | −.335*** | −.341*** | −.242** | | |
| | | | | | | |
| .291* | | | | | | |
| | .057 | | | | | |
| | | .025*** | .025* | | | |
| | | .001 | | .001 | | |
| | | | | | −.014*** | −.014*** |
| 0.969 | 0.968 | 0.968 | 0.967 | 0.967 | 0.968 | 0.968 |
| 574 | 574 | 574 | 522 | 522 | 574 | 574 |
| 64 | 64 | 64 | 58 | 58 | 64 | 64 |
| 0.44 | 0.45 | 0.457 | 0.468 | 0.456 | 0.453 | 0.448 |

represented by trade as a percent of total GDP, has a positive and significant effect on $CO_2$ emissions across all the models, lending support to the idea that economic integration in general is associated with higher $CO_2$ emissions. Our second variable of interest, proportion of exports to high-income countries, is positive and significant across most of the models, lending support to the propositions of ecologically unequal exchange theory that nations with higher levels of exports to high-income countries receive greater levels of environmental bads in return, represented here as per capita $CO_2$ emissions. This result is unchanged when manufacturing as a percent of total GDP is included (Models 8 and 9); manufacturing as a percent of GDP is not significant in either model, indicating it is not just a reliance on manufacturing that leads to elevated $CO_2$ emissions, and thus lending further support to the notion that trade relationships are a key part of the explanation for $CO_2$ emissions levels. Our third key variable of interest, EINGOs weighted by population size, has a consistently negative and significant effect across all of the models; this is also true of the EINGO raw count. These results provide support for world polity/world society theory and the possibility of the global environmental regime to have a real effect on environmental outcomes.

Turning to the interaction terms, the only significant interaction is between the LDC dummy variable and proportion of exports to high-income countries. The interaction term is positive, and thus indicates that the relationship is more pronounced in LDCs; in other words, proportion of exports to high-income countries has an even more positive effect on $CO_2$ emissions in less developed countries than it does in more developed countries. In order to get the true effect, we would need to add the coefficient for this dummy interaction with the coefficient for the main effect for proportion of exports to high-income countries. This would still give us a positive effect on $CO_2$ emissions. In other words, the vertical flow of exports to high-income nations has a much larger impact on increasing carbon emissions in less developed countries than in developed countries. Finally, the GDP per capita squared term is positive and significant in both models in which it is included. We included this quadratic term to look for a Kuznets effect, or a threshold effect in which $CO_2$ emissions would rise as GDP per capita rose, but at a certain inflection point it would begin to decouple from GDP per capita and decline as GDP per capita continued to rise. If the coefficient had been negative, this would have been evidence of a Kuznets-type relationship. However, the coefficient is positive, indicating no evidence of a decline in $CO_2$ emissions as GDP per capita rises. In fact, it suggests the opposite.

## Conclusion

In this study we engage both world-economy and world society perspectives and evaluate their theoretically derived propositions in cross-national panel analyses of per capita carbon emissions for a large sample of nations spanning the 1965–2005 period. The findings provide support for both orientations. In line with the political economic theory of ecologically unequal exchange, we find the vertical flow of exports contributes to per capita carbon dioxide emissions, particularly in less developed countries. We also find, in line with propositions derived from world polity theory, that connection to the world polity measured by EINGO presence has a negative effect on per capita $CO_2$ emissions. While world-economic integration often has detrimental environmental effects, our findings regarding the potentially mitigating influence of world society organizations on the per capita carbon dioxide emissions is potentially encouraging in terms of finding global solutions to these global problems. Although we do find evidence for the potential of world society integration to mitigate the highly unequal outcomes of world-system integration, our results for stronger effects of the vertical flow of trade in LDCs indicate that the consequences of these unequal relationships and their consequent levels of environmental degradation are felt disproportionally in the Global South, in line with other research suggesting effects of such relationships vary by zone of the world-system (Shorette 2012).

Our approach draws upon the suggestions of Jorgenson, Dick, and Shandra (2011) to integrate political economy and world society approaches. Future research would do well to examine various ways that world-economy and world society structures interact and to look for areas of overlap or disparity in different forms of structural integration, such as military power (Jorgenson and Clark 2009). Research should examine under what specific conditions civil society and trade relationships matter and how they may matter differently based on a nation's position in the structural hierarchy and for various environmental-degradation measures and human-well-being outcomes. Previous research has found an increasingly ecologically unequal effect, perhaps influenced by the increasing emphasis on export-oriented production (Jorgenson 2012). Changes over time in the effect of world polity integration on environmental outcomes are also worthy of exploration; areas for exploration include the magnitude of effects, potential threshold effects of EINGOs, how both EINGO presence and membership and their effects may change over time, and the potential for new ways to measure world polity connection, including intergovernmental organization membership and treaty participation. Research on structural integration and development and well-being impacts will be especially vital as we increasingly begin to feel the global and unequal impacts and constraints of climate change. All of these areas for future research highlight the need for more theoretically inclusive research on the human dimensions of global environmental change, especially work that considers the impacts of various forms of global integration.

# References

Boli, John, and George M. Thomas. 1997. "World Culture in the World Polity: A Century of International Non-Governmental Organization." *American Sociological Review* 62, no. 2: 171–190.

Bunker, Stephen. 1984. "Modes of Extraction, Unequal Exchange, and the Progressive Underdevelopment of an Extreme Periphery: The Brazilian Amazon, 1600–1980." *American Journal of Sociology* 89: 1017–1064.

Bunker, Stephen, and Paul Ciccantell. 2005. *Globalization and the Race for Resources.* Baltimore: Johns Hopkins University Press.

Buttel, Frederick H. 2000. "World Society, the Nation-State, and Environmental Protection: Comment on Frank, Hironaka, and Schofer." *American Sociological Review* 65, no. 1: 117–121.

Emmanuel, Arghiri. 1972. *Unequal Exchange: A Study of the Imperialism of Trade.* New York: Monthly Review Press.

Frank, David John, Ann Hironaka, and Evan Schofer. 2000a. "The Nation-State and the Natural Environment over the Twentieth Century." *American Sociological Review* 65, no. 1: 96–116.

———. 2000b. "Environmentalism as a Global Institution: Reply to Buttel." *American Sociological Review* 65, no. 1: 122–127.

Frank, David John, Wesley Longhofer, and Evan Schofer. 2007. "World Society, NGOs, and Environmental Policy Reform in Asia." *International Journal of Comparative Sociology* 48, no. 4: 275–295.

Frank, David John, Karen Jeong Robinson, and Jared Olesen. 2011. "The Global Expansion of Environmental Education in Universities." *Comparative Education Review* 55, no. 4: 546–573.

Givens, Jennifer E., and Andrew K. Jorgenson. 2011. "The Effects of Affluence, Economic Development, and Environmental Degradation on Environmental Concern: A Multilevel Analysis." *Organization and Environment* 24: 74–91.

———. 2013. "Individual Environmental Concern in the World Polity: A Multilevel Analysis." *Social Science Research* 42: 418–431.

Hadler, Markus, and Max Haller. 2011. "Global Activism and Nationally Driven Recycling: The Influence of World Society and National Contexts on Public and Private Environmental Behavior." *International Sociology* 26, no. 3: 315–345.

Hornborg, Alf. 2009. "Zero-Sum World: Challenges in Conceptualizing Environmental Load Displacement and Ecologically Unequal Exchange in the World-System." *International Journal of Comparative Sociology* 50: 237–262.

Jorgenson, Andrew K. 2003. "Consumption and Environmental Degradation: A Cross-National Analysis of the Ecological Footprint." *Social Problems* 50, no. 3: 374–394.

———. 2006. "Unequal Ecological Exchange and Environmental Degradation: A Theoretical Proposition and Cross-National Study of Deforestation, 1990–2000." *Rural Sociology* 71: 685–712.

———. 2009. "Foreign Direct Investment and the Environment, the Mitigating Influence of Institutional and Civil Society Factors, and Relationships between Industrial Pollution and Human Health: A Panel Study of Less-Developed Countries." *Organization and Environment* 22: 135–157.

———. 2012. "The Sociology of Ecologically Unequal Exchange and Carbon Dioxide Emissions, 1960–2005." *Social Science Research* 41: 242–252.

Jorgenson, Andrew K., and Brett Clark. 2009. "The Economy, Military, and Ecologically Unequal Relationships in Comparative Perspective, 1975–2000." *Social Problems* 56: 621–646.

———. 2010. "Assessing the Temporal Stability of the Population/Environment Relationship: A Cross-National Panel Study of Carbon Dioxide Emissions, 1960–2005." *Population and Environment* 32: 27–41.

———. 2012. "Are the Economy and the Environment Decoupling? A Comparative International Study, 1960–2005." *American Journal of Sociology* 118, no. 1: 1–44.

Jorgenson, Andrew K., Christopher Dick, and John M. Shandra. 2011. "World Economy, World Society, and Environmental Harms in Less-Developed Countries." *Sociological Inquiry* 81, no. 1: 53–87.

Jorgenson, Andrew K., and James Rice. 2005. "Structural Dynamics of International Trade and Material Consumption: A Cross-National Study of the Ecological Footprints of Less-Developed Countries." *Journal of World-Systems Research* 11: 57–77.

———. 2012. "The Sociology of Ecologically Unequal Exchange in Comparative Perspective." In *Routledge Handbook of World-Systems Analysis*, edited by Salvatore J. Babones and Christopher Chase-Dunn, 431–439. New York: Routledge.

Keck, Margaret E., and Kathryn Sikkink. 1998. *Activists beyond Borders*. Ithaca, NY: Cornell University Press.

Liu, Jianquo, Thomas Dietz, Stephen R. Carpenter, Carl Folke, Marina Alberti, Charles L. Redman, Stephen H. Schneider, Elinor Ostrom, Alice N. Pell, Jane Lubchenco, William W. Taylor, Zhiyun Ouyang, Peter Deadman, Timothy Kratz, and William Provencher. 2007. "Coupled Human and Natural Systems." *Ambio* 36, no. 8 (December): 639–649.

Longhofer, Wesley, and Evan Schofer. 2010. "National and Global Origins of Environmental Association." *American Sociological Review* 75: 505–533.

McMichael, Philip. 2008. *Development and Social Change*. 4th ed. Thousand Oaks, CA: Pine Forge Press.

Meyer, John W. 2007. "Globalization: Theory and Trends." *International Journal of Comparative Sociology* 48: 261–273.

———. 2009. "Reflections: Institutional Theory and World Society." In *World Society: The Writings of John W. Meyer*, edited by Georg Krucken and Gili S. Drori. New York: Oxford University Press.

———. 2010. "World Society, Institutional Theories, and the Actor." *Annual Review of Sociology* 36: 1–20.

Meyer, John W., John Boli, George M. Thomas, and Francisco O. Ramirez. 1997. "World-Society and the Nation-State." *American Journal of Sociology* 103, no. 1: 144–181.

Meyer, John W., David John Frank, Ann Hironaka, Evan Schofer, and Nancy Brandon Tuma. 1997. "The Structuring of a World Environmental Regime, 1870–1990." *International Organization* 51, no. 4: 623–651.

NASA. n.d. "NASA Scientists React to 400 ppm Milestone." NASA: Global Climate Change: Vital Signs of the Planet. http://climate.nasa.gov/400ppmquotes (accessed May 21, 2013).

Rice, James. 2007a. "Ecological Unequal Exchange: Consumption, Equity, and Unsustainable Structural Relationships within the Global Economy." *International Journal of Comparative Sociology* 48: 43–72.

———. 2007b. "Ecological Unequal Exchange: International Trade and Uneven Utilization of Environmental Space in the World-System." *Social Forces* 85: 1369–1392.

Roberts, J. Timmons, and Peter E. Grimes. 2002. "World-System Theory and the Environment: Toward a New Synthesis." In *Sociological Theory and the Environment: Classical Foundations, Contemporary Insights*, edited by Riley Dunlap, Frederick Buttel, Peter Dickens, and August Gijswijt, 167–194. Lanham, MD: Rowman and Littlefield.

Roberts, J. Timmons, and Bradley C. Parks. 2007. *A Climate of Injustice: Global Inequality, North-South Politics, and Climate Policy*. Cambridge, MA: MIT Press.

———. 2009. "Ecologically Unequal Exchange, Ecological Debt, and Climate Justice: The History and Implications of Three Related Ideas for a New Social Movement." *International Journal of Comparative Sociology* 50: 385–409.

Rockström, Johan, Will Steffen, Kevin Noone, Åsa Persson, F. Stuart Chapin III, Eric F. Lambin, Timothy M. Lenton, Marten Scheffer, Carl Folke, Hans Joachim Schellnhuber, Björn Nykvist, Cynthia A. de Wit, Terry Hughes, Sander van der Leeuw, Henning Rodhe, Sverker Sörlin, Peter K. Snyder, Robert Costanza, Uno Svedin, Malin Falkenmark, Louise Karlberg, Robert W. Corell, Victoria J. Fabry, James Hansen, Brian Walker, Diana Liverman, Katherine Richardson, Paul Crutzen, and Jonathan A. Foley. 2009. "A Safe Operating Space for Humanity." *Nature* 461, no. 24 (September): 472–475.

Rosa, Eugene A., and Thomas Dietz. 2012. "Human Drivers of National Greenhouse-Gas Emissions." *Nature Climate Change* 2: 581–586.

Schofer, Evan, and Ann Hironaka. 2005. "The Effects of World Society on Environmental Protection Outcomes." *Social Forces* 84, no. 1: 25–47.

Shandra, John M. 2007a. "The World Polity and Deforestation: A Quantitative, Cross-National Analysis." *International Journal of Comparative Sociology* 48: 5–27.

———. 2007b. "International Nongovernmental Organizations and Deforestation: Good, Bad, or Irrelevant?" *Social Science Quarterly* 88, no. 3: 665–689.

Shandra, John M., Christopher Leckband, and Bruce London. 2009. "Ecologically Unequal Exchange and Deforestation: A Cross-National Analysis of Forestry Export Flows." *Organization and Environment* 22: 293–310.

Shandra, John M., Christopher Leckband, Laura McKinney, and Bruce London. 2009. "Ecologically Unequal Exchange, World Polity, and Biodiversity Loss." *International Journal of Comparative Sociology* 50: 285–310.

Shandra, John M., Laura McKinney, Christopher Leckband, and Bruce London. 2010. "Debt, Structural Adjustment, and Biodiversity Loss: A Cross-National Analysis of Threatened Mammals and Birds." *Human Ecology Review* 17, no. 1: 18–33.

Shandra, John M., Eric Shircliff, and Bruce London. 2010. "The International Monetary Fund, World Bank, and Structural Adjustment: A Cross-National Analysis of Forest Loss." *Social Science Research* 40: 210–225.

Shandra, John, Eran Shor, and Bruce London. 2009. "World Polity, Unequal Ecological Exchange, and Organic Water Pollution: A Cross-National Analysis of Developing Nations." *Human Ecology Review* 16, no. 1: 53–63.

Shorette, Kristen. 2012. "Outcomes of Global Environmentalism: Longitudinal and Cross-National Trends in Chemical Fertilizer and Pesticide Use." *Social Forces* 9, no. 1: 299–325.

Smith, Jackie, and Dawn Wiest. 2005. "The Uneven Geography of Global Civil Society: National and Global Influences on Transnational Associations." *Social Forces* 84, no. 2: 621–652.

Solomon, Susan, Gian-Kasper Plattner, Reto Knutti, and Pierre Friedlingstein. 2009. "Irreversible Climate Change Due to Carbon Dioxide Emissions." *PNAS* 106, no. 6: 1704–1709.

Wooldridge, Jeffrey. 2005. *Introductory Econometrics: A Modern Approach.* Mason, OH: Thomson.

World Bank. n.d. "World Development Indicators." World Bank. http://data.worldbank .org/data-catalog/world-development-indicators (accessed May 14, 2014).

World Resources Institute. n.d. "Climate Analysis Indicators Tool." World Resources Institute. www.wri.org/tools/cait (accessed October 2012).

York, Richard. 2008. "De-Carbonization in Former Soviet Republics, 1992–2000: The Ecological Consequences of De-Modernization." *Social Problems* 55: 370–390.

# 10

## CLASS, CRISIS, AND THE 2011 PROTEST WAVE

### CYCLICAL AND SECULAR TRENDS IN GLOBAL LABOR UNREST

Şahan Savaş Karataşlı, Sefika Kumral,
Ben Scully, and Smriti Upadhyay[1]

**Abstract**

Drawing on a new database of newspaper articles on social and labor movements from 1991 to 2011, we examine the contemporary wave of social unrest for what it tells us about the changing contours of class and capitalism during the current crisis of historical capitalism. We argue that protests of workers are an important and underrecognized feature of the current wave of social unrest. These include offensive protests of workers advancing new demands as well as protests of workers defending previously won gains. Alongside these two types of labor unrest, which have accompanied the spread of historical capitalism, we also detect rising class-based protest by those whom Marx labeled as stagnant relative surplus population. The rise of this type of class-based protest suggests that, although the *cyclical* process of capitalism making and unmaking livelihoods continues, there is also a *secular* trend where capitalism destroys more livelihoods than it creates over time.

## Introduction

In 2011 a dramatic upsurge of social protest across the globe captured the attention of the world and turned public spaces as diverse as Wisconsin's capitol building, Cairo's Tahrir Square, and the streets of Athens into symbols of popular rebellion. There has been a widespread recognition that this wave of popular protest is an event of world-historical importance. Writing in late summer 2011, even before the Occupy movement erupted in cities throughout the United States, Gideon Rachman (2011) of the *Financial Times* asked if 2011 would come to rank alongside 1969 and 1989 as a year of global revolt. By the end of the year it seemed clear that the events of 2011 would have a lasting impact. *Time* magazine declared "The Protester" the person of the year and suggested that the 2011 wave was a final refutation of Francis Fukuyama's concept of the "end of history" (Andersen 2011). Scholars like Christopher Chase-Dunn (2013) and Paul Mason (2012) have argued that the events of 2011 should be considered alongside other historic world revolutions such as 1789, 1848, 1917, 1968, and 1989. Despite the events being recent, and in some cases ongoing, scholarly debate on the protests has already blossomed. Although analyses that examine protests as isolated case studies are still predominant in the literature, there is a wider appreciation that these diverse movements must be considered as different parts of a global wave of unrest (Badiou 2012; Burawoy 2012; Calhoun 2013; Hardt and Negri 2012; Mason 2013; Žižek 2012). In his analysis of Occupy Wall Street, for instance, Craig Calhoun (2013) explicitly criticizes narratives that analyze the movement as an exclusively American phenomenon. According to Calhoun, Occupy Wall Street was a part of an international wave of mobilization that started in 2010 in Eurozone countries such as Greece, Spain, and Portugal as a result of the 2008 financial crisis. For this reason, Calhoun contends, these movements were closely linked to the protests that emerged in Arab World countries such as Egypt, Tunisia, Libya, Algeria, and Bahrain, which later sparked protests in places as far away as China.

Calhoun is not alone in underlining the interrelationships between different types of protests all around the world and recognizing their relationship with the current financial crisis. Today, a wide range of scholars from diverse disciplines accept that the current wave of unrest has been influenced by the macrostructural dynamics of global capitalism. However, despite their commonalities, these analyses differ in two important ways. First, they give varying degrees of attention to the concept of class in explaining the current upsurge. Second, there is disagreement about whether this protest wave marks a recurrence of historical forms of unrest or whether the present period signifies a break with the past and the birth of a novel form of collective action.

In *The Rebirth of History*, for instance, Alain Badiou (2012) characterizes the present moment as the first stirrings of a global popular uprising against a worldwide erosion of the gains achieved by workers' movements, communism, and genuine socialism between 1860 and 1980. For Badiou, this erosion has led to a regression of social and economic conditions toward those in which globalized capitalism was born. According to Badiou (2012, 5), the "riots" around the globe—riots in the French *banlieues* (suburbs); youth riots in England; protests in Tunisia, Egypt, Libya, Syria, Iran, and Palestine; protests initiated by Chicano *sans-papiers* in the United States; and massive protests in China—"naturally resemble the first working-class insurrections of the nineteenth century."

For Michael Hardt and Antonio Negri (2012), however, the current wave of unrest has nothing to do with these early insurrections of modern capitalism. On the contrary, what we see is a completely novel phenomenon. Hardt and Negri analyze the social and political conditions under which the social resistance that erupted in and around 2011 took place. They argue that contemporary movements of resistance and rebellion, like the Greek and UK riots, Spanish *indignados*, the Occupy Wall Street movement, and the Tunisian and Egyptian revolutions, are made possible by *new* figures of subjectivity—*the indebted, the mediatized, the securitized*, and *the represented*—created by the triumph and the crisis of neoliberalism.

The opposite conclusions reached by Badiou and Hart and Negri with regard to the novelty of the current upsurge demonstrate the theoretical confusion that surrounds many recent analyses. It is notable that, like many observers, neither Badiou nor Hardt and Negri find it necessary to discuss the class composition of these social movements in order to explain them. There have been some analyses examining class in the global protests, but these have tended to focus on one particular class actor: the declining sections of the formerly stable middle or working classes—what Guy Standing calls "the precariat," people living and working precariously. Standing (2011, 19) associates a wide range of protests—the EuroMayDay demonstrations, riots in French *banlieues*, protests of undocumented immigrant workers, riots of local youth all over Europe, as well as ethnic violence and riots in China and South Africa—with this growing precariat, which deeply "experiences the four A's: anger, anomie, anxiety, and alienation." Standing, however, does not see this precariat as part of the "working class" or the "proletariat" in general. These terms, he says,

> suggest a society consisting mostly of workers in long-term, stable, fixed-hour jobs with established routes of advancement, subject to unionization and collective agreements, with job titles their fathers and mothers would have understood, facing local employers whose names and features they were familiar with. Many entering the precariat would not know their employer or how many fellow employees they had or were likely to have in the future. (Standing 2011, 6)

Similarly, other scholars see the declining middle classes as the main engine of the contemporary wave of unrest. In this view, the antiausterity protests of Europe, the public-workers' strike in Wisconsin, and the revolutions of North Africa all have in common middle-class workers who see their economic opportunities being limited by changes in the global economy. For Slavoj Žižek (2012, 5), for instance, these protests are, at least in part, a "revolt of the salaried bourgeoisie," whose lower levels are the "obvious candidates for a tightening of belts." Thus, although these protests are directed at the forces of marketization "they are in reality ... protesting the gradual erosion of their (politically) privileged economic position" (Žižek 2012, 11). Hence, according to Žižek, these types of events "are not proletarian protests, but protests against the threat of being reduced to proletarians." This analysis is closely linked to Paul Mason's (2012; 2013) claim that "graduates without a future" play a crucial role in these protests. For these students, Mason (2013, 45–46) emphasizes, "the jobs on offer are ... the same jobs you do while on campus: interning, barista, waiting tables, sex work. There is no way onto the housing ladder, the ladder is now horizontal; and retirement, pension schemes will be gone."

According to Michael Burawoy (2012), however, this contemporary wave of global unrest contains both old and new forms of struggles. Burawoy argues that some examples of the contemporary wave of global unrest can be conceptualized as a Polanyian counterreaction to forces of marketization. Following the work of Karl Polanyi, Burawoy underlines the change in the forms of counterreactions against waves of marketization in world history. The first wave of marketization in the nineteenth century led to a counterreaction with the formation of trade unions, whereas the second wave of marketization in the early twentieth century led to state action—such as the New Deal in the United States, fascism in Europe, and Stalinism in the USSR. From a Polanyian perspective, then, we must prepare ourselves for a new wave of counterreaction against the post-1980 wave of marketization. Burawoy cites contemporary immigrants' rights struggles in the United States as counterreaction to commodification of labor; struggles in India, China, and Latin America as counterreactions to expropriation of land; and movements such as Occupy as examples of the counterreaction to the commodification of money. Considering these changing forms of counterreactions in each wave of marketization, Burawoy also underscores the necessity of new theories of social movements that would capture the fluid nature of unrest that is taking place all over the world.

Like Burawoy, we see a need for new approaches to understanding the significance of the current protest upsurge, but we maintain that there is not only a theoretical gap in many analyses, but also an empirical one. Those like Badiou and Hart and Negri, who debate the novelty of the protests, pay little attention to the class character of the upsurge. Those who have focused on class limit their analysis to particular sections of the class structure both conceptually and geographically, namely, the declining middle class in the Global North and the middle-income countries of North Africa. These analyses have paid little attention to other important protest actors, such as the militant and ascendant working classes, especially in East Asia, and the growing sections of unemployed, excluded, and increasingly restive workers in countries around the world.

In this chapter we attempt to construct the type of new approach that Burawoy is calling for by analyzing the contemporary wave of social unrest for what it tells us about the changing contours of class and capitalism during this period of crisis and hegemonic transition, paying specific attention to the role played by different types of labor unrest. Following the work of Giovanni Arrighi and Beverly Silver (1999), we take the contemporary upsurge of social protest to be one among many signs of an ongoing crisis of capitalism. Demands from below have been an important feature of crisis and hegemonic transition throughout the history of capitalism. During past crises, the way in which popular demands have (or have not) been met has played an important role in determining changes that take place in the capitalist system as a whole. Like Ira Katznelson (1986), we see protest as more than just an expression of existing class interests. Protest, like Katznelson's "collective action," is itself a moment of class formation. Therefore, by studying the character, location, and timing of protests, we can gain a deeper understanding of the class dynamics shaping possible ways forward for the present crisis of capitalism.

This chapter draws on a database, constructed by the authors, based on newspaper reports of protests for the period 1991–2011. We searched the digital archives of five major newspapers with a high level of global coverage (the *New York Times*, the *Times* [London], the *Washington Post, Financial Times*, and the *Guardian*) for a combination of keywords that would capture different forms of social protest (e.g., protest, demonstration, uprising, unrest, revolution, revolt, riot, rebellion, upheaval, insurrection, strike). From the results of this search we drew a sample of 2,000 newspaper reports about *social protests* from all over the world. Each article is coded and categorized according to its time and location, the type of social unrest, demands, and agents. Figure 10.1 illustrates that the rise of social unrest in the world in and around 2011 is visible from all of these newspapers. The fifty countries with the highest number of mentions of social unrest can be seen in Table 10.1 in this chapter's appendix.

In addition to this dataset, we also collected a sample of 2,000 articles from the digital archives of the *Times* (London) and the *New York Times* (1,000 articles from each source) using a keyword-search string designed to exclusively capture *labor unrest* as opposed to general protest in this period (see the appendix for data-collection procedure).

Two key findings emerge from our analysis of the newspaper articles. First, protests of workers are an important and underrecognized feature of the current wave of social unrest. This includes both offensive protests of workers advancing new demands, as well as defensive protests of workers defending previously won gains. These two types of protests can be seen as a continuation of the cyclical

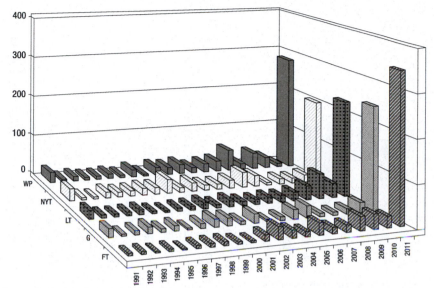

*Source:* Authors' calculations; see the appendix.

**Figure 10.1  Frequency of Mentions of Social Unrest
in the World, Five Newspapers, 1991–2011**

pattern of offensive and defensive workers' struggles that have accompanied the spread of historical capitalism across space and time (Silver 2003). Second, alongside this *cyclical* protest, we detect a *secular* trend of rising class-based protest among those who have been almost entirely excluded from capitalist exploitation. The rise of this third type of class-based protests suggests that, although the cyclical process of capitalism making and unmaking livelihoods continues, there is also a secular trend where capitalism is destroying more livelihoods than it creates over time. It is this third type of protest that gives us the most insight into the scale and scope of the crisis facing contemporary capitalism.

## The Cyclical Trends of Labor Movements

What is striking about most analyses of the contemporary global social upsurge is the nearly complete absence of attention to the classical agents of class protest: wage workers. The majority of analyses focus on youth, political dissidents, masses in general, and occasionally the declining middle classes. However, wage workers have played a more important role in the present protest wave than has been recognized. According to news reports by the *New York Times* and the *Times* (London) from 1991 to 2011, the year 2011 had the highest level of labor unrest throughout the period (See Figure 10.2).

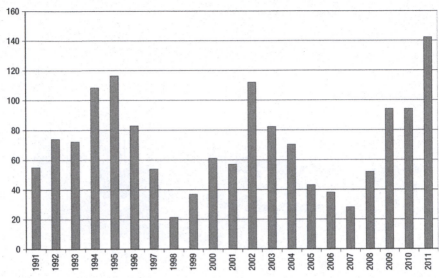

Source: Authors' calculations; see the appendix.

**Figure 10.2  Mentions of Worldwide Labor Unrest, the *New York Times* and the *Times* (London), 1991–2011**

According to our sample, France, Germany, South Africa, Nigeria, the United Kingdom, China, the United States, India, Greece, Republic of Korea, Italy, and Ireland emerged as key places with high levels of labor militancy in 2011 (see Figure 10.3). A close investigation of the events in these reports reveals that the main type of labor unrest differs between countries. In order to explicate these differences we followed a typology of labor unrest introduced in Beverly Silver's (2003) study of workers' protest from 1870 to 1996.

Silver (2003) divides labor protest into two categories: Marx-type and Polanyi-type. Marx-type unrest refers to offensive struggles of new working classes in formation, whereas Polanyi-type unrest refers to the defensive protests of workers whose previous gains are being undermined as well as resistance against proletarianization.

Our analysis of samples of newspaper reports reveals a high frequency of Polanyi-type labor unrest, especially in regions where existing working classes are being unmade through the marketization of the economy and unraveling of social compacts between capital and labor. Countries such as France, the United Kingdom, Italy, and Greece all have high levels of Polanyi-type labor unrest in our database. These protests belong to working classes that are currently being unmade in one way or another: Public-sector workers are losing their previously gained rights and privileges due to austerity politics. Workers are resisting the closing down of factories, mines, or state-owned enterprises, and are protesting the restructuring of

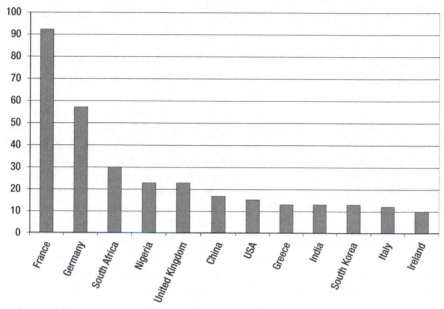

*Source:* Authors' calculations; see the appendix.

**Figure 10.3  Top Locations of Labor Unrest, the *New York Times* and the *Times* (London), Excluding the United States from the *New York Times* and the United Kingdom from the *Times* (London), 1991–2011**

the pay scales that jeopardize overtime pay, bonuses, and special allowances. These are some examples of types of labor militancy in these regions. Badiou (2012), Burawoy (2012), and Žižek (2012) have also focused on Polanyi-type unrest in one form or another in their analyses of the 2011 protest wave.

However, our data show that offensive protests by newly created working classes—what Silver has called Marx-type labor protests—have also been an important component of recent global labor protests. In analyzing the top sites of labor protest in 2011 we find that, alongside the protests of declining working classes in Europe and North America, there was widespread unrest by the working classes that have been formed in those East and South Asian countries that are undergoing economic transformations. These new working classes are putting forth offensive demands and, in doing so, have made East and South Asia global centers of labor unrest. As Table 10.1 (see the appendix) shows, China is among the top ten countries with the highest levels of social unrest in the 1991–2011 period. The majority of social-unrest events in China constitute Marx-type labor militancy, in which workers protest long working hours and low wages and demand new rights, including the right to organize.

To put it simply, in regions where capital goes, Marx-type conflicts are more likely to rise. In regions where capital leaves, Polanyi-type labor unrest is more likely to predominate. However, it is possible to find a mixture of Marx-type and Polanyi-type unrest within some countries. For instance, although in Europe we generally see the rise of Polanyi-type labor unrest, in Germany there has been a very high level of Marx-type labor unrest, especially among metal workers. Even in Asian centers of expanding production, economic transformations cause existing livelihoods to be unmade just as new working-class livelihoods are being created. Hence in China and India, for instance, together with high levels of Marx-type labor unrest, we see widespread Polanyi-type labor unrest. The growing militancy of workers in China's former manufacturing centers such as Liaoyang, or of Indian public-sector workers in Bombay, Delhi, Bangalore, or Hyderabad, fearing job losses due to privatization, are some examples of Polanyi-type labor unrest. Likewise, since the East Asian crisis of 1997, Polanyi-type labor unrest is rising along with Marx-type labor unrest in the Republic of Korea. Furthermore, in the European and North American centers of working-class decline, while old working classes still use their institutional power to put forward their Polanyi-type demands, newer sections of the working class, such as immigrants and women, are organizing and advancing their interests as workers in new and innovative ways.

Despite this complex picture, however, the character and location of this class-based protest suggest that much of the labor unrest in the recent upsurge fits the pattern of unrest expected during a period of financialization and hegemonic transition. That is, we find protests of working classes being unmade in declining centers of production, and protests of working classes being made in rising centers of production, with localized mixes of the two found across the world-economy.

## A Secular Trend of Labor Unrest? Protest of the Stagnant Relative Surplus Population

Although a combination of Marx-type and Polanyi-type labor unrest continued to take place throughout the twenty-year period under study, these movements cannot account for the rapid intensification of social protest around the world in 2011. The majority of protest activities in countries with the highest levels of mentions of social protests in 2011 (e.g., Egypt, Tunisia, Bahrain, and Yemen) cannot properly be identified as Marx-type or Polanyi-type labor protests. The 2011 upsurge encompassed a large spectrum of social and political movements, revolts and revolutions, which cannot be reduced to a single type of unrest or a single class.

Having said that, a review of the demands in these protests reveals that an important segment of protesters in these regions can be seen as parts of—if we use Marx's terms—the "stagnant relative surplus population." These are workers who, because they are superfluous to the needs of existing capital, have extremely irregular employment and thus demand primarily "more jobs." Marx ([1867] 1992, 796) defines "stagnant relative surplus population" as

> a part of the active labour army, but with extremely irregular employment. Hence it furnishes to capital an inexhaustible reservoir of disposable labour power. Its conditions of life sink below the average normal level of the working class; this makes it at once the broad basis of special branches of capitalist exploitation, [which] is characterized with maximum of working-time and minimum of wages.

The stagnant relative surplus population is an extremely heterogeneous group for Marx. While the lowest layers of this surplus population contain those unable to work, its top layers are composed of masses who can work and who demand to work, but cannot be absorbed by the productive capacity of the economy. Although the total mass of this group rises in every economic crisis and diminishes in every revival of trade, as a whole the stagnant relative surplus population increases secularly under capitalism. As Marx ([1867] 1992, 796) puts it,

> [As the] extent of [the stagnant relative surplus population] grows, as with the extent and energy of accumulation, the creation of a surplus population advances. But it forms at the same time a self-reproducing and self-perpetuating element of the working class, taking a proportionally greater part in the general increase of that class than the other elements.

It is probably the growing mass of this segment of the working class Marx and Engels ([1848] 1978) had in mind when they declared in the *Communist Manifesto*,

> the modern laborer, [in opposition to all previous forms of oppressed classes], instead of rising with the progress of industry, sinks deeper and deeper below the conditions of existence of his own class. He becomes a pauper, and pauperism develops more rapidly than population and wealth.

Interestingly, the conditions of certain segments of the "masses" that poured into the streets during the Tunisian, Egyptian, or other Arab Spring revolts and revolutions—which make up the top locations of the 2011 global social-unrest wave—closely resemble the conditions of top layers of stagnant relative surplus population defined by Marx. For these masses, the primary problem appeared to be chronic unemployment. In January 2011, for instance, when the Tunisian uprising started, protesters underlined that grievances about the lack of jobs were among the main reasons for their protests.

> Protesters say they are angry about a lack of jobs, but officials say the rioting is the work of a minority of violent extremists intent on damaging Tunisia. . . . Tunisia has recorded strong economic growth in the past decade, but it has not

been fast enough to satisfy demand for jobs. Unemployment is particularly acute among the young in the interior of the country. (Reuters 2011)

Especially in the early phases of the Tunisian Revolution, the movement was mostly portrayed as a sudden eruption of the anger of the unemployed youth with college degrees. Although unemployed college graduates who demanded more jobs were a part of these movements (Kirkpatrick 2011), the social base of the stagnant relative surplus population ranged from unemployed teachers, some of whom went on hunger strike because they were unemployed for almost a decade (Fahim 2011), to unemployed miners who occupied the halls of the headquarters of a phosphate-mining company a month after the Tunisian Revolution (Fuller 2011a). Hence, the class base of these movements was more diverse and complex than has been recognized. The story of Mohamed Bouazizi, who set himself on fire on December 17, 2010, and became a symbol of the Tunisian and other Arab Spring uprisings, is emblematic of the confusion that surrounds this issue. Initial reports stated that Bouazizi was a frustrated university graduate who had to work as a street vendor (Raghavan 2011; see Hauslohner 2011, who erroneously claimed that Bouazizi was an unemployed computer engineer). Bouazizi in fact belonged to a large mass of Tunisians who had never graduated from high school and never was able to find a secure job (Habib 2010). Thus the unemployed youth in Tunisia that played a key role in the uprisings, rather than being a part of the declining middle class, encompassed a large group of people who wanted to be employed in skilled, semiskilled, or unskilled jobs but could not find employment opportunities in their countries, often for many years. The fact that the protests did not cease to exist in the aftermath of the 2011 revolution supports the idea that the problem faced in these regions is chronic and enduring. Conflicts in Tunisia did not disappear after the fall of the Ben Ali regime. Masses demanding jobs poured into the streets and clashed with the police forces of the new regime during the post–Ben Ali era as well.

Similar patterns can be observed in other regions contributing to the 2011 upsurge. Demands for jobs were also integral to the Egyptian revolution of 2011, which led to the fall of the Mubarak regime (*New York Times* 2011). It has been argued that it is not unemployment in general but structural unemployment of the youth that made up the social base of the Egyptian Revolution:

> At the beginning of the 2011 Egyptian Revolution, the unemployment level in Egypt was about 9%, which was not very high according to global standards. However, the most important circumstance (caused just by the youth bulge) is that about half of all the Egyptian unemployed belonged to the 20 to 24 age cohort. The total number of the unemployed on the eve of the Egyptian Revolution was about 2.5 million. Accordingly, on the eve of the Revolution, Egypt had about one million unemployed young people aged 20–24 who made up the main striking force of the Revolution. (Korotayev and Zinkina 2011)

In Bahrain, the demands of thousands of people who occupied Pearl Square in February 2011 were similar: they wanted more jobs; protested against discriminatory policies prohibiting Shiite access to jobs, housing, and education; and demanded to change the political structure of their state into a constitutional regime (Slackman 2011). In Oman, protesters demanded "more jobs, more freedom of expression and less government control over the news media. In a letter to the sultan, they also requested subsidies for young people who want to get married but cannot afford the wedding expenses" (Fuller 2011b). In Morocco, "five unemployed men set themselves on fire in the capital, Rabat, as part of widespread protests over unemployment, especially among university graduates" (Associated Press 2012). Unrest in Iraq shared similar properties. Thousands of Iraqi youth organized protests against "crippling poverty, few good jobs, creaky public services, [and] an entrenched political elite" (Healy 2011). Although the scale, strength, and consequences of these protests varied, in all these regions political and economic demands were intermingled and grievances of the stagnant relative surplus population became an important force behind these movements.

Because the stagnant relative surplus population consists of segments of working classes excluded from capitalist production, their movements must be seen as distinct from Marx-type or Polanyi-type unrest. Unlike Marx-type unrest, these are not the offensive struggles of the new working classes in formation against exploitation. These segments of the working classes are excluded from production and their primary demand is to be employed in a way that would provide them some measure of dignity and security. Unlike Polanyi-type unrest, these are not the defensive struggles of workers whose previous gains are being undermined, either. This segment of the working class never enjoyed significant gains or privileges to be undermined under capitalism. As Marx and Engels ([1848] 1978, 483) put it, "the modern labourer ... sinks deeper and deeper below the conditions of existence of his own class" and reacts against this process.

Although the protest of the excluded workers is distinct from Marx-type and Polanyi-type labor unrest, it exists alongside the other working-class movements. In Egypt, for instance, there was an intensification of Marx-type labor protests even before the January 2011 protests. Egyptian workers demanding wage increases and better work conditions consistently went on strike, organized protests, and occupied factories from 2004 to 2010. From February to May 2010, there was a high number of labor protest and strikes all over Egypt by factory workers, government workers, teachers, bankers, telephone-company workers, transportation workers, ambulance drivers, and police officers who put forward demands as varied as better pay, fresh water, and political reforms. Thus, Marx-type labor unrest played a role in the Egyptian Revolution of 2011, along with the protests of the unemployed masses.

The struggle of the stagnant relative surplus population also coexists with Polanyi-type unrest. The 2010 UK riots are a stark example of how massive layoffs, benefit cuts, and shrinking of welfare provisions were paralleled by the inability of the soaring economy to produce jobs for millions of youth. The rioters who looted shops in prosperous districts of London and other UK cities were part of the 1.3 million unemployed youth who make up "one of every five 16-to-24-year-olds in the country" (Thomas 2012). England is not alone in this respect. Greece shows a similar pattern but to an even greater degree. The youth that poured into the streets in the 2008 riots and 2011 protests were angered by enduring unemployment and joblessness. As one *New York Times* article points out, they were not merely protesting against specific austerity measures, but were "feel[ing] increasingly shut out of their own futures. Experts warn of volatility in state finances and the broader society as the most highly-educated generation in the history of the Mediterranean hits one of its worst job markets" (Donadio 2011).

It is, of course, not the first time we've seen resistance by these excluded segments of the working class. However, these excluded workers appear to be a greater force and to pose a much more serious challenge to the capitalist system than before.

## Conclusion

Our analysis demonstrates that the working class, broadly conceived, has played a more important role in the 2011 protest wave than has been recognized so far. Further, the differing character of the protests in different places reveals the uneven nature of class formation (and dissolution) in contemporary global capitalism. In regions of the world where capital is leaving, we see a rapid intensification of Polanyi-type labor unrest. This is, for example, the typical form of class protest among North American and European workers who have been suffering setbacks since the 1980s. This is the type of protest that has garnered the most attention from scholars, such as Standing and Žižek, who have analyzed the 2011 upsurge in class terms. However, in regions where capital is going, especially East and South Asia, we also find high levels of Marx-type labor unrest. This presence of this type of unrest has been largely overlooked in debates about 2011. This finding confirms the continuation of the trends that Beverly Silver (2003) identified—namely, that capitalism cyclically makes and unmakes working classes across time and space, in concert with the movements of capital.

However, our analysis of class protest in the 2011 wave also extends the findings of *Forces of Labor* (Silver 2014). The rise of the third type of labor unrest that we identify shows that these cyclical processes do not offset each other on a global scale. On the contrary, capitalism's capacity to unmake livelihoods is much higher than its capacity to absorb working classes in productive activities. Thus, the global movement of capital is creating a growing mass of excluded workers. If we see increasing Marx-type unrest in regions where "capital goes" and increasing Polanyi-type unrest in regions where "capital leaves," this third type of unrest seems to be associated with regions where "capital bypasses." The ideal-typical locations for this form of unrest are geographies in which primitive accumulation processes create large segments of the population that are deprived of the means to their livelihood but have not been absorbed into capitalist production. To put it differently, these are regions that have a large relative surplus population that cannot be fully proletarianized because of capital's increasing inability to absorb labor in productive activities.

The presence of this third type of unrest has important implications for our analysis of the current conjuncture. The existing literature suggests that the protests of 2011 signal an epochal shift in the global class structure, wherein workers around the world have been weakened and put on the defensive. Our close analysis of the class character of the protests leads us to a more nuanced conclusion. For us, the defensive protests of workers whose privileges are being undermined by marketization are an important but not a novel feature of the current protest wave. These protests are a recurrence of a type of protest that, along with the offensive protests of working classes in new zones of production, has been taking place across the history of capitalism. Instead, the critical transformation in the global class structure that the current protest wave highlights is the rise of excluded workers. The secular increase in this section of the working class poses a much more serious challenge to the capitalist system. If the declining middle classes were the central feature of the crisis, then a return to twentieth-century-style welfare and developmental states would be a clear solution to the crisis. However, a solution to the problem that capitalism destroys more livelihoods than it creates will require a fundamental transformation that must be a break from rather than a return to the past.

## Appendix: Construction of the Databases

To construct the dataset of *social protest* in the world from 1991 to 2011, digital archives of the *Washington Post*, the *New York Times*, the *Times* (London), the *Guardian*, and *Financial Times* were searched via LexisNexis from January 1, 1991, through December 31, 2011, using the following search string in the full text: *(Protest! AND NOT Protestant!) OR Demonstrat! OR Upris! OR Unrest! OR Revolut! OR Riot! OR Revolt! OR Rebel! OR Upheav! OR Insurrect! OR (Strike! AND (labor! OR worker!))*. A nonrandom, high-relevance sample of 400 articles from each newspaper (a total sample of 2,000 articles) was selected and coded from each newspaper. False positives were eliminated and all mentions of social protest were categorized according to time, location, type, demands, and agents.

To construct the dataset of *labor unrest* in the world, we collected another (random) sample of 2,000 articles from the digital archives of *Times* (London) and the *New York Times* (1,000 articles from each source) via LexisNexis, from January 1, 1991, through December 31, 2011, using a keyword-search string designed to exclusively capture labor unrest: *(Protest! OR Demand! OR Demonstrat! OR Upris! OR Unrest! OR Revolut! OR Riot! OR Revolt! OR Rebel! OR Upheav! OR Insurrect!*

OR *Strike! OR struggl! OR rall!) AND (labor! OR worker! OR employee! OR wage! OR job! OR union!).* False positives were eliminated, and each article was coded and categorized according to its time, location, type, demands, and agents.

Table 10.1  Number of Mentions of Social Protest According to Newspaper Sources, by Country, 1991–2011, Top 33 Countries Shown (*N* = 2,000)

| Country | Total | Financial Times | Guardian | London Times | New York Times | Washington Post |
|---|---|---|---|---|---|---|
| Egypt | 294 | 82 | 54 | 43 | 48 | 67 |
| Tunisia | 189 | 55 | 45 | 28 | 23 | 38 |
| Syria | 183 | 38 | 21 | 56 | 34 | 34 |
| France | 167 | 3 | 48 | 64 | 32 | 20 |
| Iran | 154 | 37 | 20 | 33 | 29 | 35 |
| Libya | 145 | 37 | 27 | 22 | 31 | 28 |
| United Kingdom | 120 | 39 | 20 | 57 | 4 | |
| Bahrain | 118 | 34 | 29 | 13 | 15 | 27 |
| Yemen | 113 | 39 | 17 | 9 | 21 | 27 |
| China | 95 | 15 | 13 | 28 | 19 | 20 |
| Iraq | 76 | 11 | 9 | 15 | 21 | 20 |
| United States | 73 | 2 | 11 | 14 | 25 | 21 |
| Israel (Palestine) | 54 | 13 | 10 | 4 | 16 | 11 |
| Greece | 52 | 10 | 19 | 12 | 6 | 5 |
| Mexico | 50 | 12 | 3 | 6 | 17 | 12 |
| Jordan | 43 | 14 | 4 | 5 | 4 | 16 |
| Algeria | 39 | 10 | 3 | 6 | 9 | 11 |
| Russia | 39 | 10 | 6 | 13 | 3 | 7 |
| Germany | 38 | 7 | 6 | 16 | 3 | 6 |
| Saudi Arabia | 38 | 13 | 11 | 6 | 4 | 4 |
| Israel | 36 | 4 | 6 | 3 | 18 | 5 |
| Korea, Rep. | 33 | 16 | 3 | 4 | 7 | 3 |
| Indonesia | 31 | 2 | 4 | 4 | 6 | 15 |
| Pakistan | 30 | 3 | 5 | 4 | 9 | 9 |
| Italy | 27 | 6 | 12 | 6 | 2 | 1 |
| Kyrgyzstan | 26 | 4 | 3 | 1 | 9 | 9 |
| India | 24 | 4 | 4 | 4 | 5 | 7 |
| Spain | 22 | 4 | 10 | 5 | 2 | 1 |
| Venezuela | 22 | 8 | 1 | 9 | 4 | |
| Morocco | 21 | 6 | 5 | 4 | 2 | 4 |
| Turkey | 22 | 8 | 8 | 2 | 3 | 1 |
| Nepal | 20 | 5 | 6 | 2 | 4 | 3 |
| Uzbekistan | 20 | 7 | 4 | 5 | 4 | |

# References

Andersen, Kurt. 2011. "Person of the Year 2011." *Time*, December 14. http://content.time
.com/time/specials/packages/article/0,28804,2101745_2102132_2102373,00.html.

Arrighi, Giovanni, and Beverly Silver. 1999. *Chaos and Governance in the Modern World-System*. Minneapolis: University of Minnesota Press.

Associated Press. 2012. "Morocco: 5 Men Set Themselves on Fire, Demonstrating against Lack of Jobs." *New York Times*, January 20.

Badiou, Alain. 2012. *Rebirth of History: Times of Riots and Uprisings*. London: Verso.

Burawoy, Michael. 2012. "Our Livelihood Is at Stake—We Must Pursue Relationships beyond the University." *Network: Magazine of British Sociological Association*, Summer 2012.

Calhoun, Craig. 2013. "Occupy Wall Street in Perspective." *British Journal of Sociology* 64, no. 1: 26–38.

Chase-Dunn, Christopher. 2013. "The World Revolution of 2011: Assembling a United Front of the New Global Left." Institute for Research on World-Systems, August 10. http://irows.ucr.edu/papers/irows82/irows82.htm.

Donadio, Rachel. 2011. "Europe's Young Grow Agitated over Future Prospects." *New York Times*, January 1.

Fahim, Kareem. 2011. "In Tunisian Town of Arab Spring Martyr Disillusionment Seeps In." *New York Times*, August 6.

Fuller, Thomas. 2011a. "After Revolution, Tunisians' Concerns Turn to Everyday Matters." *New York Times*, February 14.

———. 2011b. "Rallies in Oman Steer Clear of Criticism of Its Leader." *New York Times*, March 2.

Habib, Toumi. 2010. "Man at the Centre of Tunisia Unrest Recuperating." *Gulf News*, December 31.

Hardt, Michael, and Antonio Negri. 2012. *Declaration*. New York: Argo Navis Author Services.

Hauslohner, Abigail. 2011. "After Tunisia: Why Egypt Isn't Ready to Have Its Own Revolution." *Time*, January 20. www.time.com/time/world/article/0,8599,2043497,00.html.

Healy, Jacky. 2011. "In Iraq, Protesters Seek Not New Leaders, but Jobs." *New York Times*, February 15.

Katznelson, Ira. 1986. "Working-Class Formation: Constructing Cases and Comparisons." In *Working-Class Formation: Nineteenth-Century Patterns in Western Europe and the United States*, edited by Ira Katznelson and Aristide Zolberg, 3–41. Princeton, NJ: Princeton University Press.

Kirkpatrick, David D. 2011. "Protests Spread to Tunisia's Capital, and a Curfew Is Decreed." *New York Times*, January 13.

Korotayev, Andrey V., and Julia V. Zinkina. 2011. "Egyptian Revolution: A Demographic Structural Analysis." *Entelequia, Revista Interdisciplinar* 13: 139–170.

Marx, Karl. [1867] 1992. *Capital: Volume 1: A Critique of Political Economy*. New York: Penguin.

Marx, Karl, and Friedrich Engels. [1848] 1978. "Manifesto of the Communist Party." In *The Marx-Engels Reader*, edited by R. C. Tucker, 469–500. 2nd ed. New York: W. W. Norton and Company.

Mason, Paul. 2012. *Why It's Kicking Off Everywhere: The New Global Revolutions*. London: Verso.

———. 2013. "Why It's Still Kicking Off Everywhere?" *Soundings* 53 (summer): 44–55.

*New York Times*. 2011. "Echoes from the Revolt in Egypt." February 2.

Rachman, Gideon. 2011. "2011, the Year of Global Indignation." *Financial Times*, August 29. www.ft.com/intl/cms/s/0/36339ee2-cf40-11e0-b6d4-00144feabdc0.html #axzz2f7Be8nap.

Raghavan, Sudarsan. 2011. "A Lost Generation Rises Up." *Washington Post*, January 21.

Reuters. 2011. "14 Killed in Clashes with Police as Violence Spreads in Tunisia." *New York Times*, January 10.

Silver, Beverly. 2003. *Forces of Labor: Workers' Movements and Globalization since 1860*. Cambridge: Cambridge University Press.

———. 2014. "Theorising the Working Class in Twenty-First Century Global Capitalism." In *Workers and Labour in a Globalized Capitalism*, edited by M. Atzeni, 46–69. Basingstoke, UK: Palgrave MacMillan.

Slackman, Michael. 2011. "Bahrain Takes the Stage with a Raucous Protest." *New York Times*, February 16.

Standing, Guy. 2011. *The Precariat: The New Dangerous Class*. New York: Bloomsbury Academic.

Thomas, Landon, Jr. 2012. "For London Youth, Down and Out Is Way of Life." *New York Times*, February 2.

Žižek, Slavoj. 2012. *The Year of Dreaming Dangerously*. London: Verso.

# Note

1. This chapter originates from the Global Social Protest research working group of the Arrighi Center for Global Studies at Johns Hopkins University. We would like to thank Beverly Silver, the coordinator, for her intellectual guidance and contributions to this chapter at multiple stages. We also thank undergraduate participants of the research working group: Fabio Palacio, Frank Molina, Hilary Matfess, Isaac Jilbert, and Sandhira Wijayaratne.

# 11

# SUSTAINABLE DEVELOPMENT AND POVERTY REDUCTION IN THE MODERN WORLD-SYSTEM

## SOUTHEAST ASIA AND THE NEGATIVE CASE OF CAMBODIA[1]

**Harold R. Kerbo and Patrick Ziltener**

## Abstract

There is wide variation in the prospects for economic development and poverty reduction among the Buddhist countries of Southeast Asia. Thailand has been the past leader in poverty reduction among these countries. Vietnam is now reducing poverty even faster than Thailand did in earlier decades. Conditions in Burma and Cambodia, however, are getting worse, with Laos only slowly reducing poverty. Earlier comparative-historical research (Kerbo 2005; 2006) has shown these Buddhist countries have several historical legacies that can lead to less corruption and more state efficiency in protecting them-selves in the global economy, thus sustaining economic development and poverty reduction. However, there are other factors, especially the effects of colonialism, which negatively impact these countries in differing ways.

Despite relatively high levels of gross national product (GNP) growth in recent years, poverty in Cambodia has not been reduced, and inequality and landlessness are growing rapidly. As a follow-up to earlier historical-comparative analysis, two years of fieldwork in Thailand, Cambodia, Vietnam, and Laos focused on what was or was not being done to promote economic development and poverty reduction in these countries, and the extent to which governmental institutions are able to carry out policies for economic development and poverty reduction. The present chapter focuses on Cambodia to examine why its governmental institutions are weak and corruption is high compared to the other three countries in the region.

# Introduction

Compared to earlier decades, the first years of the twenty-first century have been much better for a few Cambodians. Annual GNP growth has hovered around 8 to 10 percent (World Bank 2006b; 2007a; 2009). Every year there are more and more new hotels, casinos, and shopping malls in the capital, Phnom Penh. In Siem Reap, gateway city to the almost 1,000-year-old Angkor Wat, there is a massive building boom now that it is safe for tourists. Natural resources and textiles, however, are the only major exports.

Cambodia's economic development of recent years has left 90 percent of the people untouched, or in many cases worse off (Kerbo 2011). As we will document here, this economic development has severely harmed thousands of poor Cambodians who have been rounded up like prisoners in the middle of the night and dumped into resettlement camps in the countryside, where most have no homes, no jobs, and no agricultural land. The vast majority of Cambodians (90 percent) continue to live in villages with no fresh water or electricity and insufficient land to adequately feed their families (World Bank 2009). Thousands are losing their small plots of land to land grabs by the Cambodian elite and foreign business partners (mostly South Korean and Chinese). (For example, see Cambodian Human Rights Action Committee 2009.) As local World Bank reports (2006b; 2007a) suggested, in almost every village where interviews were conducted we found that others have been forced to sell their land to pay hospital bills to save the lives of their children. A World Bank development report (2008a) estimated that 66 percent of Cambodians live on less than $1 per day. Historians tell us the majority of Cambodians today live pretty much as they did 1,000 years ago (Chandler 1996; Tully 2006).

As we will suggest in this chapter, much but not all of the continuing tragedy for Cambodians is related to the government in place since the mid-1980s (Kerbo 2011). The 2006 annual corruption report from Transparency International ranks

Cambodia among the most corrupt countries in the world, with many other reports concurring (World Bank 2006a; 2007b).

In this chapter we will review the record of economic development and poverty reduction in Southeast Asia in recent decades, then present a model of economic development attempting to explain the reasons for this favorable record for most East and Southeast Asian nations compared to South America and Africa (Kerbo 2005; 2006; 2011). We will then turn to findings from fieldwork in four of the Buddhist countries of Southeast Asia and describe the variation within Southeast Asia to then focus on how far and why Cambodia has lagged behind the other countries, especially with respect to rural infrastructure development and poverty reduction. The final two sections of this chapter attempt to explain how and why Cambodia is not following sustainable policies for economic development necessary in today's global economy, despite having an earlier history and old civilization not so different from its neighbors'.

## Asian Economic Development

In recent decades it has become clear that nations with sustainable economic development and poverty reduction are concentrated in East and Southeast Asia (Jalilian and Weiss 2003; Jomo 2001; Kerbo 2005; Kerbo 2006, chapter 2; World Bank 2000; 2008a). Along with this trend has been the assumption that Asian values and Asian forms of social organization are responsible for these Asian success stories (see especially Pye 1985; 2000; Vogal 1991). But this assumption that Asian values are responsible neglects the variation in economic development and poverty reduction *within* Southeast Asia. Cambodia, Burma, and Laos are lagging seriously behind their neighbors such as Thailand, Malaysia, and now Vietnam, for example. As can be seen in Table 11.1, while Cambodia has had high GNP growth in recent years, the country lags behind almost all of its neighbors with respect to GNP per capita and poverty reduction. The World Bank's (2008b) new $1.25 per day income measure puts Cambodia in a slightly better position than Laos (40 versus 44 percent, though our fieldwork indicates these figures are misleading for Laos). Particularly troubling for Cambodia, however, is the rapid rise in land inequality, which now shows a Gini coefficient of .69, putting Cambodia ahead of all other Southeast Asian nations and close to most Latin American countries. The land-inequality figure for Cambodia is, of course, more recent than what we have for the other countries, but there is little reason to believe that these other countries have had dramatic increases in land inequality like those in Cambodia in recent years. In 1993, only 3 percent of rural Cambodians were estimated to be landless, whereas by 2004 that number was over 20 percent (World Bank 2006a, 85). Amnesty International (2008) in Cambodia has estimated that this landless figure had increased substantially by 2008, with some 150,000 former urban slum people evicted between 2005 and 2008.

Table 11.1 also suggests that the cultural argument (Asian values) becomes questionable when we consider that Thailand, Laos, Burma, Cambodia, and Vietnam are all Buddhist countries (though not Theravada Buddhist in the case of Vietnam) with widely varying levels of economic development and poverty rates. Indeed, Thailand and Vietnam are among the world champions of poverty reduction in recent decades, while Burma, Cambodia, and Laos remain among the world's poorest countries.

**Table 11.1  GNP per Capita, Economic Development, and Poverty Rates**

|  | GNP per Capita, US$ (Purchasing Power Parity, 2006) | Annual Percent Growth in GNP (2000–2006) | National Poverty Line (2003–2005)* | Percent Earning Less than US$1 per Day (2006)** | Percent Earning US$1.25 per Day (2003–2006) |
|---|---|---|---|---|---|
| Cambodia | 2,920 | 9.6 | 35 | 66 (2004) | 40 |
| Thailand | 9,140 | 5.4 | 12 | <2 (2003) | <2 |
| Malaysia | 5,490 | 5.1 | — | <2 (1997) | <2 |
| Indonesia | 3,950 | 4.9 | 16 | 7.5 (2002) | 21 |
| Philippines | 5,980 | 4.8 | 25 | 14.8 (2003) | 23 |
| Vietnam | 3,300 | 7.6 | 29 | — | 22 |
| Laos | 2,050 | 6.4 | 33 | 27 (2002) | 44 |

| Gini Coefficients for Inequalities | | |
|---|---|---|
|  | Income Inequality | Land Inequality |
| Cambodia | .42 | .69 |
| Thailand | .42 | .47 |
| Malaysia | .49 | — |
| Indonesia | .34 | .46 |
| Philippines | .44 | .57 |
| Vietnam | .34 | .50 |
| Laos | .35 | .41 |

*Sources:* World Bank (2008a; 2008b) and United Nations (2008).
*Notes:* * Includes estimates of value of income from family production such as family's own production agriculture, which is not the case with the World Bank $1 per day or $1.25 per day estimates.
** Based on new World Bank PPP calculations from 2005; see World Bank (2008b).

## A Model of Development Advantages

In earlier historical and comparative analysis the first author developed a historical model that attempts to explain why some countries in the world had advantages or disadvantages when trying to achieve sustained economic development and poverty reduction during the second half of the twentieth century (Kerbo 2005; 2006). Table 11.2 suggests that the presence of ancient civilizations, with somewhat complex states centuries ago, as well as less ethnic diversity and more national identity, can help make possible development states that can promote more sustained economic development and poverty reduction today. Elsewhere we have argued why such conditions are more likely found in East and Southeast Asian nations (Kerbo 2005; 2006; also see Ziltener and Mueller 2007 on the level of agricultural and state development before colonialism). The negative or positive effects of colonialism, however, are mixed within Southeast Asia, though with most of these nations now starting to overcome the negative effects of colonialism (Ziltener and Kuenzler 2013). Vietnam, for example, gained independence from the French in the north in 1953, then united the country after defeating South Vietnam and the United States in 1975. Harsh and failed economic policies dominated between 1975 and the end of the 1980s. But with the country stabilized, increasingly more free-market economic policies following *Doi Moi* (economic reform) government reforms helped produce steady economic development and poverty reduction starting in the early 1990s (Jamieson 1995; Kamm 1996; Luong and Unger 1999; Morley and Nishihara 1997; Turley and Selden 1993). Vietnam was then more open to the global economy, but with a stronger development state better able to protect the country's long-term interests, with more foreign direct investment coming into the country.

A central part of the model of development advantages is the existence of an efficient state, a development state or hard state, able to establish and carry out economic-development strategies in the face of challenges from actors in the global economy, as well as resistance from elites with short-term interests at home (veto groups), thus protecting the *long-term interests* of the country. This is also much of what is meant within economic-development circles as "state institutional capacity." Empirical research has demonstrated the importance of government effectiveness for sustained economic development and poverty reduction (Chanda and Putterman 2005; Chibber 2002; Collier 2007; 2009; Doner 2009; Evans 1995; Evans and Rauch 1999; Kohli 2004; 2012). The problem is that international agencies such as the World Bank and Asian Development Bank, and most scholars on economic development, have yet to figure out how to create government effectiveness or state capacity or even understand how countries that have these conditions today achieved them. (The origin of the development state is the subject of future analyses from our current research.)

Figure 11.1 supports the importance of an ancient civilization and a long history of somewhat complex government stressed in the model presented in

**Table 11.2  The East and Southeast Asian Advantage:
A Path to Economic Development**

| |
|---|
| *Ancient Civilizations* |
| Which help promote a sense of nationhood, national identity, fewer ethnic divisions, and more state complexity; |
| WHICH CAN PROMOTE |
| *Traditions of Elite Responsibility* |
| With norms of reciprocity and feelings of obligations toward nonelites, rooted in the development of ancient traditions codified in philosophies and religions; |
| HELPING TO MAKE POSSIBLE |
| *A Hard State* |
| Or the development of a capitalist development state with the motivation and power to enact and enforce development policies against domestic and international opposition; |
| ALL OF WHICH HAVE NOT BEEN NEGATED BY THE IMPACT OF |
| *The Specific Experiences of Colonialism* |
| Which are related to the following: |
| • The economic and political strength of the nation before it was colonized,<br>• The presence or lack of infrastructure development during colonialism,<br>• The construction of national boundaries by colonial powers (relative presence or absence of contested territory by smaller kingdoms or ethnic and tribal minorities),<br>• And how the colonial power left the country (such as the extent of planning and preparation for independence). |

Table 11.2. (Note that Khm is the UN designation for Cambodia.) Using historical data from a large dataset (we call on the Zurich dataset put together by a team of social scientists, including the second author) from all less developed regions of the world (though with less historical data from Latin America), we see in Figure 11.1 that most less developed countries with more efficient and less corrupt governments today had more complex states before the high point of colonialism 200 years ago (Mueller et al. 1999; Ziltener and Mueller 2007; also see Kerbo 2006, 35–38).[2] In essence, if a country did not have a somewhat complex state before Western colonial dominance of most of the world, the country is less likely to have efficient or effective government today. In another study with similar measures of levels of government going back to 1500, Chanda and Putterman (2005) and Bockstette, Chanda, and Putterman (2002) found much the same thing. Of underlying importance, of course, is that this Zurich dataset as well as others show that many measures of government effectiveness today are strongly related to economic development and poverty reduction (Chanda and Putterman 2005; Ertman 2005). It is also important to note that government effectiveness today is not related to the level of democracy in these countries. This Zurich dataset and other recent studies also show that levels of democracy have no correlation

to economic development or poverty reduction, nor does the lack of democracy show a negative correlation to economic development or poverty reduction (Kerbo 2006, 35–38; Rodrik 2007, 169–182; United Nations 2002, 60).

A cursory look at Table 11.2 might suggest a rather optimistic prediction for Cambodia's future. Cambodia is an ancient civilization and certainly must have had a somewhat complex state 1,000 years ago to organize the huge construction projects such as Angkor Wat as well as take care of a city estimated to contain one million people, perhaps the largest city in the world at that time (Higham 2001). But as we suggest in this chapter, historical evidence indicates that much of the effect of this ancient civilization was lost by the time of European colonialism then further eroded, if not destroyed, in the aftermath of colonialism.

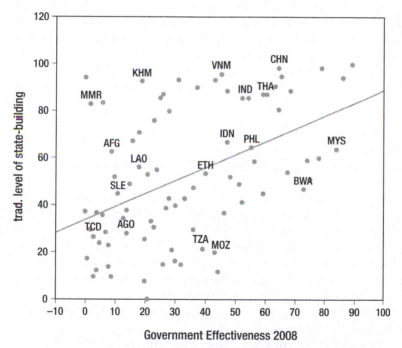

**Figure 11.1 State Complexity before the Advance of Western Colonialism (200 Years Ago) and Government Effectiveness Today**

## The Case of Cambodia and Research Methodology

After earlier historical-comparative research (Kerbo 2005; 2006), the second stage of research involved extensive fieldwork (beginning in 2006) in the rural areas and poor urban slums of the four Buddhist countries of Southeast Asia to assess evidence of any local government institutions and actual conditions of poverty, and to find out what assistance the poor were receiving (or not receiving) from their governments and foreign nongovernmental organizations (NGOs), as well as what these people need most to increase their standards of living and well-being.

The main sources of information were interviews with more than 200 poor families in a total of twenty villages across all regions of Cambodia, as well as slum areas in the capital and provincial cities. In Vietnam we interviewed dozens of families in ten villages in central and southern Vietnam, as well as in urban slum areas. In Thailand the focus was on only northeastern Thailand—Issan, the poorest region of the country, where we interviewed dozens of families in eight villages. In Laos we first encountered obstacles when trying to obtain government permission and local academic support to conduct research, but we were finally able to make progress by spring 2008. We conducted interviews in Laos with several families in three villages, but traveled through villages in three major lowland areas of Laos up and down the Mekong River to assess economic conditions and infrastructure development. (See Kerbo [2011, appendix 1] for the locations in each country.) In all four countries we had dozens of interviews with government officials and foreign NGO personnel, as well as academics who had some knowledge of poverty conditions in these countries.[3]

## A Fieldwork Summary: Economic Conditions, Infrastructure Development, and Standards of Living

The fieldwork *generally* confirmed what statistics from the World Bank, Asian Development Bank, United Nations, and several NGO surveys collected before and during the fieldwork suggest about levels of poverty. However, rural infrastructure development and standards of living in rural Cambodia appeared to be far worse than in the other Buddhist countries in the region, and worse than these reports indicate. In addition, we were able to observe and confirm through interviews with urban slum dwellers and human-rights NGOs that forced and violent evictions are far worse than so far reported by leading international agencies such as the World Bank and the United Nations.

Perhaps the most surprising observation was the almost total lack of rural infrastructure development in Cambodia compared to the other countries. There are very few all-weather paved roads in the Cambodian countryside, some 90 percent of the people have no electricity, and there are few motor vehicles. The common mode of transport and agricultural work remains water buffalos.

Observations in Laos were most unexpected. Down through the Mekong River Basin from the capital, Vientiane, to the Cambodian border, there are fewer water buffalos as draft animals than in Cambodia, and new "iron buffalos" (hand-driven gasoline engine plows for rice fields, to replace water buffalos) in most villages. The prevalence of pickup trucks and new brick houses in Laos is also striking in comparison to Cambodia. Even more striking, electric power lines can be seen in almost every village, and most main roads are paved. Discussions with academics and NGO officials in Laos confirmed our original explanation for general statistical similarities between Laos and Cambodia, which contrast with our fieldwork observations: some 40 percent of the Lao population are hill-tribe peoples primarily living in remote and at-times-inaccessible mountain areas. These people are far poorer than the lowland Lao but are, of course, included in most statistics on national poverty rates, infrastructure development, and living standards in Laos. These hill-tribe peoples in Thailand, Cambodia, and Vietnam are also poorer than lowland people but make up a much smaller percentage of the population in these countries (and have benefited from extensive development projects in Thailand). Thus, when excluding conditions for hill-tribe peoples, conditions for the lowland Lao are far better than the country statistics suggest, and are significantly above the standards of living in Cambodian peasant villages (Chamberlain 2006; Ireson-Doolittle and Moreno-Black 2004; Kerbo 2011).

As Table 11.3 indicates, Cambodia is far behind in every category and would be further behind Laos if remote hill tribes were excluded. Perhaps most striking in these Southeast Asian countries is what we found is *not* happening in rural Cambodia. In each village, and with each family interviewed in each village, we

**Table 11.3  Comparative Conditions for Agriculture and Rural Infrastructure**

| | Health Care | Fresh Water (% of Population) | Improved Sanitation | Irrigation (% Farm Land) |
|---|---|---|---|---|
| Cambodia | Almost none* | 41 | 17 | 7 |
| Thailand | Basic health care free | 99 | 99 | 31 |
| Vietnam | Basic health care free** | 85 | 61 | 45 |
| Laos | | 51 | 30 | 19 |

| | Paved Roads (%) | Fertilizer (kg per Hectare) | Electric Power (kwh per Capita) | Electricity (% of Population With) |
|---|---|---|---|---|
| Cambodia | 6.3 | 5 | 15 | 9 |
| Thailand | 98.0 | 133 | 1988 | 99 |
| Vietnam | 25.0 | 324 | 573 | 84 |
| Laos | 14.4 | — | 179 | — |

Sources: World Bank (2008a; 2009), United Nations (2008).
Notes: * Foreign NGOs have experimental health-care programs in a few regions of Cambodia. They are testing policies of funding local government clinics or funding clinics run completely by the NGOs.
** Outpatient clinic visits for minor injuries or illness costs around US$3, though hospital stays can cost around US$700. There is low-cost annual health insurance available for about $70 per year, which cuts hospital costs in half.

asked what kind of government aid program or services people were receiving. In Thailand we were offered a list of government aid programs and services, with usually spirited discussion among family members and neighbors about what was helping them most. These ranged from the "million-baht program" (about $30,000 given to village officials for economic improvement projects) to family microloans, health care, and what Americans would call agricultural extension services (see Doner 2009; Walker 2012). In Vietnam the question elicited similar discussion, with microloans, electric power, national health insurance, and irrigation projects cited most. Even in Laos we were surprised to hear of various government aid programs, and especially the new paved roads and electric lines that could be seen in most lowland villages, with government trucks putting up concrete poles for power lines in the other villages.

In Cambodia the question about government aid and services was usually answered with blank stares. We always probed for an answer: a microloan, some health care, irrigation projects? There were finally a few responses in some villages, such as wells drilled, health education about preventing dengue fever, and immunizations for children, but in almost every case we discovered with further questioning that foreign NGOs rather than the Cambodian government were the source of aid.

Another question we asked of every village family was, Are you better off today than you were five or ten years ago? Thailand has been more developed than other countries for at least a couple of decades, and the responses were mixed. Rice prices were down at the time, and rural Thais were especially angry that former prime minister Thaksin Shinawatra, who had instituted many effective rural development programs, was deposed in a military coup in 2006 (Walker 2012).

The most positive responses we received were in Vietnamese and, surprisingly, Lao villages. Improvements in their standards of living are much more recent and impressive. In a village in Quang Nam Province in central Vietnam, for example, a rice farmer described how people were given their own land after *Doi Moi* economic reforms that started in the late 1980s, and then pointed to his lush green rice field and said "and look at the irrigation system the government helped us pay for ten years ago."

## Successful Economic Development and Poverty-Reduction Policies in East and Southeast Asian Nations

While there are variations depending on the resources and conditions in less developed countries, the basic model for sustained economic development and poverty reduction is rather clear (Evans 1995; Kerbo 2006; Kohli 2004; 2012; Rodrik 2007; Walker 2012; World Bank 2008a). As a first step, in the early stages of economic development there must be infrastructure development in agriculture. With 80 to 90 percent of people in less developed countries being poor farmers or farm workers, development support in the rural areas can have the most important impact, as well as create a growing base of domestic consumers for the nation's economy. Of course, this agricultural-infrastructural development must not begin with an emphasis on capital-intensive agriculture, which puts small farmers out of business. Most countries in Southeast Asia, including Cambodia, have had an advantage among less developed countries in the world because of a predominance of small farmers who own their own land (though this advantage is diminishing rapidly in Cambodia).[4] As Table 11.1 shows, Cambodia's Gini coefficient of land inequality at .67 is far ahead of other Southeast Asian countries, where there tends to be less inequality in land ownership compared to other world regions, especially Latin America.

The second step in the basic model for sustained economic development and poverty reduction followed by successful East and Southeast Asian countries has been import substitution (Doner 2009; Kerbo 2006, 250–251; Kohli 2012). There must be policies that encourage the country to provide products and services the nation needs rather than buy them from other countries.

The third step is to encourage foreign investment for export industries that bring much-needed capital for further domestic investment. As development proceeds, the strategy is then one of moving up the scale of more value added and higher-tech export industries to expand capital accumulation coming in from the richer countries (Doner 2009).

Cambodia is accomplishing none of this. The first step, encouraging the development of domestic agriculture, is almost completely lacking (as indicated in Table 11.3). Currently Cambodia's economy is based on tourism, the export of natural resources (cheaply), and the export of very low-tech manufactured goods, almost exclusively textiles (World Bank 2009). Some 80 to 90 percent of the population are poor farmers or farm workers who cannot become significant domestic consumers to sustain the economy. The land grabs in rural Cambodia resulting in the sharp rise in land inequality are being encouraged by the policies of top politicians (Amnesty International 2008; Cambodian Human Rights Action Committee 2009). The idea is to move to large-scale farming, most often operated by foreign companies encouraged to come into Cambodia.[5] In addition to this, the natural resources are being taken out of the country very cheaply (and often illegally), with only a few of the Cambodian elite benefitting.[6] And the low-tech textile sweatshops are unlikely to remain competitive in the global economy.

There is a building boom in Phnom Penh and Siem Reap, fueled primarily by increased tourism now that Cambodia is safe (and because of the continued ban on gambling casinos in neighboring Thailand) and by the demands of the few Cambodian elites benefitting from tourism and the export of natural resources. But the biggest impact of these economic activities for the poor is their worsening economic condition because of the rising cost of living and land values. The percent of the population living on less than US$1 per day was increased in one World Bank estimate because of this cost-of-living increase (World Bank 2008b).

Much of that increase is attributed to huge amounts of foreign aid (Collier 2007, 39–43; Ear 2009; 2012, 32).

The problem is not that most Cambodian government officials are ignorant of the kinds of successful development policies already described. In interviews with rather high-level government officials we were told about (and shown) rational and sound economic-development plans. But in each case we were also told something like, "but when it gets to implementation, very little seems to happen." The programs do not work and much of the money authorized for the policies disappears.

## Government Corruption, State Incapacity, and Prospects for Cambodia

Because of years of political instability in the country, it was not until 2006 that reports finally came out with measures of government effectiveness and corruption in Cambodia. The country ranked among the bottom 10 to 15 percent of nations with respect to government effectiveness, with only Burma and North Korea ranking lower in East and Southeast Asia (World Bank 2006b). Transparency International was also able to rank Cambodia for the first time in its annual corruption report in 2006; Cambodia was among the ten most corrupt countries in the world.

We began this chapter with a model predicting that countries with ancient civilizations, somewhat complex states, and some national unity a few centuries ago have an advantage over others because they are more likely to have efficient development and government capacity, with less serious corruption today. But one must also consider how the impact of colonialism affects these potential advantages. A superficial examination of Cambodian history might suggest an optimistic future for the country. But a more careful examination of Cambodian history in the last 1,000 years suggests less optimism.

To begin with, after the high point of what some call the Angkor civilization around 800 to 1,000 years ago, the nation went into a steep decline. This decline likely began after the forests in the hills around Angkor Wat were depleted to house the approximately one million people living in that area (Higham 2001). The runoff from the hills silted up the elaborate system of canals bringing water to the rice fields that had fed those one million people. Somewhat later the Khmer empire was chipped away by the emerging Thais and Vietnamese, and the Cambodian capital was moved further and further away from Angkor Wat until it reached its current location in Phnom Penh. Historians suggest that the Khmer civilization lost much of its old government traditions and organization over these centuries (Chandler 1996; Osborne 1995; Tully 2006). As colonialism began sweeping over Southeast Asia some 200 years ago Cambodia was a weak country worried about its survival in the face of Thai and Vietnamese expansion. In the second half of the 1800s, in fact, the Cambodian king *asked* the French to come in and take the country as a protectorate. The French, of course, did so, but seeing little value in their new colony did little to develop human and physical infrastructure. To a large degree Vietnamese were brought in by the French to run their new colonial possession (Livingston 1996). In their recent quantitative analysis of the impact of colonialism in eighty-three less developed nations today, Ziltener and Kuenzler (2013) identified Cambodia as a case that has been transformed profoundly by colonialism compared to most other less developed nations, and transformed in mostly negative ways.[7] Although Cambodia was ruled indirectly by the French, French control was absolute, with only a facade of native administration, a system of camouflage (Hall 1981). A revolt in 1885–1886 resulted in heavy losses (Hall 1981, 705). In essence, development of colonial self-government had no place in French policy (Mills [1942] 2001, 310). School enrolment was low, even compared with other Southeast Asian colonies. In Cambodia as in Laos, the French preferred to employ Vietnamese in the administration and as domestic workers, and on most plantations they were the vast majority, thereby reinforcing old ethnic animosities and leaving a difficult colonial legacy (Forest 1980, 454–458).

Cambodia gained relative independence after 1953 as the French left Cambodia, Laos, and North Vietnam. But even then the French were able to enforce a rigidly protectionist trade policy (Ziltener and Kuenzler 2013). In regard to foreign investment after relative independence, France was also able to maintain one of the most one-sided dependent postcolonial economies in less developed countries, a condition that Kentor and Boswell (2003) have shown to be harmful to long-term economic development. Finally, toward the end of the US part of the Vietnam war, Cambodians were sucked into the war and devastated after a coup in 1970 brought civil war and fighting against North Vietnam (Brinkley 2011; Kamm 1998). Then, of course, the extreme communist Khmer Rouge finished off any functioning government Cambodia had before 1975. Because the Khmer Rouge tried rather successfully to eliminate all Western-educated and Western-connected Cambodians, there were only some 300 Cambodians with any education above high school left alive in the country (and some estimate less) after the Vietnamese pushed the Khmer Rouge to the fringes of Cambodia beginning in 1979 (Gottesman 2003; Kamm 1998). A few Cambodian refugees fled into Vietnam before 1979, and the Vietnamese trained them to someday take over the Cambodian government. One of the most important was the current prime minister, Hun Sen, an officer in the Khmer Rouge Army until he realized it would all self-destruct. But this handful of Cambodians guided and sponsored by the Vietnamese to form a new government from the early 1980s was not enough.

There is another understandable problem for Cambodia. In interviews with the European Union–funded Transcultural Psychological Organization in Phnom Penh and Battambang and with a reconciliation NGO in Phnom Penh, we were told by several social-service workers that 50 to 60 percent of Cambodians alive during the Khmer Rouge years experience some kind of mental-health problem today. Psychologists who have examined Cambodian refugees concluded the likely outcome of the Khmer Rouge years to be a loss of trust in their fellow Cambodians (Carlson and Rosser-Hogan 1991; 1994; Clarke, Sack, and Goff 1993). A lack of trust can mean less cooperation for common goals, and out of fear from the recent past, a greater focus on short-term individualistic goals and corruption. We were told again and again by people in all levels of the society about this lack of trust and corruption, which they claim permeates the society—corruption is not only among high government officials. Many have called the UN-led effort to rebuild political institutions in the early 1990s a dismal failure (Easterly 2001; Gottesman 2003; Kamm 1998; Livingston 1996). There was certainly failure, but given the state of Cambodia in the early 1990s the effort probably achieved as much as it could.

## Conclusion

Research associated with modern world-systems theory has been successful in identifying why and the extent to which less developed nations on the periphery of the global economy have often been harmed rather than helped economically by outside investment from the wealthy core nations (Bornschier and Chase-Dunn 1985; Bornschier, Chase-Dunn, and Rubinson 1978; Chase-Dunn 1975; 1989; Nolan 1983a; 1983b; Snyder and Kick 1979; Stokes and Jaffee 1982). More recent research has been able to better specify why and under what conditions some less developed nations can have less economic development and more inequality or more economic development and poverty reductions associated with more foreign investment from the rich core nations (Bollen and Appold 1993; Kentor 2001; Kentor and Boswell 2003; for a summary see Kerbo 2006, chapter 4). However, so far this research has primarily involved quantitative methods focused on specific independent variables measured across numerous less developed countries. Recent qualitative comparative studies focused on three or four nations have argued convincingly that a development state with some state autonomy to resist demands by foreign investors from wealthy nations, *as well as* demands by old domestic elites (representing veto groups), is necessary for sustained economic development (Chibber 2002; Doner 2009; Evans 1995; Kohli 2004; 2012). The ongoing research represented in this chapter is more focused on qualitative historical comparisons and recent fieldwork in the less developed nations in Southeast Asia (specifically Thailand, Vietnam, Laos, and Cambodia). This research focus is better able to uncover more specific historical conditions leading some nations to benefit from engagement with the richer nations in the global economy while controlling for broadly defined cultural values that might impact economic development. Several recent works have suggested the importance of historical roots of successful development states without attempting to identify the more specific nature of those historical roots (Chibber 2002; Doner 2009; Evans 1995; Kohli 2004; 2012). Only two studies we are aware of have attempted to identify the importance of the early history of current development states: Chanda and Putterman (2005) and Ziltener and Mueller (2007). Following the model outlined in Table 11.2, we have suggested that the presence of some precolonial government capacity has given some nations an advantage in achieving more government capacity and effectiveness today.

In addition, we argue that a relatively homogeneous society forged over the centuries is important for a development state to maintain development policies without veto groups blocking these policies for protection of their particular interest groups. Also, we have argued that the existence of norms of elite responsibility that have been forged through a long history are important in restraining the short-term narrow interests of elites who dominate development states today (such as by reducing the level of corruption). Continuing research from this fieldwork will focus on the possible nature and origins of these norms of elite responsibility.

These advantages, however, are still contingent upon specific experiences during the colonial period for a nation. The more devastating and long-lasting impact of colonialism in Cambodia, for example, has made that country less able than most of its neighbors to recover the advantages of an ancient civilization with some traditions of government capacity and elite responsibility.

We suggest that these factors outlined in this chapter (in particular in Table 11.2) can be applied to understanding successful or unsuccessful attempts at economic development in less developed countries today, including those in other world regions (see Kerbo 2005; 2006; 2011). Obviously, more qualitative historical research in other world regions is needed to provide support for the historical model of economic development outlined in this chapter.

## References

Amnesty International. 2008. "Rights Razed: Forced Evictions in Cambodia." Amnesty International. www.amnesty.org/en/library/info/ASA23/002/2008.

Bockstette, Valerie, Areendam Chanda, and Louis Putterman. 2002. "States and Markets: The Advantage of an Early Start." *Journal of Economic Growth* 7: 347–369.

Bollen, Kenneth, and Stephen J. Appold. 1993. "National Industrial Structure and the Global System." *American Sociological Review* 58: 283–301.

Bornschier, Volker, and Christopher Chase-Dunn. 1985. *Transnational Corporations and Underdevelopment*. New York: Praeger.

Bornschier, Volker, Christopher Chase-Dunn, and Richard Rubinson. 1978. "Cross-National Evidence of the Effects of Foreign Investment and Aid on Economic Growth and Inequality: A Survey of Findings and a Reanalysis." *American Journal of Sociology* 84: 651–683.

Brinkley, Joel. 2011. *Cambodia's Curse: The Modern History of a Troubled Land*. New York: Public Affairs.

Cambodian Human Rights Action Committee (CHRAC). 2009. "Losing Ground: Forced Evictions and Intimidation in Cambodia." CHRAC, September. www.chrac

.org/eng/CHRAC%20Statement%20in%202009/Losing%20Ground%20FINAL
.compressed.pdf.

Carlson, Eve Berstein, and Rhonda Rosser-Hogan. 1991. "Trauma Experiences, Posttraumatic Stress, Dissociation, and Depression in Cambodian Refugees." *American Journal of Psychiatry* 148: 1548–1551.

———. 1994. "Cross-Cultural Response to Trauma: A Study of Traumatic Experiences and Posttraumatic Symptoms in Cambodian Refugees." *Journal of Traumatic Stress* 7: 43–58.

Chamberlain, James. 2006. *Laos Participatory Poverty Assessment, 2006.* Manila: Asian Development Bank.

Chanda, Areendam, and Louis Putterman. 2005. "State Effectiveness, Economic Growth, and the Age of States." In *States and Development: Historical Antecedents of Stagnation and Advance,* edited by Matthew Lange and Dietrich Rueschemeyer, 69–91. New York: Palgrave.

Chandler, David. 1996. *A History of Cambodia.* Boulder, CO: Westview Press.

Chase-Dunn, Christopher. 1975. "The Effects of International Economic Dependence on Development and Inequality: A Cross-National Study." *American Sociological Review* 40: 720–738.

———. 1989. *Global Formation: Structures of the World-Economy.* Oxford: Oxford University Press.

Chibber, Vivek. 2002. "Bureaucratic Rationality and the Development State." *American Journal of Sociology* 107: 951–989.

Clarke, Greg, William Sack, and Brian Goff. 1993. "Three Forms of Stress in Cambodian Adolescent Refugees." *Abnormal Child Psychology* 21: 65–77.

Collier, Paul. 2007. *The Bottom Billion: Why the Poorest Countries Are Failing and What Can Be Done about It.* New York: Oxford University Press.

———. 2009. *Wars, Guns, and Votes: Democracy in Dangerous Places.* New York: Oxford University Press.

Doner, Richard. 2009. *The Politics of Uneven Development: Thailand's Economic Growth in Comparative Perspective.* New York: Cambridge University Press.

Ear, Sophal. 2009. "The Political Economy of Aid and Regime Legitimacy in Cambodia." In *Beyond Democracy in Cambodia: Political Reconstruction in a Post-Conflict Society,* edited by Joakim Ojendal and Mona Lilja, 151–188. Copenhagen: Nordic Institute of Asian Studies.

———. 2012. *Aid and Dependence in Cambodia: How Foreign Assistance Undermines Democracy.* New York: Columbia University Press.

Easterly, William. 2001. *The Elusive Quest for Growth: Economist's Adventures and Misadventures in the Tropics.* Cambridge, MA: MIT Press.

Ertman, Thomas. 2005. "Building States—Inherently a Long-Term Process? An Argument from Comparative History." In *States and Development: Historical Antecedents of Stagnation and Advance,* edited by Matthew Lange and Dietrich Rueschemeyer, 165–182. New York: Palgrave.

Evans, Peter. 1995. *Embedded Autonomy: States and Industrial Transformation.* Princeton, NJ: Princeton University Press.

Evans, Peter, and James Rauch. 1999. "Bureaucracy and Growth: A Cross-National Analysis of the Effects of Weberian State Structures on Economic Growth." *American Sociological Review* 64: 748–765.

Forest, Alain. 1980. *Le Cambodge à la Colonization Français*. Paris: L. Harmattan.

Gottesman, Evan. 2003. *Cambodia after the Khmer Rouge: Inside the Politics of Nation Building*. New Haven, CT: Yale University Press.

Hall, D. G. E. 1981. *A History of Southeast Asia*. 4th ed. London: Macmillan.

Higham, Charles. 2001. *The Civilization of Angkor*. London: Weidenfeld and Nicolson.

Ireson-Doolittle, Carol, and Geraldine Moreno-Black. 2004. *The Lao: Gender, Power, and Livelihood*. Boulder, CO: Westview.

Jalilian, Hossein, and John Weiss. 2003. "Foreign Direct Investment and Poverty in the ASEAN Region." *ASEAN Economic Bulletin* 19: 231–253.

Jamieson, Neil L. 1995. *Understanding Vietnam*. Berkeley: University of California Press.

Jomo, K. S. 2001. "Globalization, Liberalization, Poverty and Income Inequality in Southeast Asia." OECD Development Center, Technical Paper 185.

Kamm, Henry. 1996. *Dragon Ascending: Vietnam and the Vietnamese*. New York: Arcade Publishing.

———. 1998. *Cambodia: Report from a Stricken Land*. New York: Arcade.

Kentor, Jeffrey. 2001. "The Long Term Effects of Globalization on Population Growth, Inequality, and Economic Development." *Social Problems* 48, no. 4: 435–455.

Kentor, Jeffrey, and Terry Boswell. 2003. "Foreign Capital Dependence and Development: A New Direction." *American Sociological Review* 68: 301–313.

Kerbo, Harold. 2005. "Foreign Investment and Disparities in Economic Development and Poverty Reduction: A Comparative-Historical Analysis of the Buddhist Countries of Southeast Asia." *International Journal of Comparative Sociology* 46: 425–460.

———. 2006. *World Poverty: Global Inequality and the Modern World-System*. New York: McGraw-Hill.

———. 2011. *The Persistence of Cambodian Poverty: From the Killing Fields to the Present*. London: MacFarland and Company.

Kohli, Atul. 2004. *State-Directed Development: Political Power and Industrialization in the Global Periphery*. New York: Cambridge University Press.

———. 2012. *Poverty amid Plenty in the New India*. Cambridge: Cambridge University Press.

Livingston, Carol. 1996. *Gecko Tails: A Journey through Cambodia*. London: Phoenix Books.

Luong, Hy Van, and Jonathan Unger. 1999. "Wealth, Power, and Poverty in the Transition to Market Economies: The Process of Socio-Economic Differentiation in Rural China and Northern Vietnam." In *Transforming Asian Socialism: China and Vietnam Compared*, edited by Anita Chan, Benedict J. Tria Kerkvliet, and Jonathan Unger, 120–152. New York: Rowman and Littlefield.

Mills, Lennox A. [1942] 2001. "French Indo-China." In *Southeast Asia: Colonial History*. Vol. 3: *High Imperialism: 1890s–1930s*, edited by P. H. Kratoska, 309–313. New York: Routledge.

Morley, James W., and Masashi Nishihara, eds. 1997. *Vietnam Joins the World*. Armonk, NY: M. E. Sharpe.

Mueller, Hans-Peter, Marti Kock, Claudia Seiler, and Brigitte Arpagaus. 1999. *Atlas vorkolonialer Gesellschaften. Sozialstrukturen und kulturelles Erbe der Staaten Afrikas, Asiens und Melanesiens* [Atlas of pre-colonial societies: Cultural heritage and social structures of African, Asian and Melanesian countries]. Berlin: Reimer.

Murdock, George Peter. 1986. *Ethnographic Atlas: A Summary*. Pittsburgh, PA: University of Pittsburgh Press.

Nolan, Patrick D. 1983a. "Status in the World-System, Income Inequality, and Economic Growth." *American Journal of Sociology* 89: 410–419.

———. 1983b. "Status in the World Economy and National Structure and Development." *International Journal of Contemporary Sociology* 24: 109–120.

Osborne, Milton. 1995. *Southeast Asia: An Introductory History.* London: Allen and Unwin.

Pasuk, Phongpaichit, and Chris Baker. 1995. *Thailand: Economy and Politics.* New York: Oxford University Press.

Pye, Lucian W. 1985. *Asian Power and Politics: The Cultural Dimensions of Authority.* Cambridge, MA: Harvard University Press.

———. 2000. "Asian Values: From Dynamos to Dominoes?" In *Culture Matters: How Values Shape Human Progress*, edited by Lawrence E. Harrison and Samuel P. Huntington, 244–254. New York: Basic Books.

Reid, Anthony. 1988. *Southeast Asia in the Age of Commerce, Volume One: The Lands below the Winds.* New Haven, CT: Yale University Press.

———. 1993. *Southeast Asia in the Age of Commerce, Volume Two: Expansion and Crisis.* New Haven, CT: Yale University Press.

Rodrik, Dani. 2007. *One Economics, Many Recipes: Globalization, Institutions, and Economic Growth.* Princeton, NJ: Princeton University Press.

Snyder, David, and Edward Kick. 1979. "Structural Position in the World-System and Economic Growth, 1955–1970: A Multiple Analysis of Transnational Interactions." *American Journal of Sociology* 84: 1096–1128.

Stokes, Randall, and David Jaffee. 1982. "Another Look at the Export of Raw Materials and Economic Growth." *American Sociological Review* 47: 402–407.

Transparency International. 2006. "Corruption Perceptions Index 2006." www .transparency.org/research/cpi/cpi_2006 (accessed June 26, 2014).

Tully, John. 2006. *A Short History of Cambodia: From Empire to Survival.* Sidney: Allen and Unwin.

Turley, William S., and Mark Selden, eds. 1993. *Reinventing Vietnamese Socialism: Doi Moi in Comparative Perspective.* Boulder, CO: Westview Press.

United Nations. 2002. *Human Development Report, 2002.* New York: Palgrave Macmillan.

———. 2008. *Human Development Report, 2008.* New York: Palgrave Macmillan.

Vogel, Ezra. 1991. *The Four Little Dragons: The Spread of Industrialization in East Asia.* Cambridge, MA: Harvard University Press.

Walker, Andrew. 2012. *Thailand's Political Peasants: Power in the Modern Rural Economy.* Madison: University of Wisconsin Press.

World Bank. 2000. *World Development Report, 2000/2001.* New York: Oxford University Press.

———. 2006a. *World Development Report, 2006: Equity and Development.* New York: Oxford University Press.

———. 2006b. *Cambodia: Halving Poverty by 2015? Poverty Assessment 2006.* Report No. 35213-KH. Phnom Penh: World Bank. www-wds.worldbank.org/external/default /WDSContentServer/WDSP/IB/2006/02/22/000012009_20060222102151 /Rendered/PDF/352130REV0pdf.pdf (accessed May 16, 2014).

———. 2007a. *Cambodia: Sharing Growth: Equity and Development Report, 2007.* World Bank, June 4. https://openknowledge.worldbank.org/handle/10986/7722.

———. 2007b. *A Decade of Measuring the Quality of Governance.* AMARC. www.amarc .org/documents/articles/booklet_decade_of_measuring_governance.pdf.

———. 2008a. *World Development Report, 2008.* New York: Oxford University Press.

———. 2008b. *2008 World Development Indicators: Poverty Data: A Supplement to World Development Indicators 2008.* New York: Oxford University Press.

———. 2009. *Sustaining Growth in a Challenging Environment: Cambodian Country Economic Memorandum.* World Bank, January. https://openknowledge.worldbank.org /handle/10986/3142 and www.hks.harvard.edu/fs/drodrik/Growth%20diagnostics %20papers/Cambodia.pdf.

World Food Programme. 2005. *Food Security Atlas of Cambodia, 2005.* World Bank, December. http://documents.wfp.org/stellent/groups/public/documents/ena/wfp099145 .pdf.

Wyatt, David K. 1984. *Thailand: A Short History.* New Haven, CT: Yale University Press.

Ziltener, Patrick, and Daniel Kuenzler. 2013. "Measuring the Impact of 19th/20th Century Colonialism in Africa and Asia." *Journal of World-Systems Research* 19, no. 2: 290–311.

Ziltener, Patrick, and Hans-Peter Mueller. 2007. "The Weight of the Past—Traditional Technology and Socio-Political Differentiation in African and Asian Societies: A Quantitative Assessment of Their Impact on Socio-Economic Development." *International Journal of Comparative Sociology* 48: 371–415.

# Notes

1. Most of the focused fieldwork for this research between June 2006 and June 2008 was funded by a generous research fellowship to the first author from the Abe Foundation, a division of the Japan Foundation in Tokyo, with administrative assistance on the US side from the Social Science Research Council in New York. California Polytechnic State University, in San Luis Obispo, also helped make this fieldwork possible through a sabbatical spanning most of this period, as well as through an International Scholar award that provided funding in spring 2008. Follow-up observations and interviews continued until 2011.

2. The dataset includes more than 400 coded variables from the World Bank, United Nations, and other international organizations, all of which can be accessed on the Web. The unique part of the dataset is indicators of the state and social complexity of precolonial societies. These indicators were constructed from several sources to indicate the level of social, political, and cultural diversity before European colonialism took over much of the world. This dataset includes the hundreds of ethnic groups in the Ethnographic Atlas between 1940 and 1980 (Murdock 1986). These data have been transformed into population-weighted variables on the national level. These original data are published in the *Atlas of Pre-Colonial Societies: Cultural Heritage and Social Structures of African, Asian and Melanesian Countries* (Mueller et al. 1999; hereinafter referred to as Atlas). See Ziltener and Mueller (2007) and Kerbo (2005; 2006; 2011) for further details about coding and variables.

3. We should note again that the research focus was on lowland peoples, who are the majority in these countries (though only a slight majority in Laos; see Chamberlain [2006]), rather than hill-tribe peoples. In every Southeast Asian country hill-tribe peoples experience more poverty and are certainly worthy of much more attention. But because of many different issues relating to their poverty compared to lowland peoples, hill-tribe peoples were mostly ignored in this research.

4. With the exception of Vietnam, there has never been a significant landed aristocracy in Southeast Asia. In fact, in theory the king of each kingdom owned all the land, allowing families in each village to work a plot of land for multiple generations (Osborne 1995; Pasuk and Baker 1995; Reid 1988, 1993; Tully 2006; Wyatt 1984). And in reality, many small villages throughout mainland Southeast Asia were often free of any intervention of a kingdom as boundaries were always shifting and were unclear for centuries. Under communist governments in Vietnam, Laos, and Cambodia,

from 1975 (though earlier in north Vietnam) land was collectivized but then it was redistributed on a fairly equal scale in the 1980s to early 1990s.

5.  Information based on interviews with NGO personnel in Cambodia. Information on this can also be found in the pages of *Phnom Penh Post*: www.phnompenhpost.com/. We also interviewed village peoples who had lost their land and/or were working on the new large-scale farms in the southern and eastern regions of Cambodia. In the east-central region we found most of these new large-scale farms were operated by Vietnamese companies. The Cambodian government is also currently working on deals with Middle Eastern countries for them to establish large-scale farm projects in Cambodia.

6.  Our information about the legal and illegal selling of Cambodia's natural resources cheaply is based on various NGO reports (for example, see World Bank 2006b, 2007a, 2009). But our information also comes from unpublished documents shown to me in interviews with European and American NGO officials from three NGOs tracking and documenting the theft of natural resources and rural land in Cambodia.

7.  Their methodology was to ask several academic specialists on each of these nations to rank how colonialism had an impact on these countries in several economic, political, and social dimensions.

# ABOUT THE AUTHORS

**Manuela Boatcă** is professor of the sociology of global inequalities and principal investigator of the research network desiguALdades.net at Freie Universität, Berlin, Germany. She is author of *From Neoevolutionism to World-Systems Analysis: The Romanian Theory of "Forms without Substance" in Light of Modern Debates on Social Change* (2003) and coeditor of *Decolonising European Sociology: Transdisciplinary Approaches* (with Encarnación Gutiérrez-Rodríguez and Sérgio Costa, 2010).

**Patrick Bond** is director of the University of KwaZulu-Natal Centre for Civil Society, Durban, South Africa. His chapter is a part of the research on globalization and changes in accumulation system and class structure organized by the Institute for Social Sciences at Gyeongsang National University. Research was supported by a National Research Foundation of Korea Grant funded by the Korean Government (NRF-2010-413-B00027).

**Christopher Chase-Dunn** is distinguished professor of sociology and director of the Institute for Research on World-Systems at the University of California, Riverside. He is the author of *Rise and Demise: Comparing World-Systems* (with Thomas D. Hall), *The Wintu and Their Neighbors* (with Kelly Mann), and *The Spiral of Capitalism and Socialism* (with Terry Boswell), and is the founder and former editor of the *Journal of World-Systems Research*. Chase-Dunn is currently doing research on transnational social movements. He also studies the rise and fall of settlements and polities since the Stone Age, and global state formation.

**Gary Coyne** earned his PhD in sociology from the University of California, Riverside, in 2013. His dissertation focused on the political economy of language education, particularly the place of the languages of core power as second languages in national school systems around the world. His current research focuses on the institutionalization of languages other than English as majors and academic departments in US higher education. He is currently interim director of evaluation and assessment at the University of California, Riverside.

**Raymond J. Dezzani** is associate professor in the department of geography and affiliate associate professor in the department of statistical sciences at the University of Idaho. His primary research interests are in probabilistic political economy and the development of world-systems perspective in geography and the social sciences so as to produce a coherent integrative explanatory framework for human interaction. He is involved in the use of stochastic spatial models for the analysis of political and economic processes using the world-systems perspective and has contributed numerous articles and book chapters on these topics.

**James V. Fenelon** is professor of sociology and director of the Center for Indigenous Peoples Studies at California State University, San Bernardino. A revised version of his book *Indigenous Peoples and Globalization: Resistance and Revitalization* (with Thomas D. Hall) is forthcoming from Paradigm Publishers.

**Colin Flint**, a geographer by training, is professor of political science at Utah State University. His research interests include geopolitics, world-systems analysis, and just-war theory. He is the author of *Introduction to Geopolitics* (2011) and coauthor, with Peter J. Taylor, of *Political Geography: World-Economy, Nation-State and Locality* (6th edition, 2011). He is editor of *The Geography of War and Peace* (2004) and coeditor (with Scott Kirsch) of *Reconstructing Conflict: Integrating War and Post-War Geographies* (2011). His books have been translated into Spanish, Polish, Korean, Mandarin, Japanese, and Farsi.

**Jennifer E. Givens** is a doctoral candidate in comparative international sociology and environmental sociology at the University of Utah. Her research examines environmental concern, coupled human and natural systems, and factors that impact environmental and social sustainability across nation-states in terms of their carbon intensity of well-being. Her work has been published in venues such as *Social Science Research, Organization and Environment,* and *Environment and Behavior.*

**Lindsay Marie Jacobs** is a PhD candidate in sociology at Ghent University. Her research focuses on the impact of globalization on the changing power relations between countries and the structural evolution of the world-system. Her related research interests include the BRICS countries, international conflict, state power, and cultural globalization.

**Andrew K. Jorgenson** is professor and director of graduate studies in the department of sociology at the University of Utah. He conducts research on coupled human and natural systems, with a focus on the political economy and human ecology of global environmental change. His research appears in such journals as *American Journal of Sociology, Nature Climate Change, Social Problems, Social Forces, Social Science Research, Energy Policy, Global Environmental Politics,* and *Ecological Economics.*

**Şahan Savaş Karataşlı** is a postdoctoral research fellow at the Arrighi Center for Global Studies, Johns Hopkins University. His research focuses on the ways in which changes in the global political economy affect social and political movements, class, gender, and ethnic-based hierarchies, and various issues surrounding social change and development at global and local levels.

**Jeffrey Kentor** is associate provost for graduate studies and research and professor of sociology at Eastern Michigan University. His research is located within the broad area of macro-level social change. His work focuses on long-term processes and structures of the world economy and its impact on economic development, income inequality, health, international migration, and the environment.

**Harold R. Kerbo** has been a professor of sociology at California Polytechnic State University since 1977. He has been a Fulbright professor in Japan, Thailand, and Austria, and a visiting professor in Great Britain, Germany, Austria, Switzerland, Thailand, and Japan. From June 2006 to August 2007, he was the recipient of an Abe Fellowship to conduct fieldwork on poverty and poverty programs in Thailand, Vietnam, Laos, and Cambodia. The first book from this fieldwork, titled *The Persistence of Cambodian Poverty: From the Killing Fields to Today*, was published in 2011. Kerbo has published several books and numerous articles on the subjects of social stratification, comparative societies, and economic development and world poverty, including *Stratification and Inequality*, which is now in its 8th edition.

**Sefika Kumral** is a PhD candidate in the department of sociology at Johns Hopkins University. Her research interests include the relation between ethnic violence and democracy; far-right movements, fascism, and militarism; international development; and macro-comparative study of labor movements.

**Ben Scully** is a lecturer at the University of the Witwatersrand in Johannesburg, South Africa. His research focuses on labor and social welfare in South Africa and across the Global South.

**Matthew R. Sanderson** is associate professor of sociology at Kansas State University. His main interest is global social change. Much of his work has focused on population and environmental dynamics as interrelated aspects of development in the context of globalization.

**Jason Struna** is a PhD candidate in sociology at the University of California, Riverside. His dissertation is titled "Handling Globalization: Labor, Capital, and Class in the Globalized Warehouse and Distribution Center" and is based on ethnographic research on warehouse workers in Southern California. He is the 2012 recipient of the Society for the Study of Social Problems Harry Braverman

Award: Best Graduate Student Paper, Labor Studies Division, for "Global Chains, Global Workers: Warehouse Workers' Experience of Globalized Labor Processes and Transnational Class Relations."

**Christian Suter** is professor of sociology at the University of Neuchâtel and president of the World Society Foundation in Zurich, Switzerland. His research has focused on global debt crises, social inequality, globalization, and political transformation in Latin America, as well as on social indicators and quality of life. He is coeditor (with Mark Herkenrath) of *World Society in the Global Economic Crisis* (2012) and coeditor (with Christopher Chase-Dunn) of *Structures of the World Political Economy and the Future of Global Conflict and Cooperation* (2014).

**Smriti Upadhyay** is a PhD candidate in the department of sociology at Johns Hopkins University. Her research interests include labor and development in contemporary India and labor and social movements in comparative, world-historical perspective.

**Ronan Van Rossem** is associate professor in the department of sociology of Ghent University and head of the research group Participation, Opportunities, Structures (POS+). He is a member of the Ghent Centre for Global Studies. His research interests include macro-sociology, structural sociology, and reproductive health.

**Immanuel Wallerstein** served as distinguished professor of sociology at Binghamton University (State University of New York) until his retirement in 1999, and as head of the Fernand Braudel Center for the Study of Economies, Historical Systems and Civilizations until 2005. Wallerstein held several positions as visiting professor at universities worldwide, was awarded multiple honorary degrees, intermittently served as Directeur d'études associé at the École des Hautes Études en Sciences Sociales in Paris, and was president of the International Sociological Association between 1994 and 1998. In 2000 he joined the Yale sociology department as senior research scholar. In 2003 he received the Career of Distinguished Scholarship Award from the American Sociological Association.

**Patrick Ziltener** is associate professor at the University of Zurich, where he teaches courses on globalization, world society, and world poverty. From 1994 to 2000 he was assistant at the Sociological Institute of the University of Zurich. From 2000 to 2002 he was a researcher at the Max Planck Institute for the Study of Societies in Cologne, Germany. From 2003 to 2005 he worked in Japan, Indonesia, Thailand, Malaysia, Vietnam, Laos, Cambodia, and the Philippines for the research project Regional Integration in the World Society: East Asia. From 2006 to 2009 he was a senior advisor for Swiss-Japanese economic relations for the State Secretariat for Economic Affairs at the Swiss Ministry of Economy.

# POLITICAL ECONOMY OF THE WORLD-SYSTEM ANNUALS SERIES

## Immanuel Wallerstein, Series Editor

I.      Kaplan, Barbara Hockey, ed., *Social Change in the Capitalist World Economy*. Political Economy of the World-System Annuals, 01. Beverly Hills/London: Sage Publications, 1978.

II.     Goldfrank, Walter L., ed., *The World-System of Capitalism: Past and Present*. Political Economy of the World-System Annuals, 02. Beverly Hills/London: Sage Publications, 1979.

III.    Hopkins, Terence K., & Immanuel Wallerstein, eds., *Processes of the World-System*. Political Economy of the World-System Annuals, 03. Beverly Hills/London: Sage Publications, 1980.

IV.     Rubinson, Richard, ed., *Dynamics of World Development*. Political Economy of the World-System Annuals, 04. Beverly Hills/London: Sage Publications, 1981.

V.      Friedman, Edward, ed., *Ascent and Decline in the World-System*. Political Economy of the World-System Annuals, 05. Beverly Hills/London/New Delhi: Sage Publications, 1982.

VI.     Bergesen, Albert, ed., *Crises in the World-System*. Political Economy of the World-System Annuals, 06. Beverly Hills/London/New Delhi: Sage Publications, 1983.

VII.    Bergquist, Charles, ed., *Labor in the Capitalist World-Economy*. Political Economy of the World-System Annuals, 07. Beverly Hills/London/New Delhi: Sage Publications, 1984.

VIII.   Evans, Peter, Dietrich Rueschemeyer, & Evelyne Huber Stephens, eds., *States versus Markets in the World-System*. Political Economy of the World-System Annuals, 08. Beverly Hills/London/New Delhi: Sage Publications, 1985.

IX.     Tardanico, Richard, ed., *Crises in the Caribbean Basin*. Political Economy of the World-System Annuals, 09. Newbury Park/Beverly Hills/London/New Delhi: Sage Publications, 1987.

X.      Ramirez, Francisco O., ed., *Rethinking the Nineteenth Century: Contradictions and Movements*. Studies in the Political Economy of the World-System, 10. New York/Westport, CT/London: Greenwood Press, 1988.

XI.     Smith, Joan, Jane Collins, Terence K. Hopkins, & Akbar Muhammad, eds., *Racism, Sexism, and the World-System*. Studies in the Political Economy of the World-System, 11. New York/Westport, CT/London: Greenwood Press, 1988.

XII.    (a) Boswell, Terry, ed., *Revolution in the World-System*. Studies in the Political Economy of the World-System, 12a. New York/Westport, CT/London: Greenwood Press, 1989.

XII.    (b) Schaeffer, Robert K., ed., *War in the World-System*. Studies in the Political Economy of the World-System, 12b. New York/Westport, CT/London: Greenwood Press, 1989.

XIII.   Martin, William G., ed., *Semiperipheral States in the World-Economy*. Studies in the Political Economy of the World-System, 13. New York/Westport, CT/London: Greenwood Press, 1990.

XIV.    Kasaba, Resat, ed., *Cities in the World-System*. Studies in the Political Economy of the World-System, 14. New York/Westport, CT/London: Greenwood Press, 1991.

XV.     Palat, Ravi Arvind, ed., *Pacific-Asia and the Future of the World-System*. Studies in the Political Economy of the World-System, 15. Westport, CT/London: Greenwood Press, 1993.

XVI.    Gereffi, Gary, & Miguel Korzeniewicz, eds., *Commodity Chains and Global Capitalism*. Studies in the Political Economy of the World-System, 16. Westport, CT: Greenwood Press, 1994.

XVII.   McMichael, Philip, ed., *Food and Agrarian Orders in the World-Economy*. Studies in the Political Economy of the World-System, 17. Westport, CT: Greenwood Press, 1995.

XVIII.  Smith, David A., & József Böröcz, eds., *A New World Order? Global Transformations in the Late Twentieth Century*. Studies in the Political Economy of the World-System, 18. Westport, CT: Greenwood Press, 1995.

XIX.    Korzeniewicz, Roberto Patricio, & William C. Smith, eds., *Latin America in the World-Economy*. Studies in the Political Economy of the World-System, 19. Westport, CT: Greenwood Press, 1996.

XX.     Ciccantell, Paul S., & Stephen G. Bunker, eds., *Space and Transport in the World-System*. Studies in the Political Economy of the World-System, 20. Westport, CT: Greenwood Press, 1998.

XXI.    Goldfrank, Walter L., David Goodman, & Andrew Szasz, eds., *Ecology and the World-System*. Studies in the Political Economy of the World-System, 21. Westport, CT: Greenwood Press, 1999.

XXII.    Derluguian, Georgi, & Scott L. Greer, eds., *Questioning Geopolitics*. Studies in the Political Economy of the World-System, 22. Westport, CT: Greenwood Press, 2000.

XXIV.    Grosfoguel, Ramón, & Ana Margarita Cervantes-Rodriguez, eds., *The Modern/ Colonial/Capitalist World-System in the Twentieth Century: Global Processes, Antisystemic Movements, and the Geopolitics of Knowledge*. Studies in the Political Economy of the World-System, 24. Westport, CT: Greenwood Press, 2002.

XXV.     (a) Dunaway, Wilma A., ed., *Emerging Issues in the 21st Century World-System, Volume I: Crises and Resistance in the 21st Century World-System*. Studies in the Political Economy of the World-System, 25a. Westport, CT: Greenwood Press, 2003.

XXV.     (b) Dunaway, Wilma A., ed., *Emerging Issues in the 21st Century World-System, Volume II: New Theoretical Directions for the 21st Century World-System*. Studies in the Political Economy of the World-System, 25b. Westport, CT: Greenwood Press, 2003.

XXVI.    (a) Reifer, Thomas Ehrlich, ed., *Globalization, Hegemony & Power*. Political Economy of the World-System Annuals, 26a. Boulder, CO: Paradigm Publishers, 2004.

XXVI.    (b) Friedman, Jonathan, & Christopher Chase-Dunn, eds., *Hegemonic Decline: Present and Past*. Political Economy of the World-System Annuals, 26b. Boulder, CO: Paradigm Publishers, 2005.

XXVII.   Tabak, Faruk, ed., *Allies as Rivals: The U.S., Europe and Japan in a Changing World-System*. Political Economy of the World-System Annuals, 27. Boulder, CO: Paradigm Publishers, 2005.

XXVIII.  Grosfoguel, Ramón, Nelson Meldonado-Torres, and José David Saldívar, eds., *Latin@s in the World-System: Toward the Decolonization of the Twenty-first Century U.S. Empire*. Political Economy of the World-System Annuals, 28. Boulder, CO: Paradigm Publishers, 2005.

XXIX.    Samman, Khaldoun, and Mazhor Al-Zo'by, eds., *Islam and the Orientalist World-System*. Political Economy of the World-System Annuals, 29. Boulder, CO: Paradigm Publishers, 2008.

XXX.     Trichur, Ganesh K., ed., *The Rise of Asia and the Transformation of the World-System*. Political Economy of the World-System Annuals, 30. Boulder, CO: Paradigm Publishers, 2009.

XXXI.    Jones, Terry-Ann, & Eric Mielants, eds., *Mass Migration in the World-System: Past, Present, and Future*. Political Economy of the World-System Annuals, 31. Boulder, CO: Paradigm Publishers, 2010.

XXXII.   Reifer, Tom, ed., *Global Crises and the Challenges of the 21st Century: Antisystemic Movements and the Transformation of the World-System*. Political Economy of the World-System Annuals, 32. Boulder, CO: Paradigm Publishers, 2012.

CPSIA information can be obtained
at www.ICGtesting.com
Printed in the USA
LVOW01s0008220317
528034LV00032B/830/P

9 781612 056883